Isabel Kaeslin

Emotion, Cognition, and the Virtue of Flexibility

Practical Philosophy

Edited by
Herlinde Pauer-Studer, Neil Roughley,
Peter Schaber and Ralf Stoecker

Volume 26

Isabel Kaeslin

Emotion, Cognition, and the Virtue of Flexibility

—

DE GRUYTER

ISBN 978-3-11-221409-1
e-ISBN (PDF) 978-3-11-078093-2
e-ISBN (EPUB) 978-3-11-078097-0
ISSN 2197-9243

Library of Congress Control Number: 2023940472

Bibliographic information published by the Deutsche Nationalbibliothek
The Deutsche Nationalbibliothek lists this publication in the Deutsche Nationalbibliografie;
detailed bibliographic data are available on the internet at http://dnb.dnb.de.

To my son Noan.

I wrote this book exactly during the first six years of your life. Thank you for filling every single day of it with the happiness that comes from looking into your eyes.

Acknowledgments

This book is, like any intellectual endeavor, a product of collective effort. Many people have been generous with their time, knowledge, and wisdom in helping me put to paper what was before a hunch or a thought in my mind.

I wish to especially thank Davide Bordini, Mathias Birrer-Käslin, and Katja Vogt for their insight, encouragement, support, and help as I was completing this project, both during the dissertation stage and as I later developed it into a book. Many more people have played a crucial role in completing the book and supporting me throughout the process. They are, in alphabetic order: Monika Betzler, Borhane Blili Hamelin, David Charles, Maria Dätwyler, Max Hayward, Matt Heeney, Manuel Käppler, Verena Käslin, Franz Käslin, Sarah Käslin, Philip Kitcher, Joshua Knobe, Mariana Noé, Donnchadh Ó Conaill, Carol Rovane, Carmela Schumacher, Gianfranco Soldati, Kathryn Tabb, and Fabrice Teroni.

I thank the Columbia University Philosophy Department for having provided me with an incredibly rich and diverse philosophical environment to pursue my PhD studies, which broadened my philosophical outlook and methods in unforeseen ways.

I would like to thank Susanne Schmetkamp and the *Aesthetics and Ethics of Attention* project at the University of Fribourg, funded by the *Swiss National Science Foundation*, for having given me an academic home for the last three years. Further thanks go to the *Swiss National Science Foundation* for having funded my one-year grant at the Yale University Philosophy Department in 2017, as principal investigator of the project *Flexibility of Character: Ancient and Contemporary Approaches*.

Finally, my thanks go to Christoph Schirmer, Mara Weber, and Ulla Schmidt from de Gruyter for their professional realization of this book, and to the editors of the *Practical Philosophy* series and the anonymous reviewer for their insightful comments.

https://doi.org/10.1515/9783110780932-002

Contents

Introduction

Should we let ourselves be guided by our emotions in our ethical and epistemic considerations? In this book, I will give a positive answer to this question. This is not a new proposal. However, this book lays out a novel argument, one that involves positing a kind of mental state that has so far not been attended to in this debate. I will argue that there is a kind of emotion that is not cognitive, and nevertheless object-directed. If I am right, the question of normative guidance must revise its philosophy of mind. In other words, when we ask ourselves which mental states can play roles in normative guidance, we are starting from an account of what mental states there are; if there are more and different mental states than we have so far considered, we have reason to take a fresh look at longstanding questions.

By showing that there is a kind of emotion that is object-directed and yet non-cognitive, I argue that the debate has so far not proceeded on the right assumptions. So far, philosophers have mostly proceeded from the assumption that emotions are in some way already cognitive. Accordingly, even if they do play a role in normative guidance, this role is to be explained by their cognitive dimensions. Other philosophers reject cognitivism about the emotions. On their view, however, assuming that the emotions are indeed not cognitive, it is inconceivable that they could play any role in practical or theoretical guidance. I show that this latter idea stems from the assumption that not to be cognitive necessarily means for the emotions to not be object-directed, that is, to not be able to refer or relate to objects. Hence, I argue, if we can show that non-cognitive emotions can nevertheless be object-directed in some way, it is possible that they play a role in practical and theoretical guidance. This is precisely what I aim to show. Non-cognitive emotions are object-directed in their own way, and can thus be normative guides in a special way.

The way in which non-cognitive emotions can be normative guides, I argue, is by disrupting engrained habits and beliefs.[1] This is the second new suggestion

---

[1] Throughout the book, I will often speak of "disrupting and changing habits and beliefs" without making a distinction in how this would work for habits on the one hand, and beliefs on the other. Of course, there are important differences in how we change habits and how we change beliefs. One plausible difference is that we have less voluntary control over our beliefs than over our habits. I will leave out these complex differences for the purposes of the argument in this book. It would be an interesting follow-up investigation to ask exactly how the adjustment of beliefs and habits must be thought of, respectively, when they are disrupted by non-cognitive emotions. We will, however, get a rough idea about the commonalities and differences in these two cases in

https://doi.org/10.1515/9783110780932-003

I make in this book: that an important aspect in normative guidance has been neglected so far, namely, the importance of being able to reconsider one's ways. If it is important that at times we stop in our tracks and reconsider our ingrained ways of acting and believing, there is a question of how we achieve such a moment of pause. What makes us pause and question our ways? Philosophers have put a lot of effort into showing how we can have stable commitments and beliefs over time. But not much has been said about how we can break open such commitments and beliefs again if they are not appropriate anymore. I argue that this is a far-reaching omission: we need to ask which mental capacities are involved—and which mental states may be crucial—in enabling reconsideration and adjustments of our ways of life. We live in a constantly changing world,[2] and our circumstances demand of us different kinds of habits and beliefs as time goes by. Once we dwell on this, it is indeed surprising that not more work has been done asking how our stable commitments and beliefs over time can also be held flexible enough to be able to change according to these changing demands on us.

Bringing these two hitherto neglected strands of thought together, I argue that non-cognitive emotions play the significant role of disrupting engrained beliefs and habits when necessary, giving the agent a way to see things outside of her regular mindset, and giving her the needed starting-point to reconsider her ways when necessary.

By arguing that non-cognitive emotions play this significant role in normative guidance, I deliberately aim to stay within a modest frame of what I can argue in the scope of a short book. There is a bigger picture, however, and I wish to briefly frame the book by speaking to this bigger picture. I take the argument of this book to be a first step toward the larger hypothesis that, in the practical sphere, how an action feels can *per se* be an ethically justifying reason to do it or not to do it, no matter what other (prudential or otherwise) advantages this could bring. That is, the larger hypothesis is that feelings should be given a more substantial role in ethical decisions per se. The idea is that there is something to be lost in ethics—or rather, in our lives, and correspondingly, in theories about well-lived human lives—if we do not allow feelings to play this role in our moral decision-

---

Chapter 5, when we ask whether the account established in Chapters 1–4 can also be extended to the theoretical sphere of what it is to think well, beyond ethical decision-making.

2 As Aristotle would say, the sublunary world is always subject to change, in contrast to the celestial world. This is a metaphysical commitment that is, as it were, Platonic and Aristotelian, and that, though with revised physics, in my view captures a deep insight about human life. For Plato, our lives play out in the domain of becoming and change. For Aristotle, we are creatures who live in a domain that only displays for-the-most-part regularities. Vogt (2017) calls this the metaphysics of the sphere of action.

making. A defense of this claim would ultimately require a debate about the nature of ethics. That is, it would require me to say more—*much* more—about what we ask when we pose the question "what should I do?". Some assume that this question asks what moral principles we should follow. But I would argue that this question aims at the same time at more and at less. It aims at more in the sense that I— qua human being—want to go beyond just following moral principles when I ask what I should do. It aims at less in the sense that moral principles might demand of me to act in a way that goes beyond what one can demand of a human being if it asks me to disregard my feelings. Or so I would argue. But it is too large a theme to re-think the nature of ethics here. So, I cannot and will not argue for this larger hypothesis in this book. Rather than taking this larger point as a demonstrandum, I keep it as a framing hypothesis. My demonstrandum, then, is that non-cognitive emotions help us attain the virtue of flexibility, which makes them important in ethical decision-making.

This larger, framing hypothesis also has its parallel in the theoretical sphere, on the question what "good thinking" (beyond ethical decision-making) is. That is, we can think of the account in this book as a first step toward the larger hypothesis that, in general, feeling-based thinking is *per se* better than thinking where no such feeling-states are involved, no matter whether this has any epistemic advantages. But I will restrict myself here too not to argue for this larger hypothesis, which would require a debate about the nature of epistemology, and it is too large a theme to re-think the nature of epistemology here. Instead, I will argue —as a first step toward the larger hypothesis—that we need these non-cognitive emotional responses in order to be creative thinkers who can move beyond their current conceptual framework. This will turn out to be the epistemic aspect of the virtue of flexibility.

Since this book makes claims about the nature of emotions, I will also engage with some empirical work in psychology. My main methodology, however, remains within the confines of conceptual analysis and construction of conceptual models to clarify the questions at hand. The main result of the book will be the introduction of a hitherto neglected kind of mental state, the non-cognitive but still object-directed kind of emotions, on the one hand, and the introduction of a hitherto neglected kind of virtue, namely, the virtue of flexibility, on the other.

In the first and in the fourth chapter, I will present my two proposals, respectively, while in the second and in the third chapter, I will take a step back in order to offer the conceptual analysis to corroborate these proposals. In the fifth chapter, I will extend the framework I have developed in the practical sphere of ethical decision-making to the theoretical sphere—asking whether the hitherto neglected mental state we have discovered also plays a role in what it is *to think well*, beyond decision-making on what to do.

In the first chapter, I will make the proposal that there is a kind of emotion that is not cognitive, but nevertheless object-directed. In the second chapter, I will then defend a framework in the philosophy of mind in order to better understand the distinction between cognitive and feeling states. In Chapter 3, I will offer an account of the relevant notion of normativity; we often, though in my mind too quickly, equate normativity with rationality, which leads to the cognitivist bias I argue against. My argument against this identification of normativity with rationality will then open up the conceptual space to make my second proposal in Chapter 4, the proposal that we need to recognize a virtue that has not been considered so far, the virtue of flexibility. The virtue of flexibility can only be recognized once we allow for the idea that cognitive or rational control over our emotions can also be detrimental. That is, only once we do not equate normativity with rationality or cognitive control anymore, we can see that there is such a thing as a virtue of flexibility that allows us to make changes to our beliefs and commitments over time. Having completed my account with this chapter, I will then ask in the fifth and last chapter whether this account can also be extended to the theoretical sphere of what it is to think well, beyond ethical decision-making. I will argue that the virtue of flexibility is also a virtue in the theoretical sphere. I will hence complete the picture in this last chapter, by showing how we can think of the role of the feeling states in thinking and believing. With the distinctions in mind that I introduced in Chapters 1–4, I will argue that if we took "the best way of thinking" to be only done by our cognitive capacities, it would amount to the claim that the best way of thinking is "maximally coherent thinking". However, as I will argue, the norms of good thinking are not exhausted by maximally coherent thinking. Other norms, even such that go *against* coherence, are just as required for good thinking. And for some of them, we need our (well-trained, strong) feeling states to get there. Hence, the feeling states play an analogous role in thinking well as they do in ethical decision-making. The overall arc of argumentation in this book will thus move from the practical sphere to the theoretical sphere, showing the important role of non-cognitive emotions and the virtue of flexibility in both. At the end of Chapter 5, I will make a final observation: that these considerations also show us something about what it means to be a good philosopher. Good thinking, and thus good philosophy, is not done only with our cognitive but also with our feeling capacities. That means, in turn, that in order to be good philosophers, we not only have to train our cognitive capacities, but also our feeling capacities. Considering the role of feeling capacities and the virtue of flexibility, thus, also in the end will lead us to have an insight into our own activity and methodology as philosophers.

Chapter 1: Emotional Response as a Normative Guide

Should we let ourselves be guided by our emotions in our ethical and epistemic considerations? We can find various responses to this question in the history of philosophy.[3] Today, several philosophers reply affirmatively. However, I shall argue in this chapter that these affirmative responses have not gone far enough. They assign normative roles to the emotions merely in virtue of emotions being belief-like or cognitive (Nussbaum, 2001), imbued with reason (McDowell, 1998a; Sherman, 1989), or as a second-best and fast way to decide whenever there are no better options (Brady, 2013).[4] By contrast, I want to consider a *non-cognitive* kind of emotion, a kind that is basic or primitive, and ask whether even such basic, non-cognitive emotions can guide moral and ethical decisions. I will call these basic, non-cognitive emotions "emotional responses", while I call the other ones "sophisticated emotions". I will not be concerned with whether the sophisticated emotions entail some sort of cognition, belief, or reason; I will defend the position that basic emotional responses, my present focus, do not.

For basic emotional responses to play a normative role, they must be object-directed. In defending my position, I thus need to address a fundamental issue in the theory of emotions; I need to show that emotional responses can be object-directed and yet not cognitive. If my argument is sound, then this combination of object-directedness and non-cognitiveness is possible. I take this to be a significant result. Building on this result, I will then show how this object-directedness is sufficient for the basic emotional responses to play a unique role in normative guidance, namely, by giving us negative reasons to act against established beliefs and habits.

In a first step, I will clarify the notion of basic emotional responses (§ 1) and propose that basic emotional responses come in (at least) two modes, as a spontaneous aversion or a spontaneous attraction (§ 1.1). Then I will argue that such emotional responses are best understood as bodily feelings (§ 1.2). As feelings, they are not representational but nevertheless object-directed (§ 1.3 and § 1.4). Based on these preparatory steps, I address the question of how basic emotional responses can guide us normatively in a unique way, that is, in a way that makes it *necessary*

---

[3] The very different responses Aristotle and Kant give, as well as disagreements among ancient thinkers, have received much attention (cf. Engstrom and Whiting, 1998).

[4] There is also an influential view in psychology, Appraisal Theory, one version of which argues to the same effect. According to Richard Lazarus, we first assess a situation cognitively, in ways that are automatic and unconscious, and emotion occurs in a second step (Lazarus, 2003).

https://doi.org/10.1515/9783110780932-004

for us to rely on them (§ 2). I will argue that emotional responses can normatively guide us in our actions by giving us *negative* reasons to act against our established habits and beliefs. That is, they play a negative role in guiding our actions, by telling us what *not* to do (§ 2.1). I will then address why I think that basic emotional responses do not play a substantive *positive* role in normative guidance, thereby illustrating the limits of my proposal (§ 2.2). At the end, I will confront four challenges to the proposed account (§ 2.3): an objection from rigid emotional responses, an objection against the necessity claim, an objection against the two-mode view, and an objection against the importance of the capacity to reconsider.

1.1 What is an Emotional Response?

When the question of the relationship between morality and emotions is posed, philosophers often focus on paradigmatic so-called 'moral emotions', such as anger, courage, love, jealousy, and more. These are complex entities (cf., for example, Ben-Ze'ev, 2000) whose roles in our moral lives deserve careful analysis. But I will not be concerned with such *sophisticated* emotions (as I call them). Instead, I am interested in two basic forms of emotional response, namely, in what I will call *spontaneous aversion* and *spontaneous attraction*. We can ask some of the same questions about them that have been asked about the sophisticated emotions. Are they mere feelings? Are they object-directed? And ultimately, do they show us anything about *how good or bad* the involved action or situation is? To illustrate, here is an example of a spontaneous aversion and a spontaneous attraction.

1.1.1 Emotional Response as Spontaneous Aversion and Spontaneous Attraction

Imagine that you have always enjoyed eating meat, so much so that you indulge yourself in eating a substantial amount of meat every week. Suddenly, today, when you are about to bite into your steak, it just does not feel right. You are unable to tell what might be wrong about it. That is, you do not experience *cognitive* aversion, but you *feel* an aversion against having another bite of your steak. This aversion, we might say, is a spontaneous experience. It is an emotional response without any cognitive or belief-like content, and it appears suddenly. This emotional response will give you occasion to reflect on your usual pattern of acting, which until this moment was taken for granted. In this way, such a basic emotional response makes you question a previously unquestioned pattern of acting.

The same reflective attitude can be prompted by a spontaneous attraction. Let us imagine that you have been a confident vegetarian for the last ten years of your life. Today, just when you are about to bite into your vegetarian sandwich, you experience a sudden desire for some meat in it: you experience a spontaneous attraction. Again, you cannot tell what you like about the idea. In other words, there is no *cognitive* attraction. But you *feel* the attraction for some meat in the sandwich. Again, this emotional response will give you prima facie occasion to reflect on your usual pattern of acting, which until this moment was taken for granted. So, again, a basic emotional response can disrupt a given pattern of acting.

I am thus proposing a two-mode view. Emotional responses come in the form of either an aversion or an attraction. Note that these two modes share one core characteristic: they are directional in an immediately motivating way. If I experience a spontaneous aversion, this disrupts my habits and beliefs by *pulling* me away from my current doings. Similarly, if I experience a spontaneous attraction, this disrupts my habits and beliefs by *pulling* me away from my current doings. This is thanks to their directionality together with its motivating force. Note also that, though one response is an aversion and the other an attraction, the directionality, as described in my examples, is the same: both pull me *away* from something. That is, though the attraction to meat is a motivational movement *toward* something, this positive movement is not the phenomenon I am concerned with. Rather, alongside this movement toward something the subject experiences a movement away from something – from the established habit.

I will argue that emotional responses of this kind have the unique capacity to disrupt longstanding patterns of action (what I call here "habits") and beliefs, thereby playing a role in motivation that rational or cognitive mental processes can only play indirectly when they follow from such a response. While we might think that a new rational consideration can also give the agent pause, prompting her to reflect anew on her patterns of acting, I will argue that this reflective reconsideration of given habits cannot take place without a prior emotional response as described above.

1.1.2 Emotional Response as a Felt Bodily Response

Let us first make the characterization of the emotional responses more precise. How can we think of such spontaneous aversions and attractions? We can borrow from the literature on what I call sophisticated moral emotions. Consider what David Charles says about the experience of fear. The subject he considers is affected by the prospect of what will happen in the future, and thus experiences fear. Charles says that

(...) how it seems to him to be is not to be accounted for in terms of what he *believes* or is inclined to *believe*. In both, what is important is the *impact* the imagined or perceived scene makes on the subject: the relevant states cannot be understood except by reference to the subject's *disposition to act or react physiologically* in given ways. (Charles, 2004, 122–123; my emphasis)

Here, Charles shares with me the idea that a certain emotional response is to be thought of in a non-cognitive way – what the subject *believes* is not relevant. Instead, he suggests, what is relevant is the impact a situation makes on the subject, and specifically, how the subject *reacts physiologically.* Hence, we have here the suggestion that an emotional response is not only non-cognitive, but moreover, includes or is constituted by a *physiological* response.[5] This, I think, is a promising way to understand the kind of emotional response I sketched: a spontaneous aversion or attraction is (partially) constituted by a physiological response to the situation. Indeed, I think this is more clearly so in the case of a spontaneous aversion or attraction than in the case of the sophisticated emotions, like fear. While one might argue that fear is, beyond being a physiological reaction, the thought or the awareness of (presumed) danger, a spontaneous aversion, in which one is unaware of why one is averse to something, is more comprehensively a physiological response: one feels it *with*[6] *one's body*; something about it makes one's body feel unwell. This thought is also captured in the vocabulary of a "movement away from" that I used earlier. Insofar as the emotional response makes one stop in one's tracks, it prompts a physiological kind of "shrinking back" from whatever one is en route to doing, such as biting into one's sandwich.

Generally speaking, how we should account for the physiological basis of emotions has long been considered a hard question in the field.[7] For present purposes, I cannot go into this debate in detail. But it is worth noting that there are different ways to conceive of the idea that emotional responses are partially constituted by a physiological response. Minimally, one can distinguish a position according to which this physiological response must be conscious, such that the subject is aware of the physiological response and, as I put this, *feels* it, from a position according to which this does not have to be the case. On the latter view, according to which the

---

5 Also in Charles (2009, 2011), he argues that the emotions are always and inextricably both psychological and physical.

6 I deliberately do not say "one feels it *in* one's body" – this spatial metaphor suggests a Jamesian representational picture (cf. Whiting, 2011, 281). This seems implausible, as one does not feel displeasure in one discreet area of the body and pleasure in another, for example. Hence "feeling *with* one's body".

7 Some examples are: James (1884); Laird and Lacasse (2014); Prinz (2004); Reisenzein and Stephan (2014); and Teroni and Deonna (2017).

subject can be unaware of her physiological response, there are sub-personal emotional responses. Something goes on in the subject, the thought goes, but the subject as a whole cannot deliberately act in accordance with it (though she might *involuntarily* act in accordance with it). It is obvious that this latter kind of account would not work well with my proposal. It is imperative for my proposal that the subject *does* experience the emotional response. Only insofar as she experiences the response she can be prompted to reconsider, and perhaps modify her behavior based on it. Hence, what is important for my conception of emotional responses as physiological responses is that they are *felt*, conscious responses.[8]

However, the emotional responses that concern us here are also importantly different from other physiological, consciously-felt reactions. Let us consider the case in which someone comes down with a cold after they have gone through a stressful situation. The symptoms of the cold are a conscious, felt physiological reaction to an event, and it is felt on the personal level, not on some sub-personal level. But nevertheless, this seems importantly different to the experience of an emotional response in the form of a spontaneous aversion or attraction. The symptoms of the cold, the physiological response involved here, do not have any *psychological* content. They are *just* physiological reactions to the circumstances. By contrast, a spontaneous aversion has a minimal, albeit not cognitive, psychological content: a form of displeasure that directs the subject away from the object. In this way, the emotional responses here considered go beyond mere conscious physiological responses. But we should not read too much into the involved psychological content, or else we run the risk of understanding the emotional responses as if they were sophisticated, cognitively penetrated emotions. We will explore the nature of this minimal psychological content more in the next two sections.[9]

It is important to note that keeping the notion of psychological content at a minimal level does not force me to conceive of the emotional responses as quasi-automatic, passive reflexes. Rather, we can think of them as ways of engaging with what happens in the subject's surroundings and doings. Emotional responses are *responses*, and they are *prompted* by things that happen. In this sense, there is a passive dimension. But they are not simply causally triggered by their objects. Rather, the subject encounters the world – a steak, a sandwich, etc. – in a given state of mind. This way, her emotional responses are shaped by her prior doings and experiences. Depending on her overall state of mind at a given moment, a subject processes external promptings differently. And while the subject does not have

---

8 For a defense of the idea that it is *the phenomenology on the personal level*, as opposed to a sub-personal level, that essentially matters for a conception of the emotions, cf. Teroni and Deonna (2020). **9** See Plato's *Philebus* 35c-d (in: Plato, 1997a) for the insight that any phenomenon of the mind needs to have some minimal psychological content.

voluntary control over her emotional responses in a given situation, over time she can mold her responses in a certain way. Thereby she prepares the ground for the way in which she processes promptings. That is, a subject can have indirect active influence on her emotional responses.[10]

1.1.3 Distinguishing between Two Kinds of Object-Directedness

It may seem unclear, however, how emotional responses of the kind I presented can be object-directed.[11] But if they are not, it will be difficult to explain how they could play a role in moral decision-making – if they do not relate to objects, how could they be normative guides, or indeed any guides, at all? How could they give one occasion to reconsider, and an indication of how (not) to act, if they do not relate to objects? In what I have suggested so far, it is natural to think of the emotional responses as "mere" feelings – a feeling of aversion or attraction. To conceive of mental states as "mere" feelings is often taken to be incompatible with the thought that they are also object-directed. In what follows I will argue that emotional responses *are* mere feelings, but that they are nevertheless object-directed, even though they are *neither* cognitive *nor* representational.

Demian Whiting conceives of emotions as mere feelings. Emotions, Whiting says, "form a distinct class of feeling state" (2006, 261) and "differences in emotions simply correspond to differences in how emotions feel" (2006, 262). In his view, this has the consequence that emotions cannot be object-directed.[12] Their very nature precludes them from having what he calls a representational structure, and such a representational structure is necessary to mentally represent objects, he argues (cf. Whiting, 2011, 285). Whiting thus concludes that the only way emotions can be di-

---

10 This is an interesting similarity to Strawson's notion of *reactive attitudes* (Strawson, 1962): He also thinks that it is inconceivable that we do not have these attitudes, while we can modify and habituate them up to a point, so that we have indirect control over them. But in contrast to the emotional responses considered here, Strawson is explicitly interested in "moral" emotions narrowly conceived, namely, such emotions that figure in interactions with others, where we hold others responsible.

11 Quite in contrast to the sophisticated emotions, where it is taken by some to be a banal statement that they are object-directed: "The basic and perhaps banal observation has first to be made that when we speak of emotions, those states of mind which we speak of in this way – such as fear, anger, jealousy, etc. – always imply some reference to an object." (Peters and Mace, 1961, 117).

12 This is what Whiting argues in his later paper (2011), while he did not take object-directedness to be incompatible with conceiving of emotions as mere feelings in his earlier paper (2006) mentioned at the beginning of the paragraph.

rected at objects is through their inherent link with a thought (cf. Whiting, 2011, 285).

I argue, by contrast, that emotional responses[13] are *themselves* object-directed, even though they do not have a representational structure. A link with thought is thus not necessary in order for them to be object-directed. To clarify, let us distinguish between two kinds of object-directedness, a sophisticated and a less sophisticated one:

Object-Directed 1: a mental state is Object-Directed 1 in virtue of having a representational structure, that is, it can represent the object in a sophisticated way (to be clarified further on). This kind of representation might be conceptual or non-conceptual. The non-conceptual representation is also sophisticated, in the following sense. Its content is "thick", in the sense that it can have proper parts, and an internal structure between its parts. It is, as it were, not just a mere presentation of the object as a whole (a form of mere acquaintance), but a *structured* representation of the object. Given this, it is also more sophisticated in the sense that it can be directed at, among other things, a proposition[14] or even the inferential structure of several propositions.

Object-Directed 2: a mental state is Object-Directed 2 by providing a felt pull toward or a push away from an object, in a motivating way (there might be a kind of pleasure and displeasure involved), but not more. This way of being object-directed still requires some minimal psychological content for the push-or-pull response to count as object-directed (and as being a mental state). That is, it is not a mere knee-jerk reaction of the subject without any "inner" feeling going on, that is, without any what-it-is-like to be pulled or pushed in this way. It is a less sophisticated form of being object-directed because it cannot represent the object as having proper parts, or with an internal structure. It might be akin to mere presentation (acquaintance), but with a motivating pull.[15]

---

13 Note that Whiting uses the notion "emotions" in Whiting 2006 and 2011, and thus makes a statement about sophisticated *and* basic emotions in my terms, while I only make statements about "basic" emotions.

14 I use the term "proposition" roughly as synonymous with "sentence" or "sentence-structure". If something has propositional content, it has content that is propositionally structured, that is, structured in a language-like way. I take it that, roughly, propositional content is conceptual content. However, non-conceptual content can be structured too (that is, it can also have proper parts that are structured in a particular way among each other), but not in this language-like way.

15 So what I am suggesting here as a form of object-directedness might share many features with the acquaintance-relation Russell described, but with the added feature of feeling *pulled or pushed in a certain direction* by that relation.

Here is how Russell contrasts presentation from judgment: "I say that I am *acquainted* with an object when I have a direct cognitive relation to that object, i. e., when I am directly aware of the

If a mental state is object-directed merely in this sense, it can be directed at states of affairs, events, physical objects, and so on. But in virtue of not having what I call a representational structure (a structure that allows it to also represent the object with its proper parts and the internal structure of its parts), it cannot represent a proposition (or the inferential structure of several propositions) *as* a proposition. That is, even a mental state with only this kind of object-directedness might be directed at a proposition *in some sense*. That is, one can have a feeling of being pulled away or pushed toward a certain proposition. In that case, however, the proposition is presented as an *indiscernible whole*, without parts and relations, thus as something that one can only be related to as a whole in this binary way. This does not really do justice to the (sophisticated) kind of thing a proposition is: a something with proper parts that have (sometimes complicated) relations to each other. In a more sophisticated representation, one might have different responses to different parts of the proposition. This is not possible when only being directed at the proposition in this less sophisticated way described here. So, in a sense a mental state that is object-directed in this second way *can* take a proposition (or an inferential structure of several propositions) as its object, but not *as* a proposition.

One might worry about whether presenting a whole without presenting it as having parts is possible. On this, I agree with Russell when he says: "Whether it is possible to be aware of a complex without being aware of its constituents is not an easy question, but on the whole it would seem that there is no reason why it should not be possible." (Russell, 1917, 153)

Emotional responses, as I will argue, can be object-directed in this second sense, while they cannot be so in the more sophisticated way of Object-Directed 1.

---

object itself. When I speak of a cognitive relation here, I do not mean the sort of relation which constitutes judgment, but *the sort which constitutes presentation.* [my emphasis] (...) That is, to say that S has acquaintance with O is essentially the same thing as to say *that O is presented to S."* (Russell, 1917, 152).

It is noteworthy, however, that Russell thought that sense-data (at least the ones of which we have knowledge by acquaintance) are usually complex, that is, containing parts: "The sense-datum with which I am acquainted in these cases is generally, if not always, complex. This is particularly obvious in the case of sight. I do not mean, of course, merely that the supposed physical object is complex, but that the direct sensible object is complex and contains parts with spatial relations." (Russell, 1917, 153).

1.1.4 Emotional Response as Object-Directed 2

The example of the habitual meat eater illustrates, on my analysis, the kind of case that Object-Directed 2 describes. While seeing my steak in front of me, I suddenly feel an aversion against eating it. This emotional response to the meat arises as a specific response to a specific object. The object in question is "the meat in front of me". The response is directed at the meat. This response does not need any sophisticated representation of the meat in my mental state of aversion, despite having some minimal psychological content. It is, of course, conceivable that in addition to having a spontaneous aversion the subject *also* has richer and more complex mental states; but for present purposes we are only concerned with the spontaneous aversion by itself. Here, the subject just *feels* the aversion. Such a spontaneous aversion has the meat as a necessary presupposition. It is specific to *this* object at this moment. Hence, it counts as object-directed in the second sense. This is all the more evident when we consider cases of doubt. A subject may be unsure what precisely it is that prompts that response, and so, be in doubt about the specific object of a given response. But in a situation like this, she can vary the objects in front of her until she figures out at what specifically her response is directed.

The example of a spontaneous aversion against the meat in front of me illustrates that an emotional response can be object-directed without representing the object. As I have mentioned before, these emotional responses do not need to be conceived of as passive reflexes. They can be molded and educated over time to respond in certain ways. Thus, even though they are *responses*, we do not have to think of their object-directedness as merely passive causal reactions. In this way, emotional responses are less sophisticated than cognitive or belief-like emotions, precisely insofar as they do not represent their object and cannot take an inferential structure as their object. But emotional responses still establish a relation to objects that subjects take to be relevant to their moral and ethical attitudes and motivations.

It is worth noting that this undermines a view to the effect that *because* all emotions are object-directed, they *must* be representational, and thus cognitive in some sense. If we can show, as I think I have, that object-directedness is possible *without* representational structure (at least for *some* kinds of emotions, the basic ones), then the prevailing view that *all* emotions must be cognitive simply on account of being object-directed is a non-sequitur.

The view presented so far could be confused with a mere rejection of cognitivism about emotions. But it is distinct from mere non-cognitivism about emotions in two ways: First, the view presented here does not make any claims about emotions more generally, but only about a specific kind of emotions, the spontaneous emotional responses. Hence, it is in principle compatible with cognitivism about all other emotions (but not with cognitivism about emotions *tout court*). Second, we have to make sure to distinguish the *three* terms involved here: being object-directed, representational, and cognitive. Cognitivism about emotions claims that emotions are 1. object-directed, which (according to them) entails that 2. they must be representational, which (according to them) then entails that 3. they must be cognitive. Non-cognitivists about emotions deny the step from 2 to 3: just because emotions are representational, does not mean that they also need to be cognitive. Certain perceptualists about emotions (e. g., Tappolet (2016, 2015, 2012, 2011, 2000), Rossi and Tappolet (2019), Tappolet and Rossi (2015)), for instance, claim that while emotions are representational, they are *not* cognitive (because they are a kind of perception, rather than a kind of belief). This is a paradigmatic non-cognitivist view of emotions. My account, by contrast, targets the cognitivists' view even a step *earlier*, from 1 to 2: just because these mental states are object-directed, does not mean that they also need to be representational. Spontaneous emotional responses show us that there is a way of being object-directed without being representational (never mind being cognitive). Thus, emotional responses in the sense here question the cognitive views on emotions in a more radical way than mere non-cognitivism. By suggesting that there is a kind of object-directedness that works without representation, the view here is thus more general (and more radical) than mere non-cognitivism. At the same time, it is narrower than non-cognitivism about emotions *tout court*, because it only makes this radical claim about a certain kind of emotions, the spontaneous emotional responses.

Now, a lot hangs on the precise understanding of representational here. Perhaps a better way of putting it is that emotional responses do not entail a *sophisticated* form of representation (a propositional one, or one that is internally structured and has proper parts), but only a weak or simple form of representation (the feeling of aversion or attraction). This would amount to the minimal psychological content required for them to even amount to a mental state at all, as mentioned before. That form of representation merely consists in the felt pull toward or push away from the object. In some sense, the object is then represented by these mental states, in the form of a felt push or pull. That is, there is a psychological content that is triggered by that object, which has a directional motivating force. But this is quite different from the kind of representations with which, for instance, standard perceptual states furnish our minds. In a visual representation, for instance, one can have discernible proper parts, a certain internal structure of the represented parts, and so on (and this even when assuming it to be non-conceptual content). All that the less sophisticated form of representation has, in contrast, is a felt pull or push; a felt, motivated moving in a certain direction.

That there is more to the phenomenology of mental states than their representational content is, for instance, defended by Ned Block in his account of mental paint.[16] Having that distinction between representational content and (other) phenomenal aspects of a mental state available, one is then able to distinguish, of one and the same mental state, between the "proper" representational content, and the phenomenology of that mental state that goes beyond any representations, the mental paint, according to Block. This is applicable also to what I have called sophisticated forms of representation (such as in perception). And such a distinction is all that is needed for my account: that there is a what-it-is-like of being in a mental state which does not amount to (sophisticated) representations.[17]

The above considerations now open up two ways of talking about representations, and with it, two ways of how my account (of the nature of object-directedness of emotional responses) can be put: either by using the distinction between representational content and non-representational phenomenological aspects of mental states (in agreement with Block) or by using a distinction between simple and sophisticated forms of representation. In other words:

Either we say that

a) the what-it-is-like of emotional responses is not representational at all. *Their phenomenology*, which is what is operational in their normative guidance, is something like the mental paint Block argues for. Mental paint, again, is a phenomenological aspect of a mental state that is not representational.

In this line of reasoning, we then argue (in addition to Block's non-representationalism) that *that phenomenology alone* is enough to make emotional responses object-directed, and thus candidates for normative guidance.

Or we say that

b) the emotional responses are representational in some sense, but in a much less sophisticated way than how representation is usually thought of (e. g., in perception), i. e., with representing proper parts, inner structure, and so on. Then, what we argue is that this less sophisticated form of representation is enough to make emotional responses object-directed, and thus candidates for normative guidance.

---

16 Block (1996, 2003)

17 Besides Block, there have been others that argued that there are phenomenological aspects of mental states that are not representations (non-representationalists). See for example Kind (2013) and Bordini (2017) who argue this specifically for the case of moods. Moods, they argue, are undirected mental states, and therefore are not well described as representations. At the same time, there is a what-it-is-like to be in a certain mood. Therefore, there is a least one kind of mental state that has a phenomenology that is not reducible to its representational contents, they say.

This also shows why emotional responses as described in this book are not the same as moods. Moods are usually thought of as undirected affective states (the undirectedness being what distinguishes them from emotions). Emotional responses are, as I argued, object-directed, while still not being representational.

I think both ways of putting it work for my account, and a debate on which way of talking would be the better one amounts to a verbal debate. That is why I mainly refer to this way of relating to objects as "Object-Directed 2".

One open question remains. It is the question of whether what I argue for here is a different, hitherto un-recognized kind of intentionality, or a way of being object-directed that does not amount to a form of intentionality. Again, a lot hangs on the precise understanding of intentionality here. In one way of understanding intentionality, it is simply a synonym for "being object-directed". That is, any mental state that stably relates to objects (be they formal objects, objects in the world, and so on), is an intentional mental state. In that sense of talking, by arguing that emotional responses are object-directed (but in a less sophisticated way), I introduce a new kind of intentionality. In another (narrower) sense of intentionality, not every kind of object-directedness amounts to a form of intentionality. For example, a mere knee-jerk reaction to an object which does not entail a felt aspect by the subject of the reaction, but that is still a stable way of reacting to the same kind of object, might be a way of being object-directed but not amount to intentionality. In such a case, however, we would not be sure whether we should call this a mental state (with at least minimal psychological content) at all. But it could be a way in which the subject relates to objects in a non-intentional way. This was to illustrate that this narrower sense of intentionality (which is not synonymous with *any* kind of object-directedness) includes the idea of somehow meaningfully 'taking the object' into one's mental life. If intentionality is understood in this narrower sense, then it is not entirely clear whether I introduce a new, as of yet not recognized form of intentionality by introducing Object-Directedness 2. This is so because it really depends on how this "taking the object into one's mental life" is thought of. If, for instance, intentionality is always a sophisticated form of representation (a very narrow sense of intentionality), then Object-Directedness 2 does not amount to a new form of intentionality, as we have seen. If some minimal psychological content, for example a phenomenology akin to mental paint or a non-sophisticated form of (non-conceptual) representation, is enough to amount to "taking the object into one's mental life", then even in this narrower sense of intentionality, I am introducing a new form of intentionality with the Object-Directedness 2, namely, a less sophisticated form of intentionality.

Now, before I move to the normative side of my proposal in § 1.2, let me first contrast the here presented concept of emotional responses from the concept of desires and from conative mental states more generally, and then consider two potential objections to the view presented so far.

Many different theories of desire have been discussed (e.g., action-based,[18] pleasure-based,[19] good-based,[20] attention-based,[21] learning-based,[22] functionalist and interpretationist[23]). For the purposes of this book, I look in more detail at three of them and show how in each of them desire is different from our emotional responses: the Ancient (Aristotle and Plato), the good-based, and the pleasure-based.

In Ancient philosophy (particularly Aristotle and Plato), desire was thought of as the "lowest", that is, the least intellectual part of the soul. In Aristotle, for example, what is translated as "desire" is the term *epithymiai*, and its only possible objects were food, drink, and sex. Desire is that which ensures the physical maintenance of human beings (both of the individual and the species), and thus is that soul-part which even plants share with us (roughly, metabolism). Desire might play a role in explaining *akrasía* (weakness of will) as that which makes us act against our better judgment (for example, if desire is taken as first premise rather than practical reason in the practical syllogism). In a normative context it can only be a force toward the good in its *transformed* form (by *logos*, the intellect, and by *thumos*, the social or sophisticated emotions), for example by providing the motivational force (that which makes one actually move physically) to pursue the good end. Hence, desire in this Ancient sense could not correspond to our concept of emotional responses, as the emotional responses are (as we will see in more detail in Chapter 3) subject to affective learning, and therefore can be a force toward the good by themselves, without inculcation or transformation by the intellect.

In good-based theories of desire, the idea is that desires need to be closely linked to judgments (cf. Schroeder, 2020). Sometimes this is thought to have been Socrates' view (and thus to have Ancient origins too), in its simple formulation that "to want something is simply to think it good" (cf. Schroeder, 2020). That is, the idea is that:

"For an organism to desire *p* is for it to believe *p* is good." (Schroeder, 2020)

---

18 Anscombe 1957, Smith 1987, 1994, Stampe 1986, Davis 1986, Marks 1986, McDowell 1978, Scanlon 1998, Millikan 1984, Papineau 1987, Schroeder 2004, Wall 2009.
19 Schueler 1991, Vadas 1984, Davis 1986, Strawson 1994, Morillo 1990, Davis 1982, Schroeder 2004.
20 Price 1989, Byrne and Hájek 1997, Broome 1991, Lewis 1988; 1996, Stampe 1987, Oddie 2005, Scanlon 1998.
21 Scanlon 1998.
22 Morillo 1990, Schroeder 2004, Butler 1992, Dretske 1988, Bratman 1990, Brook 2006, Latham 2006.
23 Lewis 1972, Davidson 1980, Jaworska 2007a, 2007b, 1999.

Schroeder goes on to elaborate:

> Recommending such a theory is the intuition, shared by many, that we are motivated to do what we judge good just because we judge it good (and the intuition that, if I am motivated to do something, I desire to do it). If I judge it good to go to a meeting of the PTA, then that suffices to motivate me to go to the meeting, it would seem, and thus (perhaps) to desire it. (Schroeder, 2020)

Lewis (1988; 1996) dubbed this the "Desire as Belief" view (and raised problems against it). With this likeness to belief, we can already recognize that our concept of emotional responses cannot correspond to desires understood in this way. Beliefs are paradigmatic for mental states that are cognitive (as we will see in more detail in Chapter 2), that is, for mental states that can be object-directed in the more sophisticated sense of Object-Directed 1. There is a less belief-oriented version of the good-based view of desire, however, namely, the perception-based view. According to Stampe (1987) and Oddie (2005), "desires are a kind of high-level perceptual state: a perception of goodness" (Schroeder, 2020). That is, desires are "complex, high-level perceptual states that are nonetheless distinct from belief states." What the proponents of this view are aiming at is to say that the appearance of goodness is something quite distinct from the belief or judgment that something is good.

Our account has some overlaps with this view, in that it also emphasizes that the appearance (or the quality, or the phenomenology) given by a mental state is importantly different from the content of a judgment or belief, and in that that appearance alone can be normatively guiding. And our account has already shown some overlaps with a subclass of non-cognitivists about emotions, namely, exactly those who take emotions to be (a special kind of) perceptual state. Note, however, that to take desire (or emotions) as a form of "high-level perceptual state", as these accounts do, is still to assume a different nature about them than we do for our concept of emotional responses. We pointed out that, in contrast to perceptual theories of emotion, we not only reject that any representational state must be cognitive (because there are non-cognitive perceptions), but we also reject that any object-directed state must be representational. In other words, these perceptual understandings of desire and emotion still take desire or emotion to be representational, and in a sophisticated sense. Our concept of emotional responses is more primitive. Hence, because emotional responses only have a less sophisticated form of object-directedness (the non-representational, or the one with less sophisticated representation), they cannot be desires in the sense of "perception of the good" either.

That is why we shall also compare our concept of emotional responses to pleasure-based accounts of desire. These accounts come closest in their characterization of desire as something quite primitive, to make it similar enough to the primitiveness of the emotional responses. Proponents of this view defend a theory of desire "according to which dispositions to pleasure (and displeasure) are all there is to desire. (...) For an organism to desire p is for the organism to be disposed to take pleasure in it seeming that p, and displeasure in it seeming that non-p" (Schroeder, 2020). That is, in these accounts it is a contingent feature of desires whether they move us to action, and the essential feature is that they give rise to certain feelings (of pleasure and displeasure) (cf. Schroeder, 2020). Strawson (1994), for instance, holds that "pleasure and displeasure are the states of consciousness most closely linked to desire", and that it is conceivable that even creatures that lack the capacity to act would have desires, in the form of experiencing feelings of pleasure and displeasure.

Our account of emotional responses again shares something with this view. That is, we said that the Object-Directedness 2 of the emotional responses consists in a felt pull toward or push away from the object in a motivating way, where there might be a kind of pleasure and displeasure involved, but not more. So far, emotional responses seem very similar to desire in a pleasure-based account. In contrast to desire in a pleasure-based account, however, emotional responses *are* inherently connected to acting in a way that desire is not. That is, in emotional responses, the felt pull toward an object that involves a form of pleasure is, as we said, experienced *in a motivating way.* The subject who experiences a spontaneous attraction, thus, is inclined *to move* toward the object (or to maintain the current state of affairs that gives pleasure, and so on), and will thus move. Emotional responses do not make sense if we think of them as mere "stationary" feelings, as it were, that do not essentially move the subject toward or away from something. One *already acts* (in some sense) just by experiencing them. For emotional responses, in other words, it does not make sense that the movement toward action is a contingent feature about them, as it is for desire in pleasure-based accounts. A creature who does not have the capacity to act would thus still be able to experience desire according to these accounts, but it would not make sense to say that it can have emotional responses.[24]

---

[24] Of course, it depends on exactly how we think of this fictional creature. If we, for instance, take it to be a human being who once had that capacity and lost it, then she could perhaps still have emotional responses, similar to the phenomenon of phantom limb pain as a function of the memory of how it felt to have that limb. In such a case, she might remember how it felt to act, and can thus still have emotional responses that *would* make her act if she still had that capacity.

But if we imagine this creature to be one that *inherently* lacks the capacity to act (if such a creature makes sense at all), it seems inconceivable how this creature could experience emotional responses because one already acts (in some sense) just by going through emotional responses.

Now that we have distinguished emotional responses from desire, there is one more group of mental states that it seems very similar to: conative states more generally. Do emotional responses belong to the group of conative mental states? Often, the paradigmatic member of this group is taken to be desire. We have already shown how emotional responses differ from desire. Hence, let us look at an account of conative states that does *not* take desire as its paradigmatic member. Kriegel (2015) argues that the "field of conative phenomena is much larger" (Kriegel 2015, 72) and then lists some mental phenomena that must be included in it: "desiring to φ, wanting to φ, intending to φ, choosing to φ, deciding to φ, being willing to φ, planning to φ, needing to φ, having φ-ing as a project, performing (doing) φ, trying to φ, striving to φ, pursuing φ-ing, having a volition to φ, wishing that *p*, hoping that *p*, approving of *x*, valuing *x*, preferring *x* (over *y*)." (Kriegel 2015, 72–73) He then clarifies that "this list focuses on *positive* conative states, but there are negative counterparts that qualify equally: disliking, being unwilling, disapproving, refusing to try, and so on" (Kriegel 2015, 73).

Kriegel is interested in arguing that conative phenomenology – the what-it-is-like of being in one of these states – is irreducible to other kinds of phenomenology, such as cognitive or affective phenomenology. For this aim, one desideratum is to find a "phenomenal feature common and peculiar to their occurrences" (Kriegel 2015, 73), which would amount to the "phenomenal signature of the conative" (Kriegel 2015, 73). He ends up arguing that the conative is a "nonsensuous representing-as-good" (Kriegel 2015, 74) and that the "fundamental form of our conative experience is a proprietary phenomenology of deciding-and-then-trying" (Kriegel 2015, 72)

Should we think of emotional responses as a non-sensuous representing-as-good that has the phenomenology of deciding-and-then-trying? The following reasons speak against this: 1) emotional responses are not non-sensuous, 2) they do not include a deciding (or the phenomenology of deciding), and 3) as argued before, they are not well described as having representational content. What they do share with conative states, then, is the phenomenology of "trying". Let me elaborate each of these points a bit. 1) We described emotional responses as a felt pull toward the object in a motivating way, where there might be a kind of pleasure and displeasure involved, but not more. That felt pull, which includes a form of pleasure, seems quite sensuous. And that seems to go against it being a conative state, in Kriegel's sense. Kriegel seems to agree that when there is pleasure involved, it cannot be conative: "pleasure seems too sensory, or sensuous to qualify as conative." (Kriegel 2015, 74).[25] That is, one of the main differences between emotional

---

25 He then adds: "To enjoy something is not an act of the will!" (Kriegel 2015, 74). This second com-

responses and conative states is that emotional responses *are* sensuous, as they include a form of pleasure (or displeasure). 2) Emotional responses clearly do not include a form of deciding (and do not have the phenomenology of deciding either). We said that they are spontaneous, exactly in the sense that they are an immediate response to an object, event, or state of affairs. It is exactly because they are not belief-like, cognitive, or connected to thought that they do not include a form of deciding. 3) Emotional responses are not a form of representing-as-good, because they do not have (sophisticated) representational content. Having a spontaneous attraction does mean that the object is taken to be good by the subject *in some sense*, but not in the sense of representing-as-good. Note that Kriegel also distinguishes between "representing-as-good" (conative states), and a more cognitive form of representation, namely "representing-as-true *p*'s being good" (beliefs). (Kriegel 2015, 74) The difference lies in the fact that a conative state does not have the goodness as part of the representational content, but as part of the attitude. In belief, the attitude is about truth, and the representational content about the goodness of *p*. In a conative state, the goodness is part of the attitude, and the representational content is *p*. Now, our point here is that emotional responses do not even have a representational content of *p*, in contrast to the conative states. Again, they have some kind of phenomenology (that includes pleasure, and thus in that sense make the object seem good), but that phenomenology is not representational. With an emotional response one is drawn toward the object (in a sensuous way), and this feels a certain way, but one does not represent the object. This is a clear contrast to conative states.

If one were to allow for a less sophisticated form of representation, however, one could say that in emotional responses, a form of "representing-as-good" *is* involved (while the other contrasts to conative states would still remain). That is, in that case, one could understand emotional responses to involve a *different* kind of representing-as-good than conative states (a more primitive one). And lastly, emotional responses seem to share the phenomenology of "trying" with conative states. We said that (in contrast to desire in a pleasure-based account), emotional responses are inherently connected to acting. The subject who experiences a spontaneous attraction *moves* toward the object. Thus, one *already acts* (in some sense) just by experiencing emotional responses. Hence, emotional responses do have some over-

---

ment only makes sense if one realizes that Kriegel understands conative phenomenology along the lines of "the phenomenology of doing". That is, the what-it-is-like of doing something (or of causing something, etc.) is an essential part of conative phenomenology according to him, as he ends up thinking that the conative has the phenomenology of deciding-and-then-trying. Hence, he sees a deep difference between "enjoying something" and "doing something", the latter involving an act of the will (and the former involving pleasure).

lap with the "phenomenal signature of the conative". They are a (more primitive) felt way of taking the object to be good, and they share the phenomenology of "trying" with conative states, in the sense that by experiencing an emotional response, one *already acts* by moving toward it.

Let us now consider two potential objections before we move on to the normative proposal in § 1.2.

First, one may wonder whether my account works better for aversion than for attraction. We already noted that the latter kind of case requires a slightly different description than the former because, even though attraction is in some sense also a movement *away* from something (the vegetarian sandwich), we are *attracted* to something else. This contrast to aversion may seem to raise a complication for my claim that spontaneous attraction is object-directed only in the minimal sense that I called Object-Directed 2. Namely, it may seem that when I bite into my vegetarian sandwich and have a spontaneous attraction to meat, I respond to an object that is not there: the meat. And now it may seem that the meat just has to be mentally represented (in a sophisticated way) in the case of attraction in order for the emotional response to happen. In response to this objection, let me specify the view that in cases like this, it is precisely speaking not a current object that elicits the emotional response, but rather a perceptual memory, which is in turn elicited by the current state of affairs. In the case of a spontaneous attraction to have meat in one's vegetarian sandwich, it is the perceptual memory of eating meat prior to having become a vegetarian. A perceptual memory of this kind, elicited by a current state of affairs, does not need to include a mental representation. We can think of it as a form of spontaneous association between the current and the former perception. Once the perceptual memory has elicited the spontaneous attraction, the habit (of avoiding meat) is disrupted.

Note also that not all cases of spontaneous attraction have to rely on perceptual memory. A vegetarian subject might also be attracted to a steak that is in front of her right now without ever having tried meat before and without necessarily representing the steak as a steak in her mental state. But the perceptual memory helps us make sense of cases like the one where a vegetarian sandwich, in the absence of any meat, has a similar effect. This has interesting consequences for the ethics of how we train our emotional responses: perhaps one can only be a fully consistent and happy vegetarian if one never tried and enjoyed meat in the first place (or fully forgot about the properties of meat that were experienced as enjoyable or satisfying). For present purposes, I cannot pursue this line of argument further, but I think it has interesting consequences for how we think of the role of emotions and memory in ethical habituation.

Second, someone may object that the object of spontaneous aversion and attraction is a *particular*, and it might thus be mysterious how the emotional response can be generalized without some cognitive mental operation. The emotional response is to *this* steak, to *this* meatless sandwich. And this may seem to be in conflict with my claim that what is disrupted is something general: the (habit of) eating meat, for example. Would it not seem, the objection runs, that for the disruption to apply to something general, the subject must move from the particular object to some general content, and that this involves mental representation? To respond to this objection, let me first make the involved problem of generalization more detailed. It seems that there are *two* generalizations involved in the move from a current aversion to a steak in front of me to the habit of eating meat in general: first, the aversion is relevant not just *right now* but for eating steaks more generally, also in the future. Second, the aversion is not just against *steaks* but against a broader class of things, namely, against meat. How can I explain these two generalizations without resorting to a representation of some concepts involved, such as the concept of acting over time and the concept of, let us say, meat as the broader class under which a steak is subsumed?

Let me concede that the subject might have to experience the aversion several times in order to realize that this is not just a one-off or temporary dislike, but a general aversion. She might also have to experience the aversion to several different kinds of meat in order to realize that the aversion is not just directed at steak but at meat in general (or at several kinds of meat). This concession is not to downplay or preclude the idea that we can sometimes also come to such general insights in one instance of experiencing an aversion. It is just to say that one might sometimes need to experience several instances of the aversion in order to get the scope of the aversion right. But even if one needs several such instances, this does not show that one needs a representation or other cognitive content in order to get the scope of the aversion right. In other words, if one does not react properly to an experience of aversion, the problem involved is merely an epistemic one, namely, the epistemic problem of knowing the scope of the aversion.

But this response might not go far enough. One might claim that I have now simply posited that the aversion has a certain general scope (over time and over a class of things), and that it is a matter of epistemic skill to get the scope right (sometimes through multiple attempts). But the challenge was to presume that the aversion is to a *particular*, not a class of things (or to a certain scope), and thus that some cognitive operation is needed to generalize from this. Ultimately, I think, then, the challenge relies on the assumption that the aversion picks out a particular, while my response relies on the assumption that the aversion already picks out something more general, while we do not always know the scope of generality in the moment of the response. Without being able to go into much detail, it is worth noting that this parallels an open debate within the philosophy of perception, namely, on the question whether perceptual experiences pick out particulars as particulars, or as something more general. A Humean would claim that what we perceive in a particular are several *general properties* that come together, and these properties can, of course, then be repeated in future particulars, in various combinations. A Kantian would claim that we perceive particulars *as particulars* with our sensibility, while they have to be subsumed under a concept in order to be a unit. A rationalist would claim that we understand each particular to fall under a range of predicates, and thus perceive its particularity as the unique combination of some predicates. It seems that I need to subscribe to some form of Humean account of *general properties* as described here if I want to say that the non-cognitive emotional response, when it responds to a particular in a certain moment, nevertheless picks out something more general, whose scope can be discovered over time.[26] I am not able to defend this Humean account of general properties in the scope of this short book, but do not see any obvious difficulties in subscribing to it.

---

26 Note that with this commitment I foreclose on a different route of arguing for a unique role of emotions in normative guidance, which has been more prominently defended in philosophy. That is, it has been argued that emotions, or more generally the affective capacities, pick out the particulars in a situation, while the rational capacities pick out the general or universal.

Toulmin (1981), for example, while arguing that a casuistic ethics that considers each situation separately is superior to applying general rules, implicitly assumes that the first is achieved by cultivating a *feeling* for the particular cases at hand, while applying a general rule would be done by *cognitive* capacities (The Tyranny of Principles).

This assumption Toulmin shares with Broadie (1991, 198) when she argues against the "Grand End" view of practical wisdom (which would make practical wisdom into a kind of cognitive following of general rules). And the same idea of emotions being particularist and cognitive capacities universalist is implied when McDowell (1998b) argues that *because* the virtuous agent can rely on her emotions rather than having to think about her actions, she can act appropriately in every situation instead of rigidly applying a rule.

Such arguments that proceed from a particularist account of emotions usually rely on a quasi-perceptual account of emotions, that is, they see emotions as a capacity for value-perception. This is made explicit, for example, in Achtenberg (2002), who claims that what distinguishes "mere" (that is, sensory) perceiving from the perception of value is that the latter is accompanied by pleasure or pain (thus affective), while they are otherwise the same kind of mental act. While this analogy between sense-perception and emotion seems intuitive, I think it is too simplified if we do not attend to the disanalogies. One of them, I would argue, is exactly that while sense-perception is directed at particulars and can only be generalized with the help of rational capacities, emotional responses can themselves be directed at general properties (hence I would not accept the Humean account of general properties for sense-perception, but for emotional responses). See Whiting (2012) for a more thorough argument why emotions should not be equated with the perception of value, and see Burnyeat (2002) and Caston (2015) for a more general account of how the affections are related to sense-perception.

Now, equipped with this characterization of emotional responses as non-cognitive object-directed feeling states, we can turn to the question of how they can guide us in moral and ethical decisions.

1.2 How Can an Emotional Response Be a Normative Guide?

Emotional responses, I argue, can normatively guide us in our actions in a distinctive way, namely, by giving us *negative* reasons, to act against our given habits and beliefs. That is, they play a negative role in guiding our actions, by telling us what *not* to do. They do not, my argument continues, play a substantive *positive* role in normative guidance. In making this specification, I explore the limits of the normative role of emotional responses.

Let me first clarify what I intend to capture by the distinction of a positive and negative role in normative guidance. A mental state can play a negative role in normative guidance in the sense that it *disrupts* a held belief or a habit. It prompts us to act *against* a belief or habit to do otherwise, or to act *without* a specific belief or habit. By contrast, a mental state can play a positive role in normative guidance in the sense that it helps the subject come up with a *new* belief or course of action, once the established beliefs or habits are not available anymore. In contrast to both of these we can also imagine a neutral case, where the mental state is not disruptive and not suggesting anything new, but rather "in agreement" with the current doings and beliefs of the subject. This neutral case might also play a significant normative role in some contexts. But by focusing on the positive and negative roles alone, I restrict myself to contexts where *change* is needed for moral and ethical behavior. Thus, I am stipulating here a premise that I defend later on: that it is in some cases normatively important to be able to reconsider one's beliefs and habits as one goes along. But first, I will consider how emotional responses could play negative and positive roles in normative guidance.

1.2.1 The Negative Role

How can a spontaneous aversion or a spontaneous attraction be a negative normative guide for us? Let us imagine our habitual meat eater again. Until now, she has habitually eaten a substantial amount of meat every week. After experiencing the spontaneous aversion I sketched earlier, she must reconsider her habit. Recall, the aversion is not in any way cognitive. Any kind of rationalization and formulation of reasons would come *after* she is prompted by the emotional response to reconsider. So, what does the work here is instead the *disruptive nature* of a spontaneous aversion. The subject *cannot* simply continue with her previous habit, at least not in an undisturbed way. She might very well decide, after reconsideration, that she still wants her amount of meat every week, unchanged. Or she might decide to change her habit after just one occurrence of an aversion, or after several occurrences of the aversion. What she decides is not so much of importance here (although I do think that there are right or wrong answers to such questions). What is of importance is that *she is prompted to reconsider* due to the disruptive nature of the emotional response. Without the emotional response, there would not have been *occasion* to reconsider her meat consumption (I will turn to potential objections to this necessity claim below). It was a well-established habit that, absent this occasion for reconsideration, would have rigidly shaped her conduct.

Compare again the case of aversion and the case of attraction. How is it that a spontaneous *attraction* plays the kind of *negative* role I describe here? Does an attraction not rather do the opposite, positively suggesting new kinds of actions? However, consider the vegetarian subject again. Her spontaneous *attraction* to meat in her sandwich prompts her to reconsider her habits and beliefs too. Hence, even a spontaneous attraction plays a negative role: a previous habit is *disrupted.* The attraction prompts the agent to act *against* a belief to do otherwise, or to act *without* a specific belief at all.

Before I consider potential objections, let me sketch the potential positive role of emotional responses.

1.2.2 The Positive Role

Let us imagine you have experienced a spontaneous aversion to a given steak, and thereby prima facie to your habitual steak eating in general. In most cases, this is not yet sufficient to know *what you should do instead.* In this example, you could cut down on meat by cutting out your lunch altogether, or you could replace the meat with vegetarian products, or you could replace it with other proteins, and so on. There is often a myriad of ways of responding to such a situation, and so far, the only thing you know is that your habit has been stopped in its tracks. This gives you room to reconsider. What you need, then, is a new way of regulating some domain of your life. But how do you come up with the appropriate new actions and beliefs? Presumably, the capacity of imagination is necessary in order to come up with anything new.[27] In other words, if you have to figure out a new course of ac-

---

27 There is a longstanding debate in Aristotelian approaches in what way reason is involved in imagination (*phantasia*) and in what way, if at all, non-rational capacities, such as emotions,

tion, then what you do, roughly, is to imaginatively explore. You may mentally simulate various options, aiming to get clear about which ones you like in which ways.[28]

Let us take this as our starting point. We can set aside the question of how precisely we are to think of the relation between imagination and reasoning. They seem to be intertwined (cf. Schellenberg, 2013) and at least some modes of imagining might be describable as counterfactual reasoning (and thereby as cognitive) (cf. Byrne, 2005, 2016). Hence, we cannot plausibly argue that imagining is exhausted by non-cognitive emotional responses. Indeed, it seems difficult to argue that they play a central role at all in this process: they are, after all, *responses*, and as such, they need something to respond to, rather than coming up with a course of action by themselves. But we might find a smaller-scale role for them to play. Once we have imagined different potential new courses of action, our emotional responses to them can play the same role they play when they disrupt old habits: a feeling of spontaneous aversion might be an indication that something about this new course of action is not right. A feeling of spontaneous attraction might be an indication that we are on the right track. And in this way, they still play a negative role "within" the process of positively coming up with something new: we have good reason to listen to such emotional responses when imaginatively coming up with a potential new course of action, even if the spontaneous aversion or attraction goes *against* other reasons, or even if there is no reason to find for the spontaneous aversion or attraction at all.

In other words, I am not claiming that the emotional responses play a substantial role in the process of coming up with a new course of action. But they do play a smaller-scale role within the process of imagining oneself in the various new courses of action, thanks to the same capacity they have in their negative role: in giving a bodily felt feedback of aversion or attraction, which might be valuable even if one has reasons to the contrary.

Now, let me consider four objections to this view.

---

might be involved. For an account of how imagination enables us to come up with new actions and beliefs, see Vogt (forthcoming-a).

28 Paul (2014) conceives of decision making as "running simulations" of choice scenarios and assigning values to them.

1.2.3 Objections

The Objection from Rigid Emotional Responses

So far, I have argued that basic emotional responses can prompt reflection on established habits and beliefs, and that this is their distinctive contribution to normative guidance. Recall, further, that I argued that our emotional responses are not simply causal and passive, but instead reflective of ways in which we, in the long run, indirectly shape our emotional attitudes. This latter line of thought, however, may give rise to an objection. Against my view, one may hold that I ascribe too much potential for disruption to emotional responses. On the contrary, one may think, emotional responses support engrained habits, to the extent that we may call these emotional responses rigid. If our emotional responses are reflective of long-term ways in which we shape habits, the thought goes, they are likely to support these very habits. Rather than be disruptive, they may seem to be stabilizing. For example, emotional responses may typically reflect a preference for the familiar and the convenient. If so, this may undermine their power to disrupt given habits and beliefs as described above.

Against this objection, let me first acknowledge that many emotional responses are indeed reflective of a preference to continue in one's set ways. My claim is not that emotional responses are always disruptive; instead, it is that they *can* be disruptive. Second, let me introduce a distinction between a weak and a strong preference for the familiar and convenient. A weak preference of this sort may simply be part of the nature of habits and beliefs, by which we regulate many of our ordinary actions. To habituate oneself, say, to regularly run in the park is, to some extent, to habituate oneself to *like* running in the park. This preference now stabilizes the habit: we feel like running in the morning if we usually run in the morning, and we look forward to having a cup of tea at moments where typically we drink tea. This kind of *weak* preference for the familiar, however, hardly undermines the ability of emotional responses to disrupt given habits and beliefs. A spontaneous aversion to running may still suggest to the subject that, in given circumstances, running may not be good for her.

However, emotional responses that *strongly* prefer the familiar or convenient seem defective. We may even think that a strong preference for the familiar and convenient is characteristic of psychological disorders. For example, our runner may realize that her reliance on having the opportunity to run is getting out of hand. She can no longer feel good about herself or go through a normal day if she does not have the chance to run extensively. Her emotional responses support this: she is upset if a schedule is set by others that prevents her from running, and so on. In her case, reconsideration cannot come from her rigidified emotional responses. Such cases, however, ordinarily count as pathological. If we find ourselves in these kinds of conditions, we realize that we need help. In non-pathological conditions, the thought is, we ourselves are able to readjust and renegotiate habits as we go along, prompted by emotional responses of the sort that interest me.

Non-defective emotional responses, then, are not able to disrupt *strong and pathological* rigidity. Instead, the weak rigidity that emotional responses can disrupt simply is the stability of established non-pathological habits and beliefs. Here the emotional responses offer a sort of input that distinctively supplements "mere" intellectual thought.

Our runner, say, may have *thought* about the fact that regular exercise is a good thing. No utilitarian calculus or other theoretical method, however, can do the job of identifying for the agent which kind of exercising she likes sufficiently for her to actually come to like it in a non-pathological way – a way that permits flexibility rather than rigid control. For these kinds of "steering" – the identification of options that one likes, to the extent that one can adopt them as habitual ways of regulating some domain of one's life – agents rely on their emotional responses. These emotional responses, I submit, thereby play a distinctive role in normative guidance, one that, I argue, *necessarily* supplements the roles of reflection, deliberation, and so on.

The Objection against the Necessity Claim

It is one thing, however, to ascribe to emotional responses a distinctive contribution to our normative lives, and another thing to claim that without them, certain kinds of normative guidance are impossible. It is the latter, stronger claim that I want to defend. Emotional responses, the claim goes, are *necessary* for us to reconsider our habits and beliefs. Against this, someone might claim that we can also arrive at such a reflective attitude by reasoning alone. However, consider this: Have you ever, without also feeling an adverse feeling, been moved to say: "I am going to change my habit or my mind about this matter x now"? This does not seem very plausible. In other words, it seems that reasoning by itself does not create the kind of motivation to reconsider one's ways. An adverse feeling, by contrast, will stop you in your tracks in this way. An objection to this could be: even though one might not "out of the blue" have occasion to reconsider one's habits without an emotional response, sometimes we *think through* certain matters and come to the conclusion that we have to change our ways. Or we hear a report about, let us say, how bad meat consumption is for the environment, and thus, again, come to the (purely intellectual) conclusion that we have to eat less meat. However, I am challenging this with the claim that even in such a scenario, the change would not come about without an emotional response entailed in the complex of mental states going on. Let us say you watch a documentary on TV. Your usual meat consumption is a deep habit, so it is not like you have nothing to lose, as it will take some effort for you to stop eating so much meat. The report lingers on in your mind, first without changing anything. But slowly, you start feeling unwell about the thought of eating so much meat. The next time the steak lies in front of you, it hits you: a definite aversion against eating so much meat again. Whatever role the report played in the coming about of your aversion, you would *not* have stopped eating so much meat if you had not experienced this aversion too.

But what about other *affective* ways of disrupting habits and beliefs? For example, *courage* might demand of you to change your mind in a given situation and to go against your habit. In this case, a sophisticated emotion leads you to reconsider, and thus *basic* emotional responses are not necessary for this capacity. My response to this is similar: this sophisticated emotion would not have been possible without entailing a basic emotional response. For you to realize that you need to be courageous right now (for example, to eat the synthetic protein in your sandwich instead of real meat), you *also* have to feel a certain aversion against simply going on with your habit: you feel unwell to just continue. Once you feel this spontaneous aversion, you can build up the courage to do the action against your habit. This argument is not unheard of: Hume claimed that "reason alone cannot be a motive to the will" (Cohon 2018). Our account agrees with Hume on this point. We will address in more detail at the end of Chapter 3 in what ways our account is to be understood as agreeing and disagreeing with sentimentalist moral theories.

The Objection against the Two-Mode View

Now, both for their negative and for their smaller-scale positive role, one might ask whether the emotional responses really only have these two "modes" of operating: an aversion or an attraction. Do we not also have other basic feelings, such as, for instance, fearful or sad responses, which perhaps still do not include any beliefs or other cognitive processes? And would not such other modes of basic emotional responses perhaps change the way we view their capacities to play a negative or a positive role in normative guidance? I will claim that it makes sense to stick to the "two-modes model" of emotional responses, but that it would not change my account of normative guidance by emotional responses in its basics if we allowed for more such modes.

Whiting argues that there are at least four more emotions that can be individuated by their phenomenology alone (without referring to any thoughts or beliefs attached to them): fear, anger, joy, and sadness (cf. Whiting, 2006, 267). Together with spontaneous attraction and spontaneous aversion, we would thus have a six-modes view, a view in which there are six basic emotional responses. Again, none of them has a representational structure, but they all are object-directed, and can thus be normative guides. How would this affect my account? I think it would not change the basic tenets: if there are more than two basic emotional responses, then there would be *more ways* in which the emotional responses could play their mainly negative role in normative guidance. But there would not be *more roles* for them to play. In other words, an old habit could perhaps be disrupted not only by the feeling of a spontaneous aversion or attraction, but *also* by a fearful, angry, sad, or joyful feeling. But the contribution itself would still be the same: the disruption of a habit or belief, allowing the spontaneous response to have the negative role of giving reason *not* to do something. Most pertinently, the new modes of basic emotional responses would not give the emotional responses the capacity to make a more substantive contribution to the *positive* role in normative guidance. Just to also have the option of a sad or angry spontaneous emotional response, not just an aversive or attractive one, does not give us the option of coming up with a new course of action through the emotional responses alone. But that does not make the six-modes view an untenable one, according to my account: we might well have these differently "flavored" kinds of emotional responses that disrupt our beliefs and habits in different ways. I will stay agnostic regarding whether we should adopt more such modes or not.

However, remember that there is something specific about the two modes of aversion and attraction that might not be satisfied by other potentially basic forms of emotional response: they are directional in an immediately motivating way. If I experience a spontaneous aversion to a certain object, this disrupts my habits and beliefs by *pulling* me away from my current doings. Similarly, if I experience a spontaneous attraction to something I usually do not consider, this disrupts my habits and beliefs by *pulling* me away from my current doings. This is thanks to their directionality together with its motivating force. It is hard to see how other potentially basic forms of emotional responses could satisfy this criterion: feeling sad, fearful, or joyful does not pull me away from my current doings, at least not by itself. Hence, perhaps these other modes would be lacking an important prerequisite for the specific kind of object-directedness involved in the normative guidance of emotional responses, a prerequisite that is given in aversion and attraction due to their motivating directionality.

The Objection against the Importance of the Capacity to Reconsider

But is it really the case that *the capacity to reconsider* is of such normative importance? I would suggest so: imagine someone who is able to reconsider their old habits and beliefs, versus someone who is not. If we encounter someone who lacks the capacity to feel bad about their habits, we blame them *for that incapacity alone.* This blame is independent of the blame we might direct at someone for not changing their ways, or of the blame we might direct at someone for having bad habits or beliefs in the first place. Hence, we expect morally good agents to be at least able to *consider* the possibility that their habits are bad, or that their beliefs are wrong. This corroborates an important assumption of this chapter, for which I will argue more thoroughly in the fourth chapter of the book: minimally, good moral and ethical behavior includes an ability to reconsider. And I have argued that emotional responses are uniquely qualified and necessary for us to be able to do so.

Conclusion of this Chapter

I have argued in this chapter that emotional responses, understood as basic and non-cognitive, can be independent normative guides in our moral and ethical lives. They make a unique contribution to decision-making and to the ways in which we shape and re-shape our habits. On this account, emotional responses are non-representational, object-directed feelings. In order to defend this view, I needed to show that there is a kind of object-directedness that does not depend on a representational structure in the mental state.

The contribution of the emotional responses consists in giving us *negative* reasons in our acting, namely, in disrupting engrained habits and beliefs. While they cannot play a positive role in the sense of coming up with new courses of action, they still play a smaller-scale role within imagination when doing so, namely, by helping us assess potential choice scenarios as we imagine them. I also argued that this general structure of the normative guidance of basic emotional responses would not change if we had to assume additional modes of emotional responses besides spontaneous aversion and attraction. And yet, on the account I offered, aversion and attraction are of special interest for the theory of normative guidance.

In the next chapter, I will take a step back in order to offer a framework in the philosophy of mind that corroborates a distinction that was implicitly introduced in this first chapter: the distinction between feeling and cognitive states. I will argue that this distinction is fundamental, in the sense that all mental states can be divided into these two classes, no matter what else can be said about them. That is, this distinction is not supposed to be the *only* fundamental distinction one can make in the mental realm. Indeed, we will consider others in the second part of the chapter and see that they are orthogonal to our distinction. The claim is "merely" that besides these other distinctions, the distinction between feeling and cognitive states is an important and informative one, and cannot be reduced to any of those others.

I will maintain that each of these two classes of mental states has a unique feature that essentially characterizes all instances of its kind. This fundamental difference between cognitive and feeling states will strengthen my claim that the contribution of emotional responses to normative guidance cannot be replaced by cognitive capacities.

Chapter 2: Feeling States and Cognitive States

In this chapter, I take a closer look at the various instances of cognitive and non-cognitive mental states that have been mentioned so far. My proposal will be that all mental states fall into one of two general classes, either the class of feeling states or the class of cognitive states. In other words, I propose that, irrespective of what else might be true of each mental state, it belongs to one of these two classes. Some examples for the class of feeling states besides emotional responses are feeling fearful, feeling joyful, etc., and an example for the class of cognitive states besides beliefs are inferences (we will get to a more detailed description in a moment). I will argue that each of these two classes has a unique feature that essentially characterizes all instances of its kind, and that the division into these two classes highlights an important and interesting difference between all mental states in general. Similar divisions in such categories are familiar, to the extent that the distinction may appear uncontroversial.[29] Surely, the thought might be, there is a distinction of this sort. However, even a brief glance at related distinctions—between emotion and cognition, desire and belief, and so on—suggests that the specifics of how precisely we formulate and explicate the distinction matter.

My claim is that on a basic level and in rough terms, all mental states can be primarily sorted into either one or the other, feeling states or cognitive states, barring some special cases, where a mental state might be a compound of the two.[30]

---

[29] At least in psychology, such divisions are often taken for granted. See for example Gerrans and Sander (2014), who distinguish between implicit—associated with intuitive, emotional activities—and explicit—"rational"—processing of information. In philosophy too, we often find similar distinctions implied, for example when a distinction is made between an inquiry that is geared toward practical questions—in which it is maintained that affective capacities play an essential role—and a theoretical inquiry that is geared toward finding necessary truths, pursued by rational capacities only (e.g., Tenenbaum, 2007). Of course, making such a distinction has its beginnings already in Ancient philosophy, and it is occasionally revived through Ancient thinkers in contemporary philosophy. Burnyeat (2006), e.g., revives the Platonic idea that the human psyche is divided into three parts, the appetitive, the spirited, and the rational one. The first two parts are considered affective (as desires and social emotions, respectively), while the third part is what makes us capable of rational thinking. And McCready-Flora, e.g., distinguishes in Aristotle "belief (doxa), a form of rational cognition, from imagining (phantasia), which we share with non-rational animals" (2014, 394).

I will argue that my distinction between feeling and cognitive states is rather specific to one criterion per mental state, in contrast to being quite all-encompassing, as the here mentioned divisions seem to be.

[30] An example of such a compound would most notably be what I have called "sophisticated emotions" so far—but we will only get to the nature of the unity of sophisticated emotions and similar mental states in Chapter 4.

https://doi.org/10.1515/9783110780932-005

But what exactly does that mean? What is the unique feature that essentially characterizes either kind of mental state?

I will argue that what essentially characterizes feeling states is their phenomenology, that is, each feeling state is best characterized and individuated through asking how it *feels* to be in this mental state.[31] This is best understood, I propose, in terms of phenomenal consciousness as opposed to access consciousness: What counts is the *experience* of the mental state that characterizes and individuates each of the feeling states, not the subject's mere consciousness *that* she is in some feeling state (access consciousness).[32] That is, what characterizes feeling states is that there is a specific kind of *quality or phenomenology* to being in that state. So, the idea is:

1) Any mental state that is best characterized by how it feels to experience this mental state is a *feeling state*.

By contrast, a cognitive state is not essentially characterized by its phenomenology.[33] What unites cognitive states and makes cognitive states what they are is their *impetus toward coherence.* That is, cognitive states essentially have an impetus toward coherence, both *among* each other, as also with *other* attitudes and states of the subject. Hence, the idea is:

2) Any mental state that is best characterized by having an impetus toward coherence (where incoherence would cause cognitive dissonance[34], that is, a form of mental stress) is a *cognitive state.*

---

31 This fits well with some parts of Aristotle's theory of emotions. According to Cooper, Aristotle's theory of emotions is to be found in the *Rhetoric* (Aristotle, 1984), and has three central aspects. Emotions 1) are affected (ta pathē) states of mind, 2) arise from the ways events or conditions strike the one affected, and 3) are at the same time desires (i. e., motivational) for reactive behaviors (1998, 422). While 1 and 2 fit well with how I define feeling states in general here, 3 only seems to be the case for a more specific kind of feeling state, namely, emotional responses.

It is worth noting that not everyone agrees that the *Rhetoric* is the best place to look for Aristotle's theory of emotions. However, notable scholars agree with this, such as Rapp (2010).

32 The distinction between phenomenal consciousness and access consciousness was introduced by Ned Block (1995).

33 This is, thus, a straightforward rejection of cognitive phenomenology. Cognitive phenomenology is the idea that cognitive states have "proprietary" phenomenal character (Pitt, 2004), meaning roughly that they have a *sui generis* phenomenal character. There is a way it feels like to be in a certain cognitive state. Various authors have argued in different ways for this (Chudnoff, 2015; Bayne and Montague, 2011; Strawson, 1994; Siewert, 1998; Horgan and Tienson, 2002; Kriegel, 2015; and Horgan and Graham, 2012).

34 The concept of *cognitive dissonance*, as psychologists understand it, was first introduced in Festinger (1957).

A premise (or a result) of Festinger's research is that human beings *very generally* strive for psychological coherence in order to function mentally. By contrast, here I argue that *not all* mental

Let me clarify what I call an "impetus" here. For, it is important not to understand this in a way that suggests that cognitive states have "a life on their own", as it were. I do not want to propose, in other words, that cognitive states somehow move toward coherence by themselves. Rather, it must always be the subject who bears these mental states who moves toward coherence in regard to them. Hence, the "impetus toward coherence" is an abbreviation for a more complicated idea. What I claim, when I say that cognitive states have an impetus toward coherence, is, in more detail, that any cognitive state is *shaped in a way that moves the subject of the mental state toward coherence.* I will clarify further below what I mean by "moving" here. The claim is that the structure of these mental states creates a tendency in the subject to aim for coherence among these mental states.

The following analogy helps clarify this idea: a cognitive mental state is a bit like a piece of a puzzle. In principle, you can stack puzzle pieces on each other, or next to each other, in *any* way you want. They do not necessarily *have to* fit into each other. But the very shape and structure of the puzzle pieces still *"suggest"* to you to stack and place them in a certain way: in a way in which they fit together. In other words, the shape of each puzzle piece creates a *tendency* toward placing them in a way so that they fit next to each other, in interlocking ways. The shape of the puzzle pieces "moves" the subject toward arranging the pieces this way, rather than in some other way. Similarly, the structure of cognitive mental states "moves" the subject of the mental state toward coherence, that is, toward relating them to each other in a way so that they fit together.[35]

---

states need to be coherent in a subject's mental life. Hence, one could also see my thesis here as a clarification of the theory of cognitive dissonance, by making it a narrower claim: *Some* mental states indeed need to be coherent with each other in order for the subject's mental life to function well. And that is an interesting finding and has profound consequences. However, there also seem to be mental states that do *not* have this character. Hence, it is not true that a human being's mental life *as a whole* needs to be coherent in order to function well (which is also an interesting finding that has profound consequences).

35 One might want to ask "who or what makes the movement here?" The way I described this process, the process of how the shape or structure of cognitive mental states creates a *tendency* for the subject to "move" in one direction rather than another, leaves it mysterious where the agency is, it might be objected.

I adopt a viewpoint here that is the starting-point of many sociological theories. The idea is that our (physical and non-physical) environment predisposes us to do certain things rather than others. For example, to put gender-markers on doors of bathrooms predisposes us to choose one door rather than the other when we go to the bathroom. There is no physical restraint for us to do otherwise. It is clearly possible to go either way. But most likely, we will conform to how our environment predisposed us to act. Here, the structure of our environment created a *tendency* for us to move in a certain way rather than another. I take the structure of cognitive states to

A caveat about this analogy: I do not want to argue that cognitive mental states are like puzzle pieces in any other respect than just described above. Particularly, I do not want to argue that there is a holism involved in cognitive mental states. With puzzle pieces, it is not just that they fit next to each other when placed the right way, it is also that they create one specific whole if all of the pieces are placed correctly. There is a finished "picture" or whole at the end. I do not think that cognitive mental states work that way—that we can arrive at a point when *all* cognitive states are placed just right in relation to each other and thus form a "perfect" whole of some sort. Relatedly, another disanalogy is that for puzzle pieces, there is usually one *and only one* piece that fits for each side of a puzzle piece. By contrast, for any cognitive state, there are *several* cognitive states that are coherent ("fit") with it, and several that are not. There is, again, no one "perfect" piece that fits for each cognitive state, or for each part or aspect of it. So, the structure of a cognitive mental state preconditions the subject in *some* respects how she can combine it with other mental states in terms of coherence, but it does not do so in as narrow a way as the pieces of a puzzle do.[36]

Nevertheless, the analogy with puzzle pieces seems helpful in thinking about how the shape of something (like the structure of cognitive states) can *precondition* how it is being combined with other instances of its kind. And this preconditioning, in the case of cognitive states, can be described as a way of *moving* the subject toward coherence, even though the "moving" here does not imply any kind of active drive or push coming from the mental state. The moving involved is rather to be described in the following way: *If* the subject moves at all in regard to this kind of mental state, she will move under the preconditions provided by this mental state, and in the case of cognitive states, these preconditions are concerns of *coherence*. And this way of preconditioning the subject in how she combines these mental states, namely, that she combines them in a way that aims for coherence, I call

---

work similarly. They cannot force us to seek out the most coherent beliefs, but they strongly predispose us to do so. It would be amiss to ask exactly who or what is the subject and who or what is the object of the movement here. It is an interaction between the given structure (of the cognitive mental state) and the subject's mind's susceptibility of acting according to it.

36 Considering these caveats about the analogy with puzzle pieces, a more fitting analogy would perhaps have been one with Legos: as with cognitive mental states, there is no necessary holism involved with Legos, where a final picture would be achieved when all pieces are arranged the right way. And as for cognitive mental states, there is usually not one exclusive piece of Lego that fits into another piece of Lego, but rather, several pieces are compatible with several other pieces. I still stayed with the analogy of puzzle pieces, however, because these caveats about the analogy brought to light interesting considerations about cognitive mental states that would otherwise have remained implicit.

the "impetus toward coherence" of cognitive states. Even though in the following I say that cognitive mental states "have this impetus", I want it to be clear that this is only shorthand for the more complex phenomenon described here.

Now let us go back to the more general claim that on a basic level, all mental states are either feeling states or cognitive states. How far does this claim go? I argue that the essential features of each kind of mental state are *exclusively essential* to its kind. In other words, feeling states do not essentially have an impetus toward coherence, while cognitive states do not essentially have a unique phenomenology when one experiences them.[37] Either kind of mental state might have some instances that also have features of the other kind but without playing an essential role in what they are.

An obvious critical question would be to ask whether there are not any mental states that are *equally well* characterized by both distinctive features, that is, by how it feels to experience them, and also by having an impetus toward coherence. After all, these two features prima facie do not seem to conceptually or psychologically exclude each other conceptually or psychologically. My proposal is that at least *most* mental states fall into one or the other class, though there might be exceptions, the compounds. One such exception might be what I call sophisticated emotions, which I take to be compounds of some sort of cognition and feeling. It is interesting to ask whether we think of the compounds as a single mental state or not. That is, these compounds might be blends, as opposed to simple "additions" of a feeling state with a cognitive state:[38] their cognitive dimension and feeling dimension might be related in such a way that they cannot be disentangled. Alternatively, the compounds might be analyzable into divisible components. However, I postpone this question to the end of the book, where we can ask in what sense the sophisticated emotions might be more than just an "aggregate" of two different kinds of mental states. For now, I will say that even if there were mental states that fall into a third class, the feeling-cognition distinction would still be useful as a conceptual distinction.

For the purposes of illustration, let me now in the following two sections apply this basic distinction of two different kinds of mental states to the mental states that have been mentioned in Chapter 1 of this book. Most obviously, emotional responses are feeling states, while beliefs are cognitive states. I will henceforth use these two as the paradigmatic members for each of the kinds of mental states.[39]

---

37 This, again, is a straightforward rejection of the idea of cognitive phenomenology.

38 See Boyle (2016) for an argument against additive theories of the mental.

39 I will often go back and forth between sometimes talking about feeling and cognitive states in general, and sometimes talking about emotional responses and beliefs in particular, in the rest of the book. I do this exactly because I take emotional responses and beliefs to be "typical examples"

And because we have already investigated the nature of emotional responses and beliefs in the first chapter, we are now in a position to understand what does and does not follow from the fact that a mental state belongs to one or the other kind.

The fact that, for example, emotional responses are feeling states helps us see that at least one thing does not necessarily follow from this classification: it does not follow from being a feeling state that a mental state cannot be object-directed. In fact, very few things do necessarily follow from being an instance of one or the other kind; the only thing that does necessarily follow is that the mental state is either essentially characterized by its phenomenology or by its impetus toward coherence.

Let me also remark that while this basic distinction into two kinds of mental states, a feeling and a cognitive one, might initially look similar to Kahneman's well-known distinction between system 1 and system 2, it is quite different. Kahneman (2011) maintains that there are two systems with which we "think": system 1 is an immediate, emotional one, and system 2 is slower, deliberative, and more inclined to abide by the laws of logic. First, we should note that "think" is used in a loose sense here. Kahneman is not considering two kinds of cognition. Instead, roughly speaking, he considers two ways in which subjects "come up" with mental attitudes to some intentional object ("X is to be avoided", "Y is to be done", etc.), which he divides into what he calls system 1 and system 2.

While there are some superficial overlaps with what I am about to argue, I want to make it clear that the distinction I am introducing is based on a different thought than Kahneman's. Namely, I am saying no more and no less than the following. Whenever the core characteristic of a given state is how it *feels* to be in that state, we are dealing with one kind of state, namely, a feeling state. And whenever the state's core characteristic is to have an impetus toward coherence, we are dealing with another kind of state, namely, a cognitive one.

It so happens that Kahneman also distinguishes what one could call a feeling state (what he calls "emotional") from what one could call a cognitive state (what he calls "logical"). But as will become clear, Kahneman's distinction builds on quite a different thought than my division—his starting-point is that one system is slower and more systematic, while the other system is faster and a bit rash. An important difference to my account is that Kahneman seems to think that his division into a slow and a fast "system" implies all kinds of other distinctions, such as that one system is emotional and the other what he calls "logical", that I think

---

of their kind. However, the terms are not interchangeable, as feeling and cognitive states are a general class of mental states, while emotional responses and beliefs are specific instances of these classes.

do not follow. I do not find such "combined" claims helpful when it comes to the mental states involved here. In particular, I see no reason why one would necessarily need to assume that feeling states work in faster ways than the cognitive ones. Surely, I would argue, *some* feeling states are slow to arise and to subside again. And surely, *some* cognitive states come and go quickly. Moreover, Kahneman seems to imply with his division that *in virtue* of being slower, system 2 is more "logical". Again, this seems to combine several characterizations in a way that is by no means necessary. We can certainly imagine fast mental states being law-abiding to logic, and slow ones not. Thus, I think that equating these various characteristics with each other makes matters more confused rather than clearer, and I try to avoid such an equating of characteristics of the two kinds of mental states in my own account.

To sum up, I think there are profound differences between the kind of division Kahneman suggests and mine, despite a superficial similarity. And more importantly, I explicitly wish to reject the idea that other kinds of contrast, such as between fast and slow, can simply be inferred from my division between feeling states and cognitive states.

So, which mental states that we have mentioned in Chapter 1 are feeling states, which cognitive states, and why?

2.1 Feeling States (e. g., Emotional Responses)

To start with feeling states, let me remind the reader that we have already encountered a position in which the emotions more generally were defined as feeling states, precisely on account of their phenomenology. To repeat, Whiting argues:

> [The] view of emotion [that they just are feeling states] is strongly supported by the phenomenology of emotion—observation of which suggests that emotions are just feeling states, and that differences in emotions simply correspond to differences in how emotions feel. (Whiting, 2006, 262)

Here, Whiting not only uses the phenomenology of emotions to say most generally what they are (a class of feeling states). He also argues that this is the appropriate method to distinguish and individuate *specific* emotions. Different emotions are individuated by differences in how they feel, and they are not reducible to other kinds of feelings (they have a proprietary phenomenology):

> (...) emotional feelings are not reducible to other kinds of feelings, but rather form a distinct class of feeling state. (Whiting, 2006, 262 prior to the quotation above)

In the previous chapter, I introduced Whiting's position with a view to analyzing a specific instance of what people call an "emotion", namely, emotional responses. In this chapter, I am concerned with "feeling states." This is not a shift in terminology. Instead, my discussion at this point has a broader target: emotional responses as I conceive of them are feeling states (but not all feeling states are emotional responses). This shift allows us to analyze the issues at hand on a higher level of generality. However, a difficulty arises from the fact that the notion of "emotions" is not unitary. It includes a mixed bag of mental states, in particular "feeling states" (emotional responses), but also sophisticated emotions, which have feeling states as components.

Therefore, let us entertain the possibility that the notion of "emotions" is not a unitary concept. In such a case, one cannot infer anything necessary from having classified something as "emotion". In this book, thus, when I say "emotions", I merely refer to the "mixed bag of instances" *which are usually taken to be emotions in the literature.* And I suggested that emotional responses and sophisticated emotions are such instances.

By contrast, I am operating with the terms "feeling states" and "cognitive states" in a more technical sense. Emotional responses are an instance of feeling states among others, such as a fearful or a joyful feeling. Beliefs are an instance of cognitive states among others, such as inferences. Sophisticated emotions are a compound of feeling states and cognitive states. Hence, sophisticated emotions can be a compound of emotional responses and beliefs, but they can also be a compound of other feeling states and cognitive states.[40] So, I will try to use the notion "emotions" as little as possible. But when talking about Whiting and others, it will at times be necessary.[41]

I am concerned, then, with feeling states, and more specifically, with emotional responses. And the defining feature of this set—feeling states including emotional responses—is its phenomenology.

In a later paper, Whiting examines an important contrast, which we have drawn too, between feelings and other states, namely, the presence or lack of a representational structure. Again, he appeals to how feelings strike us phenomenologically:

---

[40] This should not be taken to suggest that just *any* concomitant feeling and cognitive states already amount to an instance of sophisticated emotions. I will say more about the unity of the two kinds of mental states in sophisticated emotions and similar compounds in Chapter 4.
[41] Whiting's own terminology, remember, is to say that emotions are a particular kind of feeling state. That is, "emotional feelings" are an instance among other feelings.

> And I now think that feelings do not have intentional properties. This is because although thoughts (and similar mental states including perceptual experiences) are representational states, feelings, including those that I take to identify the emotions, do not seem to have the sought after representational structure. Indeed, support for that view derives directly from attending to how feelings, including those I take to identify the emotions, strike us phenomenologically. (Whiting, 2011, 285)

Whiting thus appeals to the phenomenology of feelings on two levels. First, he argues that their phenomenology is what makes them what they are. Second, phenomenological investigation is his method of testing them for various features, such as whether they have a representational structure or not.

So, which of our previously mentioned mental states are feeling states? An answer to this question will help us see what the claim that a mental state is mainly characterized by its phenomenology amounts to.

Among the states that I previously mentioned, emotional responses are the most obvious candidates for feeling states. Spontaneous attraction and spontaneous aversion are paradigmatic feeling states. But we have also considered some close relatives of emotional responses, such as being angry, fearful, joyful, and sad. They too seem to be feeling states. Recall the difference between an emotional response and these four feelings I previously discussed. The emotional responses of aversion and attraction are directional in an immediately motivating way, while being sad, joyful, angry, or fearful are not necessarily so. But we are now first focusing on their commonality, namely, being feeling states.

So, what does it feel like to experience a spontaneous attraction? Again, we have a steak in front of us, and suddenly we experience an attraction to it and want to eat it. What does it feel like to be in this state? As described before, we imagine ourselves in this state as experiencing some kind of *pull* toward the steak. We can describe that pull as an experience of not being able to ignore the steak, of having one's attention and mind turned toward it. Let us build on this description of experiencing a spontaneous attraction.

This experience is immediately motivating in that it makes one want to move in a certain direction. It is basic in the sense that it does not seem to have components to it. It is primitive in the sense that it does not represent anything in a sophisticated way, it is just a directional feeling. It is felt with one's body, which comes with the pleasure and displeasure involved, and with the desire to move one's body toward an object. And we can see from its phenomenology alone that in this mental state we do not deal with any kind of inferential structures, propositions, or thinking things through, or other cognitive operations.

This is, of course, what we have already said about the emotional responses. But the point of the analysis here is to see that we can arrive at this characterization of an emotional response by looking at its phenomenology alone. By looking at how it feels to experience an emotional response, we can determine which features this mental state has and which it does not. And what makes an emotional response the kind of experience it is, is exactly that it feels like *being pulled* in one direction rather than in another, in a way that is accompanied by a mixture of pleasure and displeasure.

Let us compare this to another mental state that belongs to the class of feeling states, one that we have argued before is not an emotional response: being fearful. What does it feel like to be fearful? It seems that there is something like an edgy feeling involved, for example.[42] Further, something in one's stomach usually seems to tighten up. Even if one does not know what one is fearful of, one can experience this edgy feeling and the tightening of one's stomach area and know that one is fearful. This mental state of feeling fearful is *not necessarily* immediately motivating, although sometimes a fearful feeling comes with an immediate pull away from an object. But the pull away that we know from spontaneous aversion and attraction is not necessarily present in a fearful feeling. For example, we can imagine a situation where it is not clear what the object of fear would be. Here we would not say that there is an immediate pull away from something. But we nevertheless experience the edgy and tight feeling, thus feel fearful. The feeling is again basic in the sense that it does not have components. It is primitive, in the sense that it does not represent anything in a sophisticated way, it is just a feeling. It is felt with one's body. And again, we can see from its phenomenology alone that in this mental state we do not deal with any kind of inferential structures, propositions, or thinking things through, or other cognitive operations.

In describing these two feeling states, I have tried to illustrate that we can individuate and characterize their core features by "merely" referring to how it feels to experience them. The claim thus is that what best captures their nature is a description of their phenomenology or quality. I hope that this has become at least plausible through these two illustrations, of which one is of an emotional response, while the other is of a feeling of which we argued that it is different to an emotional response in our sense.

Now let us move on to the characterization of the other kind of mental state, the cognitive states, of which I claim that their unifying nature is that they have an impetus toward coherence.

---

42 The description of a fearful feeling as "edgy" is borrowed from Whiting (2006, 267).

2.2 Cognitive States (e. g., Beliefs)

Philosophers often take it that we aim for *coherence* between our beliefs and other epistemic attitudes, either implicitly (Betzler, 2012, 2016; Bratman, 1987), or explicitly (Worsnip, 2018a, 2018b, 2021). This claim is defended both for theoretical (Worsnip) and practical (Betzler and Bratman) beliefs. However, the claim that I introduce here in terms of beliefs is often put in terms of practical and theoretical *rationality*. Both, the thought goes, come with the commitment to or the aim of coherence. For present purposes, I shall prefer to speak of *beliefs*, setting aside the notion of rationality. For my aim in this section is to show that the commitment to and aim of coherence only governs mental states that are *cognitive*, as opposed to *all* mental states that can be normatively guiding (I will say more about this further on). And it is often unclear whether the notion of "rationality" is meant to denote just the cognitive states, or all mental states that can be normatively guiding. To the extent that I will use the notion of rationality at all within my own terminology, I will stipulate that the rational is the cognitive. In other words, cognitive states may also be called rational, and non-cognitive states may also be called non-rational.

To anticipate, in the next chapter, I return to the concerns of the first chapter, with a view to clarifying how these concerns relate to the distinction between cognitive states and feeling states. I shall argue that the domain of the normative is broader than that of the cognitive (or the "rational"). In other words, I will argue that there are non-cognitive (and so, non-rational) mental states that can provide normative guidance. On this account, then, normativity and coherence are not to be identified. The latter governs only cognitive states, not feeling states, while feeling states can also be normative, as I argue. This may strike us as a puzzling proposal. Traditionally, coherence and normativity relating to our mental states have been discussed as *inseparable* ideas (often under the, as I argue, ambiguous term "rationality"),[43] so that it seemed that the norm of coherence governs *all* mental states in general.[44]

If this is the intuition behind the traditional notion of rationality, then we can formulate the traditional position on this as follows: coherence is a basic norm of rationality. Something like this, in so many formulations, is found in any number of contributions. I depart from this picture because I want to accommodate non-

---

[43] For instance in McDowell (1998a), Nussbaum (2001), and Sherman (1989).

[44] Except perhaps in sentimentalist accounts, in which matters are reversed and normativity derives from passions and aversions alone. Hence, in a sense, in sentimentalist accounts normativity gets identified with the passions rather than with rationality, leading to an equally one-sided identification in my view.

cognitive (and so, non-rational) states that are normative. This departure generates theoretical pressure to use some familiar vocabulary in distinctive ways; hence my choice to use the distinction between the rational and the non-rational as expressing no more and no less than the distinction between the cognitive and the noncognitive, and instead to speak, where possible, of practical and theoretical *thinking* or *belief-formation*. As a first step toward the picture I want to lay out, let me show how an impetus toward coherence is a unique feature of the *cognitive* capacities. My hope is that this will capture the truth in the view I reject while still moving beyond it.

Hence, let me now illustrate how the cognitive mental states we have mentioned so far essentially have an impetus toward coherence.

Let us start with the paradigmatic member of cognitive states, beliefs. Let us imagine someone who holds the belief that it is wrong to eat meat. She also holds the belief that she is eating a steak right now. And of course, we have to imagine a host of other background beliefs in order for these two beliefs to be related to each other at all, for example the belief that a steak is a kind of meat. Now, with the two beliefs mentioned above and assuming such connecting background beliefs, we take our subject to experience a form of mental stress, one that psychologists call cognitive dissonance: the two beliefs involved are clearly incoherent with each other, absent any extenuating circumstances. It is *not easy* for the subject to hold on to both beliefs at the same time.[45] There is pressure toward abandoning one or the other: perhaps eating meat is not wrong after all, she might start to think, or perhaps she can do something so that she does not have to believe that she is eating a steak right now. If not, it will be difficult for her to endure the incoherence that arises from her current beliefs. This impetus toward coherent beliefs, many agree, is inherent in the mental state of beliefs.[46] It does not matter what the beliefs are about—as long as they are *beliefs*, it will cause a problem for the subject if they are incoherent with each other.

Of course, it would require further refinement to establish this claim fully. There have been debates about the question, for instance, whether this is also the case if one of the incoherent beliefs is merely dispositional, not occurrent, in the sense that the subject is currently not aware of the belief. For example, I might have a dispositional belief that eating meat is wrong, but at this very mo-

---

45 Indeed, Worsnip (2018a) would say it is *impossible* under conditions of transparency.

46 The impetus toward coherence of beliefs is also what makes Moore's paradox an actual paradox. The paradox concerns the absurdity if one said "It's raining, but I don't believe it's raining." (For a more thorough description of the paradox, see Moore (1942).) If we did not assume that incoherent beliefs are to some degree untenable for the subject, then thinking "It's raining, but I don't believe it's raining" would not seem to be a problem.

ment while eating the steak, this belief is quite unconscious, which is what enables me to eat the steak without experiencing cognitive dissonance at the moment.[47] I do not intend to address these more refined debates here, however. All I want to note here is that beliefs are generally seen as having an impetus to be coherent with each other. If a subject wants to hold two or more incoherent beliefs, she has *to do* something in order for it to be possible, even if this "doing" is merely to push one of the incoherent beliefs into unconsciousness.

Note that, so far, we were talking about the content of beliefs in the form of propositions. We have exclusively talked about beliefs *that* p or *that* q here.[48] I take it to be a standard way of understanding beliefs as propositionally structured. If one takes a subset of beliefs to be structured differently than in a propositional way, then the here presented account only applies to beliefs which display a propositional structure. This is so because I think that the propositional structure contributes in an important way to the impetus toward coherence inherent in beliefs. The propositional structure allows for *parts* within the mental state to be discerned, with differing functions within the proposition. These parts, then, can be compared with similar parts in other propositions and beliefs, and thus, ultimately, they can be evaluated for whether they are coherent with each other, or not. Hence, an important *precondition* for the impetus toward coherence is, as it were, the propositional structure involved in belief.[49]

Let us take our second example of cognitive states to be *inferences*—let us call this the mental process of "inferring". I should clarify here that I do not take mental *states* and mental *processes* to be fundamentally different in regard to the question that interests me here. A belief seems to be a mental *state*, while inferring seems to be a mental *process*, but both of them are a kind of cognitive state in the sense intended here. Many cognitive states also share the features we described in Chapter 1, such as being object-directed in the more demanding way that includes abstract objects, and so on. But, as I argue here, their most important unifying feature is that they have an impetus toward coherence. With a view to

---

47 This would be a situation in which the condition of transparency (the simultaneous awareness of all relevant beliefs) would not be fulfilled, according to Worsnip (2018a).

48 The Aristotelian tradition, which is in many ways present in discussions of agency and mental attitudes, also speaks of *predications*, as opposed to the propositional structure presented above. A predication has the form S is P, where S is a subject and P a predicate. For example, when we say "the sky is blue" we predicate "blue" of the sky. Today, however, we can represent predications as propositions, for example, as the proposition *that* the sky is blue.

49 Here, I am in agreement with views in the philosophy of mind that hold that thought, or cognition, is compositional in the way language is.

this dimension of cognitive states, it makes no difference whether we talk of mental *states* or mental *processes*.

When making inferences, we move from one proposition to the next. If we take beliefs to be the mental state in which we represent propositions, we can also say that when making inferences, we move from one belief to the next.[50] But the point about inferences is that we *have limits* in regard to which proposition we move to from the prior one. We are bound by some rules of logic, and often also by some considerations of likelihood. And with this, the impetus toward coherence is almost already given: The rules of logic only allow us to move between beliefs or propositions that are mutually coherent. For instance, one cannot move from "It is wrong to eat meat" to "I should eat meat now", at least not without adding other propositions that limit or cancel the first proposition. Of course, there is more involved in inferring than just to check for coherence: as mentioned, often, considerations of likelihood need to be added. The point is rather that the impetus toward coherence is already built into the process of inferring: the process of inferring does *not allow* a subject to arrive at a proposition that is incoherent with the prior propositions.[51] Of course, the same refinements as in the case of beliefs would be appropriate here: it is an open question whether there can be incoherent inferences because the subject is currently not aware of the incoherent proposition involved. But the main point is that there is an impetus toward coherence in the process of inferring, whether or not this is always fully successful. Perhaps one could think of an analogue to the cognitive dissonance when holding incoherent beliefs in the case of inferring too: perhaps there is also a specific kind of mental stress one experiences if one is going through an inference between incoherent propositions. This seems plausible. However, let me end these considerations about inferences here, in order to move on to some more general observations.

To sum up, one common feature in both examples of cognitive state is some form of *internal structure*. This internal structure, the propositional structure involved in beliefs and in inference, allows for *parts* within the mental states to be discerned, and therefore for these parts to be compared to corresponding parts of other mental states, with which the mental state then needs to be coherent. Feeling states, by contrast, do not have an internal structure. They are defined by the *quality*

---

50 For a more comprehensive treatise on what inferences precisely are, see Boghossian (2014).
51 One might say that there exists an even stronger requirement of coherence than the one I have been employing so far, namely, a kind of conceptual coherence that goes beyond logic and is not captured by probabilistic support. I do not want to claim that cognitive states have an impetus toward such a stronger kind of coherence. The claim is rather that they strive toward a minimal coherence, a coherence with at least a requirement of logical consistency and some probabilistic support.

or phenomenology of the experience when one is in that mental state, and that quality is, as it were, equally spread over the entire feeling state, with no discernible internal structure or parts. Hence, in feeling states, there would not be anything for a requirement of coherence to "latch onto", as it were: there is nothing to be compared or evaluated for coherence in a feeling state. A quality cannot be coherent or incoherent with another quality; and this is due at least in part to the fact that there are no *comparable parts* within a quality or experience due to the lack of an internal structure.

Another common feature of both examples that is a clear contrast to the feeling states is that the cognitive states are not *directional* themselves, and not *immediately motivating.* Remember what we said about the emotional responses: they *pull* us in a certain direction, in an immediately motivating way (toward the steak, away from the sandwich, and so on). While we said that other feeling states, such as experiencing fear, do not *necessarily* entail this directional motivation, we said that they *can* do so under certain circumstances (for example, when the object of fear is very clear and immediately present). By contrast, it is hard to see how cognitive states *could possibly* be directional themselves, or how they *could possibly* be motivating by themselves. Cognitive states by themselves precisely seem to be characterized by being motivationally and directionally *neutral*, in the sense that they do not pull us in one direction rather than another by themselves.

Recall that the cognitive states' "impetus toward coherence" is not a moving of the subject in this way, as I argued earlier. The movement of the subject from one belief to the next is *constrained* by the impetus toward coherence, but "moving toward coherence" is not a substantial direction itself. In other words, "moving toward coherence" is a way of saying what *limits* apply when one is pursuing a substantial direction (toward the sandwich, or toward a belief), not a direction itself.

For example, when making inferences, we *can* "move" toward a new proposition if the new proposition is coherent with the prior one, but we might simply not move there, without contradiction. There is no "motivation" or pressure one way or the other, and so there is no way, just on the basis of the cognitive state alone, to adjudicate between two or more possibilities. There is no reason (or motivation) to move at all, for all that concerns the cognitive states. So, just by being in the mental process of inferring, then, we are *not* pulled in one direction rather than another, we just stay within the limits of coherence. Hence, if there were no other kinds of mental states than the cognitive ones, we would proceed (or not) from one proposition to the next *within the limits of considerations of coherence and likelihood* alone, without substantial directional guidance.

One could object that there seems to be the phenomenon of "rational persuasiveness". That is, if I have a purely cognitive insight, for example that the sum of the internal angles of *any* triangle in a plane is always 180°, then I also *feel some pressure* to believe that. In other words, I cannot just have a cognitive insight and then withhold judgment.[52] And that, one might say, shows that cognitive mental states can also give substantive directional guidance. In this example, the constellation of beliefs "moves" one toward the belief that the sum is always 180°, away from the belief that this is not so.

I would argue that even in such a case, what the cognitive insight gives us is only a *possibility*. After having had the insight, we know that it would be coherent with our other mathematical beliefs to believe that the sum is always 180°. But I think, against the supposition above, that if it were for the cognitive insight alone, one could indeed withhold judgment in such a case. That something is "rationally persuasive" is already more than just the cognitive insight alone. A certain *attraction* to the conclusion must be involved if one actually moves there. Without such an attraction or other feeling state involved, I argue, one could indeed just go through the intellectual steps that lead to the cognitive insight, then say "well, perhaps this is so, perhaps not, who cares", and then withhold judgment. One *cannot* do that if one has an attraction to holding abstract mathematical beliefs, for example. And that is what makes such inferences feel *persuasive*, for a suitably inclined subject. And again, most of the time and for most people, there are probably such feeling states already involved *whenever* they draw inferences. That is why it might sometimes seem as if a cognitive state itself gives such substantive direction. It is hard to imagine any cognitive operation without feeling states involved. But it nevertheless makes sense to conceptually distinguish between the respective contributions of the respective mental states. And, as I argue, the persuasiveness does not come from the cognitive state itself.

Hence, not entailing such a substantial directional motivation is exactly what allows cognitive states to be neutral and thus to have an impetus toward coherence. The flip side is that they could never have an impetus toward *anything else* than coherence, which is exactly the opposite in the case of feeling states. This seems to open up space for the role of feeling states in normative guidance: by only being concerned with coherence, and by only being able to move in a direction through considerations of coherence and likelihood, the cognitive states cannot really provide the subject with substantive motivation and direction to move toward one thing rather than another (if both are coherent). They can only provide *the limits* of the movement, by saying what directions would be co-

---

52 This is, again, a version of Moore's paradox; that one cannot say: "It's raining, but I don't believe it's raining."

herent; they cannot motivate one of the coherent directions more than another.[53] Thus it is the feeling states that enable the subject to ultimately move toward one direction rather than another.[54]

One could now object that I said that being fearful does not necessarily have a pull in one direction, in contrast to emotional responses, and that this might be true of many other feeling states too. So, the thought goes, the contrast to the cognitive states seems to disappear. But the point is not that feeling states *always* give us directional guidance (it is not one of their *essential* features). The point is rather that feeling states *can* potentially give us directional guidance, while cognitive states *could not possibly* generate this kind of direction without being combined with a feeling state (hence it *is* one of cognitive states' essential features that they lack this). Thus, for example, the feeling of being fearful might *not very often* give us that directional guidance (while emotional responses *always* do),

---

53 Interestingly, coming from a different starting point, Goffin (2021) ends up arguing something similar. He proposes that, what he calls, "emotional representations" maximize the function of leading us in one direction or another, while thereby often giving us "false alarms" where we would not have had to do anything at all. By contrast, what he calls "careful reasoning" would often miss a moment where one needed to do something. But careful reasoning, in turn, aims at minimizing false beliefs, so that if both capacities work together, the false alarms are held in check by reasoning, while the missed moments of reasoning are taken up by the reaction of the emotional representations. Hence, here too, the cognitive states seem to play the role of keeping the subject's reactions within certain limits (like coherence), while not catching all the moments when one needs to act (not giving substantial direction); by contrast the feeling states tend to move the subject in a substantial direction, while they need to be held in check by the limiting capacity (by the impetus toward coherence of the cognitive capacity).

54 Harte (2014), for instance, argues that pleasure has a motivational role in making an activity worthy of pursuit. In Harte (2004), while considering Plato's *Philebus*, she asks whether pleasure can, in principle, be false or misleading at all. But either way, argues Vogt (2010), pleasure must play a constitutive role in discovering the good according to the *Philebus*. These latter positions are related to the hedonistic thesis that pleasure or other positively valenced feelings can by themselves ground normativity. See Feldman (2004) and Vogt (forthcoming-b) for a discussion of the hedonistic thesis that pleasure is the only good that does not derive its value from another good. Even more, a sophisticated form of hedonism would not be inconsistent with Aristotle's psychology, argues Rapp (2009), which is significant for us because in Chapter 4, I will borrow some parts of Aristotle's psychology to show how there can be unity between the feeling and cognitive states.

Perhaps even closer to my notion of primitive but nevertheless trained emotional responses is the premise of a version of Appraisal Theory that holds that emotions are elicited according to an individual's subjective evaluation of important events, rather than brute responses (cf. Scherer, Schorr, and Johnstone, 2001). However, the question in what sense emotions themselves might be evaluations is still an open one in the current research literature (cf. Deonna and Teroni, 2015, for discussion).

while cognitive mental states *never* give us such direction, as their nature *precludes* this possibility.

2.3 Objections

Let me now consider a few potential objections to the view presented here, before moving on to Chapter 3, where we explore what the proposed distinction means for a non-rational (non-cognitive) form of normative guidance.

2.3.1 Objection 1: Idiosyncratic Division of the Mental Realm

When I first presented the basic distinction between feeling and cognitive states proposed here, the worry was that this distinction might seem trivial (and I motivated why it is nevertheless worthwhile to spell it out in some detail). One could, however, also have the opposite worry: that this is an idiosyncratic way of dividing up the mental realm. There are various other possible ways of how to divide up the mental realm. There seems to be no strong reason to emphasize exactly this contrast as proposed here.

In response, let me first point to some allied accounts that give reason to divide up the mental in this way (A), then consider how two potentially non-fitting mental states (intention and desire) in the end do fit into our characterization of cognitive states (B), and finally compare it to some alternative topographies of the mind (C), in order to motivate the path taken here.

A) Allied Accounts

To divide the mental roughly into a feeling and a cognitive (or belief-like, propositional, conceptual, doxastic, representational) class is not a new idea. The first (known to me) accounts of this are to be found in Plato and Aristotle, and up to the 1990s and early 2000s, this was more or less the mainstream mental topography. For example, separatism is the view that intentionality and consciousness are separable from each other. It is claimed that conscious states are individuated in terms of qualitative, that is, non-(essentially-) representational properties (and the opposite for intentionality) (cf. Siewert 2022). Siewert goes on to observe that "perspectives reasonably regarded as separatist occupied the mainstream of much twentieth century analytic philosophy" (2022).

For instance, consider Sellars, Rorty, and Brandom:

the conception expressed in Wilfrid Sellars' (1956) distinction between sentience (sensation) and sapience. Whereas the qualities of *feelings* involved in the former—mere sensations—require no cognitive sophistication and are readily attributable to brutes, the latter—involving awareness *of*, awareness *that*—requires that one have the right concepts, which cannot be guaranteed just by having sensations, but needs learning and inferential capacities (which Sellars believed come only with language). Richard Rorty (1979) was not alone in taking Sellars' views to support a strict separation of the phenomenal and the intentional (see also Brandom 1994). Rorty's appropriation of Sellars (blended with Quinean eliminativism) leads him to deny not just the importance, but even the reality of consciousness. (Siewert 2022)

Siewert continues to observe that externalist positions of meaning have also seemed to support such a division, and this is still defended also in recent literature:

Externalist arguments (...) have also been taken to support the separation of the "qualitative" from meaning and content (hence the separation of consciousness from intentionality). For it has been sometimes assumed that the phenomenal character of one's experience is "fixed internally"—i. e., it has no necessary relation to the nature of particular substances in one's external environment or to one's linguistic community. Thus, if externalist arguments (like those of Putnam and Burge) show that neither meaning nor content is "in the head", phenomenal consciousness cannot imply any intentionality or content. Putnam (1981) himself drew such a conclusion, and much like Ryle, took the stream of consciousness to comprise nothing more than sensations and images, which (recalling Frege) are to be set apart from thought and meaning. (...) It seems reasonable to suppose that together they helped entrench in analytic philosophy a conception (sometimes welded to the term "qualia") that confines consciousness, in the experiential/what it is like sense, to sensations and sensory images—and thus segregates it from thought, concepts, and "propositional attitudes"—hence from intentionality. (For a recent defense of this tradition, see Papineau 2021.). (Siewert 2022)

The term "separatism" (where a separation along the lines of the division of the mental as suggested here is implied) was introduced by Horgan and Tienson (2002). They observe:

A common picture in recent philosophy of mind has been that the phenomenal aspects and the intentional aspects of mentality are independent of one another. According to this view, phenomenal character of certain mental states or processes (...) is not intentional. Examples (...) of sates with inherent phenomenal character are sensations, such as pains, itches, and color sensations. This view also asserts, (...) that the intentionality of certain mental states and processes (...) is not phenomenal. Beliefs and desires are the paradigm cases of intentional mental states. (...) We will call this picture separatism, because it treats phenomenal aspects and intentional aspects of mentality as mutually independent, and thus inseparable. Although there may be complex states that are both phenomenal and intentional, their phenomenal and their intentional aspects are separable. (...) Separatism has been very popular in philosophy of mind in recent decades, and is still widely held. (Horgan and Tienson 2002, 520)

Finally, we also find a similar observation in Pitt:

> It is a traditional assumption in analytic philosophy of mind that intentional states, such as believing, doubting or wondering that p, have no intrinsic phenomenal properties, and that phenomenal states, such as feeling pain, seeing red or hearing middle C, have no intrinsic intentional properties. We are, according to this view, of two metaphysically distinct minds, the intentional and the phenomenal. (Pitt 2004, 1)

Hence, there seem to be quite a few examples where this (or a very similar) division of the mental was assumed or argued for. This should allay the worry that the proposed division is idiosyncratic. The examples we have encountered spread over a wide range of time: Plato, Aristotle, Sellars, Rorty, Brandom, Putnam, Burge, Ryle, and Papineau—in other words, from Ancient times until now. The observation, moreover, that this is or was a mainstream position, we have encountered by four independent contemporary philosophers: Siewert, Pitt, Horgan, and Tienson. We can thus conclude that such a division is not idiosyncratic.

B) The Impetus toward Coherence is a Mischaracterization of the Cognitive
Perhaps, one could counter, what is idiosyncratic is not so much the division between a cognitive (or belief-like, propositional, conceptual, doxastic, representational) and a feeling (or qualitative, phenomenological) class, but the claim that the cognitive states are essentially characterized *by an impetus toward coherence*. While this might work well with the provided examples (beliefs, inferences), it would be quite surprising if this were true about *all* cognitive mental states.

That worry can be divided into two putative problems: that there are mental states that *both* are characterized by how they feel *and* have an impetus toward coherence (the two classes are not mutually exclusive), and that there are mental states that are *neither* characterized by how they feel *nor* have an impetus toward coherence (the two classes are not jointly comprehensive for the mental realm). The first putative problem has already been addressed: mental states that seem to have both characteristics turn out to be compound mental states, a compound between a feeling and a cognitive state. But what about those mental states which seem to not be well described by *any* of the two features? In other words, are there cognitive mental states that do not have an impetus toward coherence?

While this seems plausible, I do indeed argue that any cognitive mental state ends up having an impetus toward coherence in the sense intended here. Let me consider two examples of mental states that are sometimes taken to be cognitive but that do not obviously have an impetus toward coherence: intention and desire.

Intention is often taken to be a cognitive state. In action theory, for example, it is sometimes posited that when *S* is doing *A* intentionally, *S* knows that she is doing A.[55] As there is knowledge entailed in doing something intentionally, then at least something like true beliefs must be part of an intention. Intention then must be cognitive, as it entails the paradigmatic member of cognitive states. But in what sense can intention be said to have an impetus toward coherence?

Consider cases of practical rationality, and cases when it fails (akrasía). When practical rationality is successful, it can be described in the form of a practical syllogism:
1. One ought to eat healthy.
2. Eating salad is healthy.
3. I intend to eat the salad in front of me.

Conclusion: (I proceed to eat the salad in front of me.)[56]

When it fails, it can be described, again in the form of a practical syllogism, as a failure to form the appropriate intention or as a failure to proceed to the proper action after having formed the intention.

1a. One ought to eat healthy.
2a. Eating salad is healthy.
x I fail to intend to eat the salad in front of me.

1b. One ought to eat healthy.
2b. Eating salad is healthy.
3b. I intend to eat the salad in front of me.
x I fail to eat the salad.

That is, both the successful as also the unsuccessful cases of practical rationality can be described as a practical syllogism, where intention plays either the role of the conclusion itself, or the role of an interim conclusion that then leads to the conclusion (the action). If we understand intention in this way, it is easy to see that it has an impetus toward coherence. Intending to φ puts pressure on me to φ; otherwise, I am incoherent (akratic). Reasons to form an intention to φ put pressure on me to actually form the intention to φ; otherwise, I am incoherent.

---

55 Anscombe, 1957.

56 See Aristotle's *NE*, Kenny (1963), Geach (1956), and Anscombe (1957), who describe practical rationality in the form of a practical syllogism in this way.

There is a debate as to whether the conclusion of a practical syllogism is the intention to φ, or the action of φ-ing (as described here). This is relevant, for example, if one wants to understand whether akrasía is a failure *within* the practical syllogism (the proper intention does not get formed), or a problem that arises *after* the practical syllogism has been performed (the right intention got formed, but for some reason the body does not move accordingly).

Moreover, two intentions can clearly be incoherent with each other. If I intend to only eat healthy things, and I intend to eat the chocolate cake, and I believe that the chocolate cake is not healthy, then my two intentions to only eat healthy things and to eat the chocolate cake are clearly incoherent.

The objection might arise that with the above description, I have made intention maximally belief-like, and thus made it easy for myself to accommodate it within my twofold distinction.[57] Therefore, let us consider a view on intention that does not take it to be captured by the belief-desire model. We will consider Bratman's, which will still turn out to give cognitive states a prominent role in the constitution of intention. My aim is to show that also this notion of intention can be accommodated in our proposed twofold distinction.

Bratman (1987) takes intention to be a paradigmatic case of conative states.[58] That is, in contrast to the usual understandings of conative states that take desires as their paradigmatic member (and in contrast to Kriegel (2015), whom we discussed earlier), Bratman thinks intention is the core case of a conative state. Moreover, he argues that intention cannot be reductively accounted for in terms of desire (and/or belief). Note, thus, that in Bratman's own view of intention, it is not taken to be a cognitive state in the first place, but a conative one. So, it would not create a problem for our notion of cognitive states if intention in that sense did not fit into our class of cognitive states. But on a more general level, if there is a mental state (called intention) as described by Bratman, then it must fit into our twofold division. Let us see where it fits. Intention, according to Bratman (1987), can only be understood if we take seriously that human beings are planning creatures. That is, intention is part of a web of other human mental activities, such as making plans, deliberating, and committing to something (while it might be more accurate to describe conative states for non-human animals in a less sophisticated way (Bratman, 1987)). He takes this to be a clear reason to reject the desire-belief model of intention (cf. Bratman, 1987, 14). With this, we can already see that one way of classifying intention is not available to us: As a compound of belief (cognitive state) and desire (feeling state—to be discussed in more detail below). Roughley (2001) summarizes the emerging account well: the commitment typical of intention is "manifested in a complex set of planning mechanisms (...). These mechanisms combine causal processes and normative requirements, the latter concerning intention-belief consistency, coherence between super-ordinate and subordinate intentions and intention agglomeration" (Roughley, 2001, 265).

---

57 And indeed, Roughley (2016, 15), for instance, would argue that intention is only contingently related to belief.
58 Cf. Kriegel (2015, 72).

Bratman (1999) then developed his planning theory of intention further, later pooled in a collection of essays. There, Bratman takes shared cooperative agency to be the paradigmatic case to be studied, as opposed to individual agency, in order to understand intention (Bratman 1999). What is distinctive in the proposed account, is that it is not the *content* (of the mental state) that distinguishes intention from other mental states, but, as Roughley puts it, "something about the specific way in which the bearer of the attitude is related to that content, what we can call its *mode*" (Roughley, 2001, 267). Roughley continues by making an important aspect of Bratman's view explicit: "The structure of his theory is such that the mode of intending is reasonably construed as articulated in the concept of 'commitment': if we intend something, we are 'committed' to its realization. And what the object of such commitment might be is not, so Bratman might want to argue, fixed in any way by the concept of intending" (Roughley, 2001, 268). This commitment can extent not only to one's own actions, but also to others', according to Bratman. That is, I can intend (and thus be committed to) the realization of an action that someone else might need to perform, and thus also to something that is not under my full control, but other-mediated (cf. Roughley, 2001, 268). An example is that, as a group leader, I can be committed to actions that others in the group need to perform.[59]

With this (let us call it "more sophisticated" than the syllogistic) account of intention, where does intention belong in our twofold division? This helps us illustrate more clearly how the twofold division is to be understood. In an account of intention like Bratman's, it seems that cognitive states still play the decisive role in what intention is, while intention is arguably also bound up with non-cognitive and thus feeling states. Consider what Bratman thinks intention is composed of, and with which mental states it is inextricably bound up: beliefs, decisions, plans, commitments. Beliefs, decisions, and plans are clearly cognitive states. They have an impetus toward coherence, and their phenomenology does not seem to play an essential role in their individuation. Commitment is a bit more complicated. We can understand the term "commitment" either in a cognitive or in a feeling way, I would argue. I can be (purely) cognitively committed to, let us say, being a vegetarian. This consists in a set of beliefs of what I am (not) supposed to do. This cognitive commitment might sometimes come into conflict with how I feel in a certain moment, and then it takes some self-constraint to keep my actions coherent with the commitment. Here, a clear impetus toward coherence is

---

59 Roughley rightly points out that this account works especially well—and perhaps only—for cases where one individual has power over others or at least enjoys a certain power to decide for the group (cf. Roughley, 2001, 269).

present. By contrast, if I am committed to something (merely) in a feeling way, this impetus toward coherence ceases to apply. I might have a feeling-commitment to please my child's every wish. That is, I might have a non-reflected, standing, dispositional desire (as a feeling-commitment) to do things for him if I can. If he, for instance, urgently wants a candy in the store, I am, prima facie, automatically committed to fulfilling his wish, on the basis of this feeling-commitment. I wish to fulfill his desires, as a general feeling. This could be a case of a feeling-commitment. If I then decide to not fulfill his desire in a particular instance, this does not end up as an incoherence. I know that it is "just" a feeling-commitment that I cannot shake. I also know that it is not good for children to get every wish fulfilled. If I act on the basis of that knowledge and against my feeling-commitment, I can still fully acknowledge the simultaneous presence of my feeling-commitment, without being incoherent. Thus, it is conceivable that there can be at least three different kinds of commitment: 1) a purely cognitive commitment, 2) a mere feeling-commitment, or 3) a compound of cognitive and feeling commitment (and the latter might be the strongest kind of commitment one can have).

In other words, most of what is involved in Bratman's sophisticated account of intention turns out to be cognitive states in our twofold distinction. It seems to fit with our description of cognitive states having an impetus toward coherence. If Bratman meant to include something like the feeling-commitment just described, it would clearly be classed as a feeling state in our division. This makes it perhaps a bit clearer that our division of the mental realm—that no matter what else is true about a mental state, in general it can be classified in either one or the other class —is not meant to make an exclusive or a controversial claim. There are many other ways of dividing up the mental realm that are consistent with our twofold distinction. For example, one can distinguish conative from non-conative states —and then our twofold division is orthogonal to that distinction, that is, some conative states end up on the cognitive, some on the feeling side. If a mental state does not *purely* fall on one side or the other, it can be understood as a complex of cognitive and feeling states (such as intention, in case it includes such a feeling-commitment or another feeling state).

Let us now move on to the second mental state that might seem difficult to accommodate in our twofold distinction, desire. We have already discussed in some detail how desire is commonly understood in the literature, particularly in the Ancient, the good-based, and the pleasure-based accounts of desire. I showed how desire in each of these accounts is different to our concept of emotional responses. Now, how does desire fit into our twofold distinction of cognitive and feeling states? The short answer is: in the good-based account, desire is primarily a cognitive state, while in the Ancient and the pleasure-based account it is primarily a feeling state. Let me expand a bit. We said that in the good-based account, to desire *p* is to take *p* to be good. Lewis dubbed it the "desire as belief" account. So, if desire is to take *p* to be good, then it seems to exactly have that impetus toward coherence. That is, if we understand desire in this way, then to desire to eat a chocolate cake, and to desire to eat something healthy, while believing that the chocolate cake is not healthy, would amount to an incoherence. In such an account, thus, one cannot knowingly desire to eat something healthy and desire to eat the chocolate cake at the same time. This, however, seems to amount to an argument against the good-based account of desire—exactly because desire does not seem to be as belief-like as this account makes it out to be. Let us turn our attention to the pleasure-based account, then. In this account (just like the Ancient one that takes desire to be the *epithymiai*, whose only kind of object can be food, drink, or sex), desire is a feeling state. That is, it is individuated by how it feels to be in that state. Most of us know how it feels to desire a chocolate cake. I can have such a desire while also having a desire to eat something healthy— there seems to be no impetus toward coherence in the mental state of desire. We said that, in contrast to desire in a pleasure-based account, emotional responses are inherently connected to acting. The subject who experiences a spontaneous attraction *moves* toward the object. Thus, one *already acts* (in some sense) just by experiencing emotional responses. In desire, we do not already move toward the object just by desiring it. Desiring, as it were, can be done in a stationary sense, while an emotional response already moves me toward the object while experiencing the response. But what both of these mental states share is that they are feeling states. They are individuated by how it feels to be in them, and they do not have an impetus toward coherence. One of them moves one while experiencing it (emotional response); the other can be experienced in a stationary sense (desire).

One reason why desire has sometimes taken to be conceptual (and thus at least to entail some cognitive state) is because it might otherwise be mysterious how one can have a desire for a specific kind of object, "something healthy", for instance. It seems that there is some conceptual capacity included if I can desire "something healthy". At least, I need to have a belief about what it is for a type of food to be healthy. To fully respond to this debate would go beyond the scope of this book. Let me briefly say the following. I see two rough ways how one can make sense of the idea that one can desire "something healthy", and both of them seem compatible with our twofold division. First, one can say that the conceptual content "something healthy" is not part of desire itself, but a belief that is added to the desire. Thus, strictly speaking, if I desire (to eat) something healthy, there is a belief about what is healthy, and my (non-conceptual) desire is directed at this object. The "desire to eat something healthy" is then a specific belief-desire compound, and thus a compound of a cognitive and a feeling state. Second, one can say that "something healthy" is indeed part of the desire itself, but that it is not conceptual (if we want to keep with the pleasure-based account of desire). Of course, the non-conceptual sense of "something healthy" is not properly coughed in linguistic terms, it is just a kind of feeling. Some foods feel healthier to us than others (perhaps there is a different kind of feeling in the stomach area if I imagine or see a healthy food item than if I see an unhealthy one). Once we *talk* about this non-conceptual sense of "something healthy", however, we are bound to use linguistic means. This does not mean that the "something healthy" included in the (purely pleasure-based) desire is itself linguistically or conceptually structured. That is, it is conceivable that we would have a purely feeling based sense of "desiring something healthy". In that case, then, it is clear that desire is a feeling state.

Let us thus move on to the third response to the first objection (that this is an idiosyncratic way of dividing up the mental realm), where we consider two alternative topographies of the mind and show how they relate to our twofold division.

C) Comparison to Alternative Topographies

Let us briefly consider two other ways in which the mental has been divided up, to make it clear that our division is not a competitor to them, but orthogonal and compatible with them. Specifically, I will consider functionalism (C.1) and direction of fit (C.2).

C.1 Functionalism

Functionalism, according to Ned Block, is "the view that mentality can be characterized in terms of relations among internal states and between sensory inputs and behavioral outputs" (Block, 2007, 1) To put it in more everyday terms, functionalism is the idea that various mental states play different functions for us (they transform a particular input to a particular output for us). Mental states are then, roughly speaking, individualized by what role they play within the structure of the mental overall. Functionalism is sometimes already attributed to Aristotle, and it is also understood as one of the major responses to the mind-body problem:

> Functionalism is one of the major proposals that have been offered as solutions to the mind-body problem. (...) Cartesian dualism said the ultimate nature of the mental was to be found in a special mental substance. Behaviorism identified mental states with behavioral dispositions; physicalism in its most influential version identifies mental states with brain states. Functionalism says that mental states are constituted by their causal relations to one another and to sensory inputs and behavioral outputs. Although it is descended from Aristotle, modern functionalism is one of the major theoretical developments of 20th-century analytic philosophy, and provides the conceptual underpinnings of much work in cognitive science. (Block 2007, 15)

As such, functionalism is a thesis about the nature of mental states. Many functionalist accounts are holist, in the sense that the mind or the mental are understood as a whole with a certain purpose for its organism (usually a human being), and its proper parts take on sub-tasks, that is, sub-functions within that whole. Our twofold division of the mental between cognitive and feeling states is far from being a thesis about the nature of the mental *tout court.* As stated at the beginning of this chapter, the claim is that *whatever else can be said* about a mental state, it can be classified either as cognitive or as feeling state. As such, it is a much more minimal claim than the functionalist thesis.[60] There is, at least prima facie, no reason to think that our claim is incompatible with functionalism. Perhaps some interesting functionalist claims can be built upon our division: that feeling states, primarily giving us the what-it-is-like of being in a certain state of affairs, have the function of informing us about the quality of that state of affairs, while cognitive states, characterized by their impetus toward coherence, have the role of restricting us in our thinking and behavior in certain (functional for us) ways. For the purposes of this book, no such functionalist claims are being made. But it is not only compatible, but it would also be a welcome outcome of the claims of this book if they were developed further into a functionalist interpretation of feeling and cognitive states.

C.2 Direction of Fit

Another way of dividing up the mental is according to their direction of fit. The common paradigmatic instances of each direction of fit are belief and desire: belief has a mind-to-world direction of fit, while desire has a world-to-mind direction of fit. That is, metaphorically speaking, belief is geared toward taking what is the case in the world and makes itself fitting to that state of affairs (arriving at a true belief). Desire, by contrast, "wants" a certain state of affairs to be the case, and thus makes the world fit its content (fulfilled desire). Or as Velleman puts it:

> The term "direction of fit" refers to the two different ways in which attitudes can relate propositions to the world. In cognitive attitudes, a proposition is grasped as patterned after the world; whereas in conative attitudes a proposition is grasped as a pattern for the world to follow. The propositional object of desire is regarded not as fact—not, that is, as *factum*, hav-

---

60 One might say that to claim that *all* mental states fall within one or the other class makes it a claim about the mental *tout court.* I disagree. A claim about the mental *tout court* is a metaphysical claim—what the mental on the most fundamental level is. Our claim only goes so far as to say that —whatever the mental is—apparently, we can divide it into these two classes. Whether or not these two classes correspond to a metaphysical division of the mind is being left open by that claim.

ing been brought about—but rather as *faciendum*, to be brought about; it is regarded not as true but as to be made true. (Velleman, 1992, 8)

In short, belief has to adjust to the world, and in desire, the world has to adjust to it. They have an opposite "direction-of-fit" to the world. In rough terms, then, what is claimed is that all doxastic mental states have a mind-to-world direction of fit, while all conative states have a world-to-mind direction of fit.

In contrast to functionalism, this does not need to be understood as a metaphysical claim about the nature of the mental in general. Rather, it is an interesting observation that we can divide most (or all) mental states either into one or the other class. In this sense, the direction of fit division is much more similar to our division (as the *kind* of claim it is) than functionalism. In what relation do these two divisions stand? We have already seen that beliefs, and doxastic states more generally, belong to the cognitive states in our division. Would it thus perhaps be right to say that all states with mind-to-world direction of fit are cognitive in our sense, and have an impetus toward coherence? This is a far-reaching question, and one would need to actually test this for each doxastic state. In principle, however, it is conceivable that there is something about a state having a mind-to-world fit that makes it also have an impetus toward coherence. What is distinctive about a mind-to-world direction of fit is that the mental state needs to bring itself into accord with something else—one might want to say it needs to accord itself in coherence with the world, with the actual state of affairs. Hence, perhaps in the very idea of a mind-to-world direction of fit, there is entailed a certain impetus toward coherence. Or, put in another way, only mental states that have an impetus toward coherence have the right kind of "capacity" to accord themselves with the world, that is, to have a mind-to-world direction of fit. This is, however, quite metaphorically speaking. It suffices to say that there might be a conceptual link between cognitive states in our sense, and mind-to-world direction of it. By contrast, there does not seem to be the desired conceptual link between world-to-mind direction of fit (as found in desire) and feeling states. This might amount to the same argument as why emotional responses are not the same as (pleasure-based) desires or conative states more generally. The world-to-mind direction of fit seems to describe conative states well, but not feeling states more generally. There is nothing that makes feeling states—states that are individuated by what it is like to be in them—geared toward an impetus to make the world accord with their content. If we understand desire along the lines of the pleasure-based account, then desire does belong to the class of feeling states, and then there is a feeling state that has a world-to-mind direction of fit. There are certainly more conative states that belong to the feeling states, so perhaps there is a considerable overlap of feeling states and states with a world-to-mind direction of fit. But there are also cognitive states with a world-to-mind direction of fit (think of intention, for instance). Hence, there is no reason to think that there is a conceptual link between belonging to the feeling states and having a world-to-mind direction of fit. In sum, then, we can say that the direction-of-fit topography of the mental and our twofold division are compatible, but different. They might not be fully orthogonal to each other, because there might be a conceptual link between being cognitive in our sense and having a mind-to-world direction of fit. This link, however, would need to be further explored.

With these considerations, I hope to have established that the twofold division of the mental realm into feeling and cognitive states is not overly idiosyncratic. Let us move on to the two other objections.

2.3.2 Objection 2: Methodologically Dubious

On a more general level, one could think that it is methodologically dubious that two different mechanisms of individuation should be at work in a topography of the mind. To have one criterion to identify the cognitive states and then a completely different one for the feeling states—that could look a bit contingent and thus dubious. If the two criteria are not conceptually linked, then there is no reason to think that they are mutually exclusive and jointly exhaustive. We have addressed the issue of mutual exclusion and joint exhaustion already. But even if the two criteria now turn out to be so, a twofold division of this kind might look like it should better be reduced to a more fundamental principle of individuation.

Let me thus motivate this twofold division also on methodological grounds here. First, consider that our prior consideration of other divisions between cognitive and phenomenal states—for example in terms of the separatism between consciousness and intentionality—has shown that such a fundamental twofold division is an accepted way of individuating mental states, at least for some, from Plato until today. As Pitt put it: "We are, according to this view, of two metaphysically distinct minds (...)" (Pitt 2004, 1). Second, it is true that it would be more parsimonious if we had only one criterion of individuation for the mental, or two criteria that are conceptually linked, than phenomenology and impetus toward coherence. But sometimes parsimony leads us astray. Sometimes, a phenomenon (e.g., the mental) is too complex to be captured by one criterion alone. In such situations, we have to apply more than one epistemic standard (more than just parsimony) in order to arrive at the best explanation.[61] And third, it might very well turn out that the two criteria of impetus toward coherence and phenomenology are in the end conceptually linked. I have already hinted at some interactions between these two criteria. Remember that I pointed out that, because cognitive states do not entail a substantial directional motivation, they are (motivationally) neutral, and that *allows them* to have an impetus toward coherence. The flip side, I said, is that they could never have an impetus toward *anything else* than coherence, which is exactly the opposite in the case of feeling states. That is, there could be a substantial, conceptual reason why an impetus toward coherence and phenomenology are mutually exclusive. Perhaps we have, on the one hand, mental states (the cognitive ones) whose nature only *limits* us in the way we can move from them to other attitudes, but such a nature cannot give us a substantial direction about toward which other attitude we shall move (the limiting function of cognitive mental states in virtue of having to be coherent). On the other side of the coin are those mental states that are unrestricted, unlimited and motivationally loaded (the phenomenal states that do not abide by coherence requirements), whose function it is to give us substantial direction (motivation) to move to a particular attitude A rather than B, if both A and B are coherent.[62] In such a case, our twofold division would boil down to one criterion, which divides up the mental realm into something like a restricting and an expanding class of mental states. There is nothing in our account that precludes such an outcome. It would, however, go too far to try to argue for such a substantial claim in the scope of this book. Note that I made the example here of boiling down to a single criterion in functionalist terms—one class of mental states has one function for us, the other class has the opposite function for us. This should not be understood as claiming that a functionalist story would be the only way of bringing them under one criterion, or of conceptually linking them. It is just one interesting possibility how our account could be further developed.

2.3.3 Objection 3: A Set of Qualities Can Be Incoherent Too

The last objection we are considering is about the way I described feeling states. I said that they, in contrast to cognitive states, do not have an impetus toward coherence. I said that it is not incoherent to feel sadness and joy about the same state

---

61 Cf. literature on inference to the best explanation, e. g., Lipton (1991), Mackonis (2013), and Williamson (2018).
62 So that we do not end up like Buridan's Ass (cf., for instance, Chislenko (2016)).

of affairs (at the same time, by the same subject, etc.). To this, one could object that there are indeed qualities that are incoherent with each other. Most saliently, attraction and aversion pull one in opposite directions, so experiencing these two at the same time (about the same object, etc.) amounts to an incoherence. Similarly, experiencing pleasure and displeasure about the same event is incoherent. Hence, it seems that a set of qualities can be just as incoherent as a set of cognitive states.

To respond to this, it is important to understand the difference between incoherence and exclusion. Two qualities might exclude each other, but it would be inaccurate to say that they are incoherent with each other. The same surface cannot appear in pure green *and* in pure red at the same time. But it would be wrong to say that green and red are incoherent with each other. This is an insight that already Wittgenstein brought to our attention:

> (...) properties which admit of gradations, i.e., properties as the length of an interval, the pitch of a tone, the brightness or redness of a shade of colour, etc. It is a characteristic of these properties that one degree of them excludes any other. One shade of colour cannot simultaneously have two different degrees of brightness or redness, a tone not two different strengths, etc. (Wittgenstein, 1929, 167)

And he continues:

> The mutual exclusion of unanalyzable statements of degree (...). I here deliberately say "exclude" and not "contradict", for there is a difference between these two notions, and atomic propositions, although they cannot contradict, may exclude one another. (...) There are functions which can give a true proposition only for one value of their argument because (...) there is only room in them for one. (...) How, then does the mutual exclusion of RPT [red in a certain place at a certain time] and BPT [blue in a certain place at a certain time] operate? I believe it consists in the fact that RPT as well as BPT are in a certain sense *complete*. [It] leaves room only for one entity—in the sense, in fact, in which we say that there is room for one person only in a chair. (Wittgenstein, 1929, 168–169)

It is impossible (excluded) that I sit on a chair on which another person is already sitting if it is a one-person sized chair. Nevertheless, we would not say that it is *incoherent* if I also sit on the chair (it is simply not possible, excluded). In the same way, feeling states might sometimes exclude each other. Because they are, just like Wittgenstein says, complete. This sounds very similar to our earlier characterization of them, that is, that their quality "extends over the entire mental state" as an indiscernible whole, in the sense that their quality does not have proper parts or an internal structure. If two feeling states exclude each other, they each do it "as a complete whole" as it were—nothing "within" them could be shown as the element that makes it incoherent with an element of the other mental state.

Let us look at the kind of potential for exclusion of feeling states in a bit more detail. What does it amount to?[63] This will also help us make the notion of "impetus toward coherence" of the cognitive states sharper. It seems like not all feeling states have the same potential for exclusion-relationships with other states. An experience of pure green excludes an experience of pure red in a different way than attraction excludes aversion, and some other feeling states—like sadness and joy— do not necessarily seem to exclude each other at all. But none of these relationships amount to incoherence relationships. What is the difference?

While in the perceptual case (pure green and pure red), the two mental states seem to *fully* exclude each other (it amounts to an impossibility), it seems to be possible, but problematic, to experience an attraction and an aversion to something at the same time. Hence, attraction and aversion do not have a "full" relationship of exclusion to each other like pure color experiences. On the other hand, also with cognitive states it seems that we can be *temporarily* incoherent. Hence, the difference seems to become weaker. Cognitive states, however, have an *impetus* toward coherence, in contrast to feeling states. That is, I might be able to temporarily believe it is raining and also believe it is not raining. But the impetus toward coherence of cognitive states will *then* put pressure on me to resolve this. And *that* is what is different to the kind of exclusion that can happen with feeling states. If I experience attraction and aversion toward the same object, I might experience some tension between the two directions. There is, however, no impetus to *resolve* this tension. Hence, what is distinctive about cognitive states is not only that they can stand *in a special kind* of tension with each other (incoherence as opposed to "mere" exclusion), but that they also include *an inherent pull toward resolving* that tension. To put it in other words, incoherence is the kind of tension whose mental states move toward resolving it. Exclusion (in the form of a weaker kind of tension than impossibility) is the kind of tension whose mental states can remain in that tension, without an impetus to resolve it. What is different, then, in feeling states as opposed to cognitive states is that the kind of tension they can be in does not come with an impetus to resolve it. Cognitive states' tension comes with an impetus to resolve it.

This contrast exists, as argued, because the tension involved in cognitive states amounts to incoherence, while the tension involved in feeling states is a form of exclusion. This could exactly be explained by the more "total" nature of exclusion

---

63 Pautz argues that it is still an open puzzle for all accounts of experience (representationalism, naïve realism, perceptual confidence theories, and everything in between) that there are "certain necessary constraints on how things can visually appear" (Pautz, 2020, 257). He makes it clear that he cannot offer a satisfying solution to the puzzle either—all he argues is that the puzzle is indeed (still) a puzzle for all of us.

in contrast to incoherence. This is the thought: in incoherence, we can think of the involved mental states as still being interlocked in some way. The two mental states can relate to each other, while they each have an element that is incoherent with an element of the other mental state. In exclusion, that seems different. Exclusion is a much more total way of "not fitting together". It seems that in exclusion, the two mental states simply have nothing to do with each other. There is no comparability, and no elements or inner structure that could show some overlap. It is like apples and pears—there is no use in comparing them.[64] And as there is no way of comparing them, this can also not trigger an impetus toward resolving the tension —it is in some sense not even experienced as a tension. With cognitive states, by contrast, the two incoherent mental states still have elements, a structure, that allows them to be comparable, while incoherent with each other. This results in an impetus to resolve the tension, an impetus toward coherence.

Hence, by confronting this objection we were able to make the notion of "impetus toward coherence" sharper. First, incoherence is a different kind of tension between two mental states than exclusion. Cognitive states can be incoherent, feeling states can be in a relation of exclusion (to various degrees). What is special about cognitive states and incoherence is that *they include an impetus to resolve this tension,* in contrast to the feeling states.

2.4 Kinship with the Feeling-toward-Value Theory of Emotions

Before moving on to Chapter 3, where we explore what the proposed account means for a non-cognitive form of normative guidance, let me briefly point out that a kindred account of emotion has recently come out, the feeling-toward-value theory of emotion (Mitchell, 2021). It differs in some important respects from our account, but it shares its general spirit more than any other current theory of emotions.

To start at the strongest similarity: "The central claim of the theory of emotions as feelings-towards-values (…), is that paradigmatic emotional experiences represent evaluative properties of their particular objects *through felt valenced intentional attitudes of favour and disfavour*" (Mitchell, 2021, 106–107; my emphasis.).

That is, the feeling-toward-value theory of emotion also claims that we have a way of feelingly picking up on value, which is not mediated by cognition or cognitive

---

64 This is, of course, only true in a limited way. Two pure colors exclude each other while they both fall under the category of color. Apples and pears are in some sense incomparable, while they are both fruits. What seems true, however, is that the experience of pure red and the experience of pure green might not share anything with each other.

attitudes, and which operates in the modes of attraction (favor) and aversion (disfavor). Mitchell says that "one is affectively moved by the object" (Mitchell, 2021, 102). He then also makes clear, just like we did, that his account differs from perceptualism about emotions (cf. Mitchell, 2021, 100), and that the felt valenced attitudes are not the same as desire (or conative attitudes more generally) (cf. Mitchell, 2021, 116).

The way in which Mitchell distinguishes his account from perceptualism, however, brings to the fore the first difference to our account: the role that reason-responsiveness plays in his account. He argues that perceptualism "struggles to accommodate this idea of *being moved by value*" (Mitchell, 2021, 102). He rightly points out that "to encounter a particular object and its properties is not the same as being affectively moved by it (...)" (Mitchell, 2021, 102). What is a difference to our account, however, is that he understands this "being moved by value" as a form of reason-responsiveness. He says, "emotions are reasons-responsive in a way that arguably perception is not" (Mitchell, 2021, 98). He thinks that this reasons-responsiveness is also reflected in emotional phenomenology: "(...) such that it is a feature of emotional experience that it involves a phenomenology of affective response" (Mitchell, 2021, 100). Here and throughout the book, it becomes clear that he treats "affective response (to be moved by value)" as equivalent with "reason-responsiveness". Now, the difference to our account could in the end boil down to a terminological question, namely, to how narrow or broad we understand the term "reason". For our account, I deliberately avoided talk of reason and reason-responsiveness exactly because this sounds like reintroducing a form of cognitivism. Perhaps Mitchell understands reason in a fully non-cognitive sense. But if not, emotions' reason-responsiveness could be interpreted as reintroducing cognitivism in the following way: emotions can be a guide to value because they are reasons-responsive. That is, what really entails the normative content are *reasons*. Emotions do not themselves entail normative content, but they can guide us whenever they are responsive to normative content, in the form of reasons. By responding to reasons, then, they get cognitively penetrated. In the end, they are normative guides *by being (able to be) cognitively penetrated*. (Why and how this is not the case in our account is the main topic of Chapter 3.)

Now, importantly, this is *not* how Mitchell tells the story. I suspect that he has a more neutral, and perhaps metaphorical sense of "reasons" in mind. But no matter what we call "the thing" to which emotions respond (and thanks to which they then are geared toward value), it seems then that "that thing" is what introduces the normative guidance into the story, and not the emotions. All the emotions can do is to be good (sensitive enough) *responses* to value (or reason). In such an account, then, it is not the emotions *themselves* that are normative guides, but "the thing" (or "reasons") with which they get penetrated (or to which they respond) when everything goes well. That is why I avoided reasons-talk throughout my own account. I think there are other ways available to us of cashing out how emotional responses can be a form of "being moved by value" than reason-responsiveness, ways that do not reduce them to being a good *response* to value, but that instead make value being *partly constituted* by being part of an emotional response. Again, this sounds a bit vague and would need much more elaboration which goes beyond the scope of this book. But I think it does boil down to a difference to the feeling-toward-value theory of emotions, even if Mitchell did not have a narrow sense of "reason" in mind.

Second, Mitchell's argument why the felt valenced attitudes of favor and disfavor are not the same as desire (or conative attitudes more generally) boils down to showing that they have a different direction of fit. He says: "(...) disfavour is not the same thing as wanting some state of affairs to cease, and favour is not the same thing as wanting some state of affairs to continue. (...) Conative-attitudes (...) seek to make it such that the relevant state of affairs (...) be fulfilled. (...) Contrastingly, the affective-attitudes of favour and disfavour are valenced responses to states of affairs that have already obtained" (Mitchell, 2021, 116).

That is, Mitchell understands the affective-attitudes of favor and disfavor as having a mind-to-world direction of fit, while we understand our concept of emotional responses to share with desire that they want to bring about something in the world—thus as having a world-to-mind direction of fit. We pointed out, as a contrast to desire, that our emotional responses do entail a movement in the direction of attraction (or aversion), thus are inherently linked to action, while desire can be "stationary" in the sense that one is not already moving toward the object by desiring it. Hence, not only do we see the contrast to desire differently, but also, we assume a different direction of fit between our concept of emotional response and his concept of "affective-attitudes of favor and disfavor".

Perhaps this is related to the first difference we pointed out. The first difference consisted in the role reason-responsiveness plays in Mitchell's account. This, together with what he says about direction of fit, makes his account seem to be clearly on the side of emotions being a special kind of *responsiveness*, their goodness consisting in properly picking up on how things are, just about evaluative, that is, value-related objects. While, in his account, one is *moved* by the value (and therefore it is not a kind of perceptualism), this being moved still is a kind of "appropriate response" to the value that is already out there—hence the mind-to-world direction of fit. Thus, our accounts seem to be the same all the way up to emotional experiences having a special kind of intentionality by "being moved" in a certain direction, in a felt way. Then, it seems, our accounts come apart in how realist we are about the object that "moves" one through the emotional experience. In my account, I take it that the emotional response is not just a being moved in a direction by an already existing, objective value, but that *part of what makes* something a right response is that it feels good/right to respond that way in that situation. Mitchell is more realist than me in his account of the value-relation of emotional experiences. Hence, he suggests a different direction of fit and talks about reason-responsiveness.

The last difference is, however, perhaps the most significant one. Mitchell's feeling-toward-value theory of emotion is a theory of emotions *tout court*. That is, he takes himself to explain the nature of emotions, in general. By contrast, as I pointed out at the beginning of the book and as I repeated when I contrasted my account with mere non-cognitivism about emotions, my account is an account about *one special kind* of emotion, the (non-sophisticated) emotional responses, and I claim that (also) they play a crucial normative role in our lives. I pointed out there that my account is in principle compatible with cognitivism about all other kinds of emotions. By suggesting that there is a kind of object-directedness that works without representation, I said, my view is thus more general (and more radical) than mere non-cognitivism. At the same time, it is narrower than non-cognitivism about emotions *tout court*, because it only makes this radical claim about a certain kind of emotions, the spontaneous emotional responses.

Now, let me make my position a bit clearer. I think cognitivism about emotions turns out to be true about a vast number of emotions, the sophisticated ones. Even though this is today a minority view (but still held by Nussbaum, McDowell, Sherman, for instance), I find it convincing for many reasons. To defend this here in this book would go beyond its scope. This book is about exactly those kinds of emotions (basic emotional responses) that do *not* fit into the cognitivist account of emotions. Of those kinds of emotions, I want to give an appropriate account, and show that also they play a crucial normative role in our lives. So, cognitivism about emotions cannot be right *tout court*, in my view, but, on the other hand, a feeling-toward-value account (or non-cognitivism more generally) of emotions cannot be true *tout court*, either. In other words, if I had more space, I'd defend a view on emotions where *some* emotions turn out to be cognitive in the strong sense (belief-like as in Nussbaum, or imbued by reason as in McDowell), and *some* turn out to be non-cognitive and non-representational as described in this book. They each play important, albeit different, normative roles in our lives. Of course, if one has such a (prima facie) non-unified account of emotions, one needs to say something about their relation. This, again, would go beyond the scope of this book. Chapter 4, however, will be concerned with how we can think of the unity of emotional responses and our rational capacities – that is, how they need to be thought of as cooperatively working together for fully virtuous normative guidance. This is a first start of how to think of the unity of non-cognitive and cognitive mental states (at least in the realm of normative guidance), and thus by extension, also a start in how to think of the unity of non-cognitive and cognitive emotions.

Either way how this would have to be cashed out, this shows a clear difference in the scope of the claim being made in my account as opposed to Mitchell's feeling-toward-value theory of emotion. His account makes a claim about the nature of *all* emotions, while I stay neutral (with strong sympathies toward a cognitivist account) about the nature of a vast number of emotions not captured by my account.

Let us now move on to Chapter 3, where we explore what the here defended distinction between cognitive and feeling states means for a (purely) non-cognitive form of normative guidance.

Conclusion of this Chapter

We have seen that feeling states are those which are best characterized by how it feels to experience the mental state, while cognitive states are those which are best characterized by an impetus toward coherence. I argued that this distinction is fundamental, in the sense that all mental states can be divided into these two classes, no matter what else can be said about them. I take this fundamental difference between cognitive and feeling states to strengthen my claim that the contribution of emotional responses to normative guidance cannot be replaced by cognitive capacities. We will see in the following chapters how exactly this distinction helps understand the independent role of feelings in decision-making.

Moving on with this distinction in mind, I will now consider in the next chapter three challenges to the claim that feeling states in general, and emotional responses in particular, can be normative guides. The first challenge states that feeling states or emotional responses are too fallible, that is, that they go wrong too often or too systematically to be normative guides. The second challenge states that even if they can guide us normatively, they can only do so because they have been imbued with a cognitive structure first. As a third challenge, I consider two positions in which emotions play a crucial normative role, to the effect that they might appear close to my own position. I argue that both these positions are importantly different to mine because they fail to accommodate the role of *affective learning*, a notion I develop in response to the first two challenges.

By arguing against these three challenges, I ultimately aim to show that the identification of normativity with rationality (the cognitive) is wrong and that the ability of feeling states to guide us normatively becomes visible only once we reject this identification.

Chapter 3: Against the Identification of Normativity with Rationality

In this chapter, I ask whether the normative and the rational are the same. This question, however, is too hard to tackle directly, in particular since my answer is "no"—and this is not a traditional answer. Rather than address the question directly, then, I counter three challenges that could be mounted against my argument for normative guidance by emotional responses. The first two challenges relate to the emotional responses' ability to get things right and their relation to rationality. The third challenge is of a different sort, namely, insofar as it puts forward a claim about the nature of emotional responses. Emotional responses, the challenge goes, are akin to "knee-jerk" responses, acquired as the contingent result of evolutionary processes. Though positions of the third kind ascribe normative guidance to emotional responses, they fail to accommodate an idea that is crucial for my view. Namely, they fail to accommodate *affective learning* as a crucial aspect of the normative guidance of emotional responses, as I call learning and improving of emotional responses that works in an affective manner.

First, in § 3.1, I counter the challenge that emotional responses cannot normatively guide us because they are fallible, that is, because they can lead us astray in our moral decisions, or more strongly, because they always or systematically lead us astray. These considerations lead me to some fundamental matters: the question of whether we should identify normativity and rationality. Ultimately, if my claim that emotional responses can provide normative guidance is to be compelling, this identification must be rejected. Accordingly, as I explore and respond to the three objections, I am most fundamentally concerned with this: normativity is not to be identified with rationality, for otherwise there is no room for normative guidance by emotional responses.

Turning to the second objection, in § 3.2, I counter the challenge that even if the emotional responses play the outlined unique role in normative guidance, they can only do so because they were habituated *by reason* to respond in the right way. In other words: the challenge says that the emotional responses' unique role is not one they can really take on by themselves, as they only operate as a medium for reason to "speak through". One version of the challenge is that, even if at a given moment it really is the emotional response itself that is guiding, this is only possible because the agent's affective dispositions have, some time prior to this situation, been properly trained *by reason* to do so. On another version of this line of thought, emotional responses can function as more convenient, quicker responses to moral situations. As such, they can be used *by reason* as a first indication, helping us decide what to do. In both approaches, it is ultimately reason alone that does

https://doi.org/10.1515/9783110780932-006

the work of normative guidance. While I will be mainly concerned with the first version here, I think my response applies also to the second version.

Finally, in § 3.3, I argue that it is wrong to think of the emotional responses considered here as mere "knee-jerk responses"[65]. The notion of *affective learning* that I develop in this chapter helps us see why. Building on that, I compare my account of emotional responses to the one of "learned bodily responses" from Jesse Prinz. Prinz and others rely on an evolutionary story in order to explain the capacity for guidance of emotional responses. I argue that we need *not* pursue the route of thinking of emotional responses as products of evolution in order to argue for their capacity for normative guidance.

But for now, let us turn to the first challenge, the presumed fallibility of emotional responses.

3.1 The Fallibility of Emotional Responses

The challenge from the fallibility of emotional responses can be summarized as follows. What if my emotional responses go wrong, at least every once in a while?[66] What if they are sometimes mistaken and lead me to do a morally bad thing?[67] The challenge arises from the insight that our emotional responses are fallible. A more extreme version of the challenge is to allege that emotional responses *systematically* lead us astray. For instance, some think that implicit bias (racial, gender, class, etc.) is best explained in terms of unconscious emotional responses (cf., for example, Jost, Banaji, and Nosek, 2004). If so, then there are at least some emotional responses that are systematically misleading.[68] A more general version of this concern, not limited to implicit bias, might be ascribed to Kant. Here, the claim is that feelings or emotional responses in general are *that which needs to be overcome* in order to act in the best way. Whatever they may lead us to do, the thought goes, they *cannot* lead us to act with the right motivation, namely, the moral motivation of acting from respect for the moral law. Admittedly, the

---

65 A term coined by Jaggar (1989, 153).
66 Others call this the question of "reliability" of the emotions. (Cf., for example, Dohrn, 2008.)
67 This is a question that is tricky for anyone who argues that the emotions should play a role in decision-making. It seems that especially sentimentalist accounts, accounts that argue that normativity *mainly* or *exclusively* derives from feelings or passions, often turn a blind eye against this challenge. As I share some of the premises with sentimentalist accounts, I want to make sure to have a response to this question. See Bell (2013) for a recent version of a sentimentalist account of normativity.
68 This is also a view defended in Goldie (2008).

Kantian position does not say that emotional responses never pick out the right thing to do. Say, one's emotional response may push one to help one's friend when it is also one's duty to help one's friend. But the Kantian position says that emotional responses never supply the motivation that by itself is good. Only to act from duty is morally worthy, and when we act from duty, we are motivated by reason's regard for the moral law (and not from any emotional state). Another position that concedes nothing of any value to the emotional responses is Stoic ethics. Here, the emotions are, in all cases, tumultuous disturbances in our mind. They disturb our reasoning faculties, that is, they disturb the one and only way in which we can figure out what we should be doing.

I think of these (and other) versions of the fallibility challenge as situated along a spectrum. At one end of the spectrum, emotional responses are bona fide normative guides, though sometimes they get things wrong. A view that sits somewhere in the middle of the spectrum says that they often get things right, and often get things wrong. A view at the other end of the spectrum says that they are consistently responsible for bad decisions. My response aims to refute all versions of the challenge that are too far at this latter extreme. "Too far", for present purposes, cannot be numerically specified. We are not looking for a certain percentage of cases. Any position is too far at the latter extreme, I will argue, according to which no room is left for a significant range of instances where emotional responses get things right.

My refutation begins with the following observation. Our cognitive capacities —our capacities to deliberate and think through questions and problems—are fallible too, in the moral realm and beyond. One reason why people often seem less troubled by this, it seems, is the (unargued for) assumption that nevertheless, reason or deliberative thinking is the best we have. If sincere deliberating goes wrong, the thought goes, we have tried our best, and we just have to accept the limitations of our capacities. To strengthen the pull of this view, many moreover think that deliberating is exactly what *compensates* for the shortcomings of emotional responses. Even if we sometimes can rely on emotional responses to some degree, the thought goes, it is *as reasoners* that we find out when they go right or wrong, and it is as reasoners that we can correct any wrong guidance by the emotional responses. Hence the common usage of the notion of "rationality" as "that which is correct." "It was rational to decide to go there", "it was rational to believe he would be home"—when we talk like this, we mean that it was right to decide to go there and that it was justified to believe he would be home. In other words, our ordinary talk often presupposes that the rational is what should be done and what should be believed. We take deliberation to be the best decision-making capacity we have.[69] When we make this assumption, we often explicitly appeal to the contrast between deliberation qua rational response on the one hand, and emotional responses on the other hand. But if we do not simply grant the identification of normativity with rationality, these moves are not available. In that case it becomes a problem for our opponent that our cognitive capacities, just like emotional responses, are also fallible. The mere fact of fallibility, then, does not demonstrate the inferiority of emotional responses in normative guidance.

Perhaps our opponent will make her position more radical rather than conceding that the emotional responses and our reasoning are both fallible. That is, perhaps our opponent will opt for a position at the end of the spectrum, arguing that the emotional responses are *always* wrong. This would indeed mean that we should never follow their lead. It seems impossible to empirically substantiate the claim that the emotional responses always misguide us. Our opponent will not be able to consider all instances of a person making a decision, discerning that the person's emotional response (if any) is misleading. Perhaps our opponent would not go an empirical route. Perhaps she aims for some kind of Cartesian skepticism regarding the emotions. An evil demon, let us say, has set up our emotional responses in such a way that they consistently and systematically lead us astray. I set this option aside on account of its implausibility. If an evil demon wanted us to systematically be led astray, the demon would seem likely to misdirect both our reasoning and our emotional responses.

Perhaps our opponent could try to make the point that our cognitive capacities are *less often* wrong than emotional responses. However, note that even if it were true that purely cognitive deliberation is *less often* wrong than the emotional responses, and even if there were a conceptual reason why this is so, this would not necessarily mean that we should not rely on our emotional responses at all for normative guidance. Perhaps there are types of situations where, typically, emotional responses are the only capacity to supply normative guidance. If so, then we might want to identify these types of situations, and we would have reason to listen to the emotional responses in particular in these situations, though on the whole they are more fallible than the cognitive capacities. Perhaps, then, as I argued in Chapter 1, emotional responses supply a unique and irreplaceable kind of normative guidance. If so, we may want to avail ourselves of this guidance, even if it is not a pervasive dimension of our decision-making. This view is situated somewhere in the middle of the spectrum I mentioned earlier: at least sometimes, emotional responses get things right. So, we can safely leave the (ultimately empirical)

---

69 Or, at least, we think that going *against* our deliberated decisions is bad.

claim open whether emotional responses are *more* fallible than purely cognitive deliberation.

What I would like to do now is to propose an alternative way of conceiving of normative guidance, a way that does not identify normativity with rationality. Instead, the thought goes, we need to rely on both capacities—cognitive deliberation and the emotional responses—for full normative guidance. The proposal is that both capacities, for reasoning and for emotional responses, are fallible. They can and do go wrong at times. But in some situations, the proposal goes, we just *have to* listen to our emotional responses, namely, for example, when given habits and belief-sets need to be disrupted, no matter the fact that the emotional responses are fallible. And in some other situations, we just have to listen to our cognitive capacities, no matter the fact that they are fallible. This might sound pessimistic, as it allows for a lot of uncertainty when we make decisions. But the bright side of this proposal is that for both kinds of situations, we can make the respective capacity *less* fallible with good training (discussed in the next section).[70]

In other words, the proposal is no more pessimistic than accounts that identify normativity with rationality. On the contrary. Though it allows for mistakes, it also points to one more resource for correcting our mistakes. Insofar as we have *two* kinds of capacities when we make decisions, we have capacities that can keep a check on each other. Where reasoning goes wrong, we often can correct the mistake by more reasoning; where emotional responses go wrong, we may be able to correct the mistake by improved affective responses. But in other cases, our two kinds of decision-making abilities interact. Emotional responses can give us pause, alerting us to things we get wrong in reasoning. And reasoning can alert us to flawed emotions. In sum, my proposal aims to recognize that our decision-making activities are rich and complex. In spite of their fallibility, this means there are also various modes of improving and correcting ourselves.

This line of thought is not familiar. Let me therefore restate the main idea, aiming to make it as clear as possible. The mere fact that emotional responses are fallible (even if they are systematically so) is not an argument against the claim that they are unique normative guides that we need in our decision-making. Such an argument would also speak against the claim that our cognitive capacities are unique normative guides that we need in our decision-making. By contrast, it

---

70 However, I do not mean to suggest that the goal is to be infallible. This could seem to be implied in my framing things in terms of fallibility and how we can train our capacities to be less fallible. It is still possible, in my account, that even if both capacities are virtuously trained, there will be open questions about what to do and what to believe. In other words, there may always be something essentially creative and open about moral learning, independently of how fallible or infallible our capacities are.

is rather an argument to take the *training* of the emotional responses (and of the cognitive capacities) seriously. I shall take it to be uncontroversial that one *can* be better or worse at deliberative reasoning and reasoning in general.[71] Comparably, there are myriad ways in which we train the emotions, some of which I address in the next section.

How can this response to the challenge of fallibility explain that some people's emotional responses are more morally reliable than others' (inter-personal variation of reliability)? And why, within the same individual, are some emotional responses helpful and to be relied on, and others not (intra-personal variation of reliability)? And how can one identify the good ones and the bad ones? Again, both of these phenomena, the intra-personal and inter-personal variation of reliability of emotional responses as normative guides, are not a reason to say that we cannot rely on our emotional responses *at all* in decision-making. Again, we have to rather explain them through differences in the quality (and quantity) of the *training* of the emotional responses: within one individual, the emotional responses can be variously well trained for different kinds of situations and states the individual finds herself in (for instance: stress, nervousness, ambition). Depending on how well trained she is for these various situations and states, she will have differing moral accuracy when relying on her emotional responses. And the same holds inter-personally: person A might be well trained in one situation and one state, while person B is quite bad in such a situation: here, we should rather trust person A's emotional responses. But in a different situation and state, it might well be that person B's emotional responses are to be trusted.[72]

My proposal, as it were, accepts fallibility as a *general* condition of human decision-making. As a correlate, it puts strong emphasis on the fact that we can *train* our emotional and cognitive capacities to become better in decision-making. So, presumably, the thought goes, *all* human beings make mistakes in moral decisions, no matter what capacity they rely on. We just have to keep training *both* capacities to become better at it over time. We can make out differences between people and within individuals, and can explain them with different levels of experience and training. And this helps us resolve conflicts as to which emotional responses we should trust in what situation, and which human beings we should trust in

---

71 Vogt (2017) offers a discussion of this in her Chapter 4.

72 I do not want to suggest any kind of sum-equality between different people by making these statements about person A and B. Rather, it is plausible that some people are *on the whole* better in this than others, and one would hope that the older we get, the better we are in this in general. But note that not all of us get better at it with age. This is one of Aristotle's core examples in NE, Book I (Aristotle, 2002) for illustrating that in human psychology, things are only for the most part: for the most part, people get wiser over time, but we have all seen silly old people.

which situation. Erratic as human nature is, all of these forms of normative guidance only hold for the most part, and none of them provide any *guarantee* that one is doing the right thing (whether it be through cognitive or emotional capacities).

These considerations do not yet establish the claim that both rationality and emotional responses supply normative guidance. But they undermine characteristic lines of support for the identification of normativity and rationality. What needs to be shown—and this is the thought I shall pursue further as I go along —is that emotional responses not only give us pause and help us by prompting reflection. More than that, it needs to be shown that their normative guidance is a kind of justification. When we pause or change course based on an emotional response, the thought goes, we are *justified* in doing so. This is what the claim that emotions provide normative guidance amounts to.

3.2 Emotional Responses as a Habituated Form of Reason

The second challenge against my proposal goes as follows. The emotional responses, it is argued, necessarily need to be trained or educated *by reason* in order to play their role in normative guidance.[73] Therefore, rather than being a normative guide on their own, they are (at least sometimes) merely a medium for reason to "speak through". They are aides of reason. When moral decisions have to be made, the emotional responses may enable us to respond faster, or perhaps they supply relevant motivational states. This challenge could be mounted in an effort to show that it is always, ultimately, *reason* that guides normatively, no matter appearances to the contrary. Ultimately, the thought goes, only reason can justify. Accordingly, only reason can be responsible for moral behavior.

It is a longstanding premise in philosophy that rationality and normativity go together. This is, most notably, what cognitivists about emotions (who at the same time also take such emotions to play a normative role) would argue. That is, cognitivists' thought is that *because* emotions are belief-like or imbued with reason, they play a role in normative guidance. With this, they agree with rationalists (e.g., in the Kantian and Stoic ethical traditions) that normativity only arises through rationality.[74]

---

73 A version of this view is, for example, found in McDowell (1998a) and in Sherman (1989).
74 I take Nussbaum (2001) to be a Stoic version (belief-like) of this and McDowell (1998a) to be a rationalist version (imbued with reason), although it should be noted that McDowell himself takes this to be an Aristotelian position. A Kantian rationalist who identifies normativity with reason (besides Kant himself in his *Groundwork*) would be Korsgaard (2009, 2008, 1999, 1996a, 1996b).

Reason or rationality, the thought goes, must be the ultimate ground for anything normative. The relevant intuitions run deep, and the premise has been defended in any number of ways throughout the history of philosophy. It is thus not my aim to discredit them in a wholesale manner. But often enough, the premise has the role of an unquestioned conviction. It is assumed as a natural starting-point, as if it did not require any justification.

I want to resist this tendency, and ultimately, I want to reject the premise that normativity must be grounded in rationality. As a first step, I want to flag that the traditional starting point is not banal at all. The burden of proof is not necessarily on the side of those who aim to show that a different capacity than reason can also be a genuine, independent ground for normative guidance (or indeed, for normativity). To illustrate this point, let me take up one prominent position from the history of philosophy that has *argued* (not taken for granted) that reason or rationality must be the ultimate ground for anything normative. Kant, when putting forward an account of morality, argues in the *Groundwork* that it is reason and only reason with which we can arrive at the *necessary maxims* for our actions and intentions. Thus, it is reason (alone) that can ground morality. Any other capacity or faculty might be able to provide us with other kinds of "shoulds." But according to Kant, these "shoulds" will not have the moral *necessity* of the maxims arrived at with reason. Consequently, only that which is at least compatible with these necessary maxims can be moral. Hence, there is no morality besides the one arrived at with reason, and no place for other capacities to ground anything moral.

Let me only tentatively hint at how one could respond to such a position. First, the last point seems questionable. Does morality have to exclusively consist of that which is compatible with *necessary* maxims? What if we can have moral insights that are right only "for the most part",[75] or perhaps even "only now"? I am aware that this goes against the core of Kant's project in defending the categoricity of moral norms. He calls exactly these kinds of non-necessary shoulds, taken as a moral maxim (by acting according to them), *the morally evil (Religionsschrift)*. For present purposes, it is not possible to address this debate fully. However, it is by no means clear that Kant is right, and that categoricity is the hallmark of the moral.[76] Perhaps there are some categorical moral norms and some non-cate-

---

75 See Vogt (2017) for an account of "for the most part regularities".
76 Williams (1982), for example, shows how *practical necessity* is always a different kind of necessity than literal or physical necessity. Practical necessity, he argues, comes about partially through facts and limits *about oneself*, facts about one's capacities and incapacities (and these facts are what gives one moral character), besides facts about circumstances. Because practical necessity (of which moral necessity is a subset) is partially constituted by facts about *oneself*, Williams ar-

gorical moral norms. Perhaps there are no categorical norms at all, though there are moral norms.[77] All this is disputed and should be recognized as such.[78]

Second, Kant rejects the idea of "formal feelings" (formale Gefühle), which is an assumption also operative in his above sketched argument. In other words, he rejects the idea that feelings could provide us with anything *general or necessary*, such as the necessary moral maxims mentioned above. Rather, his thought goes, feelings only operate according to contingent facts and affections. But what if this is wrong? In other words, *even if* we accepted that morality exclusively consists of that which is compatible with *necessary* maxims, why would feelings not be able to track these necessary maxims (and without the help of reason)? What if we have various kinds of feelings, some of which can indeed track insight into necessary things, such as into moral maxims? If this is possible (which remains an open question here), then we would have another interesting route to defend, on a more conceptual level, the idea that emotional responses can be normative guides.[79]

These remarks so far against the identification of normativity with rationality have only been a rejection of possible opponents' views. Let us now turn to a positive argument for the (independence of the) emotional responses' capacity to guide us normatively.

Rather than showing how the shaping, training, and education of the emotional responses is *not* an imparting of reason "into" them, I try to show, positively, how the shaping is achieved by the emotional responses' own means, at least partially. That is, I try to show that we can train the emotional responses in a way that does

---

gues, the categoricity involved in the "must do" can only be one of not *intentionally* doing a certain thing, and "cannot mean (...) that the world will not contain his doing that thing, for it is certainly compatible with the beliefs (...) that the agent might do the act unintentionally, for instance in ignorance" (Williams, 1982, 129). In other words, any practical necessity can only amount to a necessity relative to its subject, according to Williams. And hence, any kind of categoricity of a moral command would be undermined by such facts about the subject.

77 Compare to MacIntyre: Macintyre (1957) argues that first, moral judgments are not necessarily and essentially universalizable, and second, their distinctive function is not a prescriptive one.
78 In fact, from the late 1950s all the way into the 1980s, there was a lively debate on exactly the questions of whether, for example, moral judgments must be categorical (Gewirth (1968), for instance, argues yes) and whether they must be universalizable (Hare (1955) argues yes; Macintyre (1957) and Sprigge (1964) argue no), prescriptive (again, Hare (1955) argues yes; Macintyre (1957) argues no), overriding (Frankena (1966), Taylor (1978), and Cooper (1968) argue yes), and so on. And as Stich (2018) notes, no consensus was reached in any of these questions either then or now.
79 This seems to be related to a claim I made in Chapter 1, namely, that I seem to need to subscribe to some form of Humean account of *general properties* if I want to say that the non-cognitive emotional responses, when they respond to a particular in a certain moment, nevertheless pick out something *general*. Perhaps being a Humean about this already entails that I accept the possibility of "formal feelings", that is, the idea that feelings can provide insight into *general* matters.

not, at least not exclusively, rely on deliberating and reasoning, not even indirectly, for example through the imitation of a (reasoned) teacher or role model.

The question of how emotional responses can be trained or shaped into being normative guides (in a way that is not essentially based on the guidance of reason) is partially an empirical question, or to be more precise, a psychological one. So how can this have a bearing on the philosophical question at hand at all? Like this: if the philosopher's charge is that such a training is *not possible* without an imbuement of reason, then to show empirically that such training is indeed possible *falsifies* this (strong) philosophical claim (and I do not intend to show more than that).[80] Indeed, if the philosopher were then to respond that the normativity of the here empirically considered training of emotional responses is still "in some way" grounded on rationality ("what makes this good or right is its rationality"), then his claim just begs the question.

Let me clarify the demonstrandum at hand. In the following, the goal is not to say that no cognitive, rational, reflective, or intellectual capacities are "mixed into" the processes of moral learning here described. Rather, the goal is to say that they do not necessarily always do the crucial work, the work that results in the moral learning of a child or adult. And even if they do *some* of the crucial work, my goal would still be achieved: to show that there are some *aspects* and some *parts* of moral learning that are *not* done through reasoning, not even indirectly, but that are rather done through an affective way of refining one's feelings for moral situations *itself.* The demonstrandum, then, is to show that moral learning *also* depends on some genuine contribution from the emotional responses and the feelings of a human being, without any thinking or deliberating involved in the feeling. In other words, the goal is to show that there *are some* aspects and parts to moral learning that genuinely do not come from any of the rational or cognitive capacities. And the claim is that this is not just the case as a matter of empirical fact, but that there is something about the feeling aspect of the learning process itself that is irreplaceable: if it were not learned through feeling one way or another, something would be wrong or missing.

So, after these clarifications, let us imagine a child whose capacities are not yet shaped to distinguish between good and bad. That is, the child does not have much experience in distinguishing between good and bad actions, good and bad intentions, and so on. It is a genuinely innocent kind of character that does not yet have propensities or tendencies toward one kind of action pattern or another.

---

80 Of course, a conceptual position on the intrinsically rational nature of morality like Kant's, mentioned before, is not falsified by an empirical finding of this kind. But I indicated how such a conceptual position is problematic on other grounds.

With this thought experiment I do not want to claim that the characters human beings usually start out with actually are this way, a tabula rasa, as it were. I just want to imagine a situation where *good and bad* still have to be learned to be distinguished from each other. I take it that the following thoughts would also work if one imagined that the child already had some tendencies rather than others, as long as these tendencies do not yet track morality in a systematic way. The only scenario for which the thought experiment would be invalid is one in which we would assume that human beings are already born with a finetuned "moral compass"; that they have an inborn capacity to distinguish the good from the bad. Again, I am not excluding here that we are born with evaluative tendencies, as work in evolutionary psychology suggests.[81] Such tendencies, of course, may be good and bad, altruistic, hostile, etc. I only exclude that we are born with more than that, with dispositions to correctly distinguish what is ethically and morally right and wrong, good and bad. In such a scenario, the concept of moral learning is itself invalid, and thus I exclude this scenario for the present purposes as one that seems implausible.

So now let us imagine how such a not-yet-morally-trained character can learn *just some things* about what is good and bad without necessarily always depending on intellectual or cognitive processing of what is going on. That is, how can such a character learn to distinguish good and bad not just independently of cognitive deliberation but also independently of the reflected views of a rational teacher or role model (which would be an indirect transmission of a cognitive structure[82])? Is it possible to learn some good and bad principles of human life just by *feeling* responses, such as spontaneous aversions and attractions?

Let us borrow some terms from psychology. In *embodied cognition* accounts, for example, psychologists talk about the "associative relevance of perceptual stimuli", and of the "salience of perceptual stimuli".[83] So, let us imagine that *on a feel-*

---

[81] See, for instance, de Waal (1996 and 2006), who argues that the existing evidence demonstrates that the fundamental building blocks of human moral psychology already exist in nonhuman primates, and can thus be explained well in evolutionary terms.

Stanford (2018) builds on this and similar findings to argue that we externalize moral commands (that is, we claim that they are objectively true) because this turned out to be useful for cooperation and for creating prosocial norms of interaction in former human generations, and thus got selected in the evolutionary process.

[82] Of course, in human interaction (as in the interaction of a guardian and a child) you can never fully pull apart dimensions of reasoning and feeling. But it would be wrong to infer from this that everything the child learns from interacting with the guardian originates from cognitive or rational sources. And as long as this is not the case, our thought experiment still works for our demonstrandum, even if we imagine the child interacting with adults (and with children).

[83] Azevedo, Garfinkel, Critchley, and Tsakiris (2017).

ing basis, a child can learn about the associative relevance of some perceptual stimuli and the irrelevance of others. For example, the child might start acting according to an associative relevance along the lines of "for the most part, when I encounter x, I should look out for y." This is, of course, not to be thought of as a mental rule that the child "goes through" in her mind. The associative relevance is instead operative on a feeling basis. To put it in other words, for the most part, when x happens, y becomes *salient* to the child. An example: "For the most part, when another child in the sandbox cries, I should look out whether I or someone else did something that hurt the child." Again, this is not to be thought of as a mental rule that the child consciously follows. Rather, it should be thought of as something that is operative in the background that makes the child *feel* a certain way, that is, that makes certain things more salient to the child than others.

So, the child learns that certain situations call for[84] the salience of certain stimuli. *How* does the child learn this? If it were only possible by someone *telling* him that this is so, or through a cognitive deliberation done by the child, then the child would *depend on* cognitive capacities in order to learn this. My claim, however, is that this is *not necessary.* Already a child, I submit, can *affectively pick up* when a certain situation, for example if another child is crying, calls for certain responses. Perhaps it has indeed first had to see others *show caring attitudes* in such situations. This is hardly a problem for our current demonstrandum. The demonstrandum is shown as soon as we can see a way how the child starts *feeling* caring attitudes[85] in situations where they are called for, without the need of someone having told him to do so, and without the need of the child deliberating about it. If these conditions are met, I submit, then the child picked up the right behavior *affectively*, on a *feeling* basis.

But let us say our child does not get it right from the beginning, or that he does not even get it right for the most part—that is what it means that he does not yet have an established moral character. Just every once in a while, he (perhaps sometimes even accidentally) *hits on* the right response, and other times he is confused

---

84 We can think of the situation "calling for" a certain response in similar terms again as we did when we considered the analogy of puzzle pieces for cognitive states: the structure of certain situations *creates the tendency* for us to respond in a certain way. Hence, the "calling for" need not be something like a rational or cognitive demand. Here, we might think, it is rather a "calling for the appropriate salience" that is involved. And the point is that the child picks up on this *affectively.* Through experiences of this kind, a child learns in an affective way what responses are appropriate, without thinking about them and without other cognitive operations.

85 Betzler (2014) argues that caring is a prototype of commitment, the kind of prototype of commitment that children have before their rational capacities are fully grown.

as to what is going on around him. How does he get from these chance-like situations to an established pattern of responding the right way?

There are plenty of things guardians do (intuitively or not, and not cognitively) to help the child become more secure and experienced in such situations. Imaginative role-playing, for instance, is thought to enlarge empathy for others,[86] and most guardians do this kind of role-playing without any specific moral (or deliberated) goals in mind. It is a playful role-taking that human beings do with children (and with adults) for fun and without deliberating, and nevertheless it has the tendency to *stabilize* a young character's emotional responses in moral situations by adding to the child's experiences.

And there is more. We can think of the emotional responses of a young character as operating with basic, *affective kinds of heuristics*, as opposed to anything deliberative or cognitive. These non-cognitive heuristics, I argue, are able to stabilize the normative guidance on the basis of the felt emotional responses over time. Gaut (2017) considers partially non-cognitive heuristics when he asks whether creativity can be taught. Gaut's question is similar to ours. He maintains that teaching creativity cannot consist in giving the learner *instructions* on what to do. It must be a kind of teaching that triggers the learner to figure out by herself what it is to be creative (otherwise she would not count as genuinely creative). So, any kind of cognitive instructions on what to do are already precluded from the teaching. And this is analogous to our question: How can a child learn to distinguish good from bad genuinely by himself, without cognitive instructions? Other heuristics than cognitive ones on the part of the learner are thus needed in such a situation, heuristics that are *feeling based*, rather than akin to cognitive instructions. Gaut says:

> The (…) ability to produce new things can be taught. For instance, one may look for similarities between disparate areas by *seeking analogies*; (…) One may generate new works, for instance, by constructing fictional worlds that *display analogies* with other successful works (…). One can also generate new ideas in art by a *close attention to experience*; (…) For instance, *introspective attention* to how one's mind works can be a valuable source of insight in psychology. (Gaut, 2017, 273)

To some degree, Gaut's examples are, of course, far from a young character's repertoire. However, we find helpful suggestions here: *seeing analogies* between disparate areas, and *paying introspective attention*. These two are affective processes that are already operative in a child, and can thus play a role in figuring out what to do. A child might over time and experience start to see an analogy

---

86 Rorty (1998, 111) also builds on this idea when she considers how a slide into corruption could be prevented through certain early childhood experiences.

along the following lines: "If I did not *feel well* after I snatched another child's toy (because she then cried), then perhaps I should not, *analogically*, secretly steal this other toy now from my brother." Of course, if we try to formulate the "seeing analogies" in a sentence-structure, like here, the insight seems to be in the form of a deliberative syllogism. This is only a limitation of the language in which we are trying to make sense of the idea of "seeing analogies" here. And of course, reasoning might be *part of* the picture of the learning process on the whole here, because *in between* the affective heuristics, the child might indeed already have to draw some simple inferences. The point is that there is also crucially something *affective* going on, from which the child learns moral lessons that it would otherwise not learn. And these affective parts and aspects of the learning experience do not build on anything reflective or rational. So, in other words, there is something irreducibly affective going on in the learning process, some affective heuristics that are not further reducible to anything cognitive or rational, and without which the moral learning would not happen. And this is what I call the *affective heuristics* that are involved. In the example above, we see at least two heuristics at play: the child *paid attention* to how he *felt* during one scenario, and then he *saw similarities*, so that he was able to transpose that feeling into the new situation.

And we find more about these heuristics in Gaut's suggestion of how one can teach creativity:

> The role of questions and suggestions is to *connect the problem with the student's formerly acquired knowledge and experience*, so that solutions found to be effective in similar situations can be considered in new ones. But this *spotting of similarities* requires (...) no mechanical rules. This is why, as Ian Stewart notes in the foreword to Polya's book [an influential advanced math textbook], these heuristic techniques have resisted algorithmic formulation in computer programs. The questions asked are ones that are "typically useful", but there are no guarantees. (Gaut, 2017, 277; my emphasis)

And:

> We noted differences between the heuristics employed in teaching creativity in writing and those used in mathematics; (...) [but both] learners need to *practice*, to *imitate well*, to be *highly motivated*, and to have an ability to *see likenesses* between dissimilar things. (Gaut, 2017, 282–283)

If we apply these thoughts to our case, we can say that the new situation has to be close enough to the child's former *experiences*, so that the child is able to *affectively connect* the feeling from one situation with the other. This enables a *spotting* of similarities, as Gaut calls it, which does not operate according to any mechanical rules—this is so because such similarities only happen "for the most part" in "typical" situations that are sufficiently similar. These kinds of varied experiences—situations where the learned responses are applicable and situations where they are not—*refine* a young character's affective responses *over time* (by repetition that ensures practice) and enable improvement in picking out the good and the bad.[87] What seems to be involved in all forms of learning creativity, according to Gaut, is thus also applicable to a young character's affective moral learning: a lot of repetitions (practice) are needed, some form of imitation (that is not just mere copying) is going on, some sort of pleasure or motivation is involved in figuring out what to do, and the child needs to pay attention to his feelings and to try to see analogies and disanalogies.

Interestingly, the affective heuristics we just established are surprisingly similar to Burnyeat's Aristotelian suggestions of what is involved in learning to be good. Burnyeat also emphasizes that we should not think of moral development as a fully rational process:

> (...) it follows not only that for a long time moral development must be a less than fully rational process but also, what is less often acknowledged, that a mature morality must in large part continue to be what it originally was, a matter of responses deriving from sources other than reflective reason. (Burnyeat, 1980, 80)

Instead of reiterating the affective ways of shaping the emotional responses that are similar in Burnyeat's Aristotle and the literature on learning to be creative, I would like to mention one that Burnyeat discusses that has *not* yet been mentioned: the role of the feeling of *shame*. Burnyeat discusses the distinctive role of shame in moral education when he illustrates how practice can lead to moral knowledge. First, here is what he says about the step from practice to moral knowledge:

> (...) perhaps we can give intelligible sense to the thesis that practice leads to knowledge, as follows. I may be *told*, and may believe, that such and such actions are just and noble, but I have not really *learned for myself* (taken to heart, made second nature to me) that they have this intrinsic value until I have learned to value (*love*) them for it, with the consequence that I *take pleasure* in doing them. To understand and appreciate the value that makes them enjoyable in themselves I must *learn for myself to enjoy* them, and that does take time and practice—in short, *habituation.* (Burnyeat, 1980, 78; my emphasis)

---

87 There might be a question as to whether it is possible at all to improve one's feeling responses. It could be, after all, that feeling responses are something we are naturally born with, or that they are too engrained to be improved, at least from a certain age on. This would pose a significant difficulty for my account. However, Liao (2006), in his chapter *The Possibility of a Duty to Love*, argues that there is (almost) always room for improvement of our feeling responses.

The crucial difference, here, between having moral knowledge *for oneself* and "just having been told about it" seems to be a different *emotional response* to the just and noble actions. According to Burnyeat (1980, 78), only once one "has acquired a *taste* for, a capacity to *enjoy* for their own sake, things that are in fact noble and enjoyable for their own sake", has one gained moral knowledge. How does *shame* fit into this picture? In short, the difference between one who has acquired moral knowledge and one who has not is that the first will *experience shame* if she does not act according to what is noble, while the latter will not. The latter will only act according to the noble if she is forced. This force, to be sure, can also happen by way of affective influence, but it will be a different emotion: fear of punishment (cf. Burnyeat, 1980, 79). Hence, according to Burnyeat, a morally formed character and one that is not, differ fundamentally in the emotions they will give rise to vis a vis their immoral actions. This is an *affective* difference: the morally formed character will feel shame, while the other one will only feel fear of punishment.

So, now we can ask, with Burnyeat: how do these different affective setups come to be? It seems clear that when the crucial difference is an affective one, it cannot come about purely by cognitive means. At least part of the picture of arriving at a good affective setup in one's character must be an *affective* kind of learning. For example, it would be implausible that the different affective setups would come about by just *telling* each of the young persons how they should feel in these situations. How could one get someone to feel shame by just telling them to do so? We can imagine someone telling a young person "you should be ashamed!". But what does the work here, I argue, are not the words or their content but rather the emotion that is expressed by the person uttering them. If this person is genuinely hurt or angry, *this* will make the young person feel shame. And so, it is not even necessary that the words or their content contain the cognitive content of shame. One could equally say, for example, "why did you do that?" with the same emotions, and they would also have the effect of instilling shame in the young person. Indeed, one might not need to say anything at all. If one can express pain or anger as a response to the young person's action without saying anything, I argue, it would still have the effect of making the young person feel shame. And this is because the crucial learning experience here is an affective one, not a cognitive one.[88]

---

[88] A cognitivist might object that the fact that the emotion of shame in this example can be elicited without words does not suffice to show that it is not cognitively mediated. However, I have allowed in my account of affective learning that the affective aspects interact with cognitive ones. What I argue is that within this mix, there are some aspects of learning that genuinely originate in the feeling itself, rather than anything else. Hence, it depends on how the cognitivist would

We could imagine, as a contrast to the above, that the other affective set-up, acting according to a fear of punishment rather than shame, could indeed come about by just hearing the words that they did something bad. That is, perhaps the fear of punishment indeed comes about purely through cognitive rather than affective learning, and that might be the very reason why mere fear of punishment is not a genuinely moral response. For instance, if someone says "you should not have done that!", it is possible for the young person to take away a purely cognitive lesson from this, namely, the lesson: "if I do that, I have to be careful not to get punished." And it might be that this is the result of *how* the "you should not have done that" was expressed. Perhaps it was expressed with no emotion at all. Perhaps it was expressed purely with a lust for punishment. If so, it was more natural for the young person to take away the message that this is about punishment, rather than about doing the right thing. In either case, we see that the affective aspect of learning plays a crucial role.

Moral learning depends on learning *in an affective way* what is involved in the situation. It depends on being able to feel shame for one's immoral actions. When moral learning goes wrong, it is either because no affective aspect was involved at all (uttering moral commands without emotion), so that the young person was forced to take away a purely cognitive message, or it is because a wrong affective aspect was involved (uttering a moral command with a lust for punishment), which might either instill a wrong emotion (fear of punishment) or a purely cognitive message (avoid punishment) in the young person.

So, for present purposes the following is the takeaway. There are different kinds of feelings involved in the moral education and shaping of a young person's emotional responses. Not all of them lead to well-adjusted, appropriate emotional responses. We can imagine various strategies and tricks for guardians to instill one feeling rather than another in a child learning from moral situations. Crucially, once one rather than another feeling is learned, for example, shame rather than fear of punishment, this new feeling *itself* becomes the driving force behind the moral learning. The child or young person will know that whenever they feel shame, they have gone wrong, and they will be motivated to try to avoid behaving in this way again, because they are ashamed of their own actions. In this way, over time, they can learn to weed out the bad from the good ways of acting, all in an

---

understand the "cognitive mediation" of the relevant learning experience here. If the cognitive mediation is only a vehicle to help the young person remember and generalize her affective experience, for example, there seems to be no problem to allow this kind of cognitive mediation in my account. If the cognitivist's claim were rather to say that a cognitive process is always already presupposed even before the young person can feel the relevant feelings, this would indeed be incompatible with my account.

ongoing process of affective learning. Emotional responses, we can conclude, can thus be a good normative guide exactly when they went through an extensive process of affective learning of this kind.

Before we close the topic of how we can think of the training of emotional responses in an affective way, let me say a few more words about the role of *chance* and the role of *control* in this process. It has become obvious that the affective shaping of the emotional responses takes place over many cycles of *trial and error*, a kind of practicing over time. At the beginning, it might be random when the young person hits on the right or wrong action, and over time they become better at feeling the right feelings in the right moments. Hence, chance plays a big role in this process, especially at the beginning. And even after an extended training of the emotional responses, we do not expect a person to always get it right. No matter whether through emotional responses or through cognitive deliberation, human beings sometimes make mistakes. And it is often up to chance what consequences arise from our actions (and what moral questions and challenges we are faced with in the first place).[89] There are many different ways in which chance enters the picture. This could make it look like affective learning is too much up to chance. After all, in affective learning we have much *less control* over the learning process than in cognitive learning. In cognitive learning, we can state clearly what the goal of an action is. We can formulate moral maxims, and we have cognitive instructions on how to act according to these maxims. This gives us much more control over the learning process than in affective learning as described above.[90]

However, that does not make affective learning *random*. Less control does not mean it is not goal directed, in an indirect way. There are *different ways in which one can deal with chance*. One can be aware of the erratic nature of human life, for example, and be ready to spot exceptional situations that call for a new kind of

---

89 This is the phenomenon that Nagel (1979) coined "Moral Luck".

90 Indeed, a cognitivist might say that how I have described *affective* learning, it seems rather close to mere classical conditioning in the Skinnerian sense. And the topic of control in the affective learning process is an important aspect in order to respond to this objection. In classical conditioning, the learning of the subject is fully out of her control. What she learns depends fully on what a trainer, or her circumstances, confront her with. This is not how we conceptualized affective learning, however. Affective learning does depend more on aspects outside of the subject's control than cognitive learning, as we have just seen. But, as I have argued in Chapter 1, I take the emotional responses to be able to pick up on *general* properties of a situation, and I have argued in Chapter 2 that emotional responses, qua feelings, give the subject a specific kind of phenomenology of the situations she finds herself in. Hence, I argue that feelings and emotional responses are an *active* kind of mental state in the learning process, and not to be thought of as mere "affective matter", as it were, that gets shaped into a certain form by classical conditioning.

behavior. As a contrast, one could ignore the role of chance and be thoroughly confused each time things go or feel differently than expected. I argue that a propensity to respond with confusion to unforeseen circumstances gets something wrong. Namely, it gets wrong how the world is, exactly in relation to the role chance plays in it. Whatever is the case on the level of fundamental physics, the world *as agents engage with it* does not display necessary regularities. Things can go one way or another, and we are subject to contingency in myriad ways. Accordingly, attitudes which recognize this dimension of the sphere of agency are virtues (I will argue for this more thoroughly in the fourth chapter). They are ways of coming to terms with the world as the world is.

This "readiness to deal with chance", I argue, is another important capacity to cultivate in an affective way. If the guardian can help the young person realize the very fact that something happened by chance, the young person will have a better feeling of how much weight to give their various experiences. If the guardian can help the young person realize the very fact that human life has a somewhat erratic nature, they will be better prepared to use their emotional responses in exceptional situations. And all of this teaching, we can imagine, is again done in an affective way. If the guardian shows their *surprise* about a situation and is *not overly angry* at the young person's wrongdoing in light of the special situation, they have shown them that this was not to be expected. If they, by contrast, rather *merely tell* (without showing the appropriate emotions) the young person when something exceptional happened, the young person would not get a grip on how to deal with exceptions and chance. To conclude, the fact that affective learning is not as much under our direct control as is cognitive learning is not a problem. It is not random. We have ways in which we can indirectly influence the course of affective learning. And crucially, that kind of influence itself also happens in an affective way. On top of that, affective learning can give us a sense of how we can deal with the very fact that chance is involved in many ways in human life. To deal with less-than-perfect-control over happenings is an important lesson and one that can be excellently trained by way of affective learning.

Now that we see that the training of the emotional responses is not an imparting of a cognitive structure onto them, it should become clear that emotional responses can be *educated* kinds of responses, while still not being *rational or cognitively penetrated* responses. This is a significant finding. To elaborate on this, I now turn to the third challenge I mention at the outset, the view that what I call emotional responses are mere "knee-jerk responses". This proposal is typically part of a cognitivist position. Any non-cognitive emotion, the thought goes, must be a mere "knee-jerk response". This classification follows if we work with a dichotomy between cognitive emotions on the one hand, and uneducated emotions on the other. But the notion of affective learning that I developed indicated that this dichotomy is wrong. It is unable to accommodate an important class of attitudes, namely, those that involve affective learning. My argument involves a comparison with a competing position. This competing view shares my premise that emotional responses are *learned bodily responses,* rather than the outcomes of cognitive or deliberative teaching. We will see, however, that the notion of *non-cognitive learning* in this otherwise similar account is quite different. Ultimately, this leads to different assumptions about the nature of the emotions and their role in normative guidance.

3.3 *Educated* but *Non-Cognitive* Emotional Responses: Not Mere "Knee-Jerk Responses" and Not Mere Products of Evolution

Alison Jaggar argues for the vital role emotions play in the construction of knowledge broadly construed. Her notion of "outlaw emotions" plays a similar role in her ethics and epistemology to the one I suggested here. She says:

> (...) *outlaw emotions* may also enable us to perceive the world differently from its portrayal in conventional descriptions. They may provide the *first indications that something is wrong with the way alleged facts have been constructed,* with *accepted understandings* of how things are. (Jaggar, 1989, 167; my emphasis)

Interestingly, hence, we also see in Jaggar's paper the idea that emotions can play the distinct role of *seeing past* accepted understandings of things, of *going beyond* alleged facts, and of bringing up the first indications that something is wrong—in other words, emotions playing the negative role of disrupting given habits or beliefs. Besides this, however, there are quite a few disanalogies between her account of outlaw emotions and my account of emotional responses playing a negative role in normative guidance. Foremost among these differences is that Jaggar is explicitly operating with a cognitivist notion of emotions, even to the extent that she calls a non-cognitive notion of emotions the "Dumb View".[91] In her view, a non-cognitive notion of emotions is *positivist.* That is, she thinks that any kind of non-cognitive account of emotions must take them to be mere products of nature, similar to knee-jerk responses.

I argue that it is wrong to call a non-cognitive notion of emotions positivist, and that this betrays an assumption of a false dichotomy between "uneducated"

---

91 She borrows this term from Spelman (1989).

and "cognitive" emotions. This false dichotomy, I argue, can be suspended now that we have the notion of affective learning available. [92]

As I have tried to show, even if we take the emotional responses to be non-cognitive, this does not at all mean that they are unformed or pure products of nature. In other words, even if we take them to be a (partially) physiological and non-cognitive affective response, we can think of them as *formed* or *informed* responses. What is more, the discussion of early childhood education showed that emotional responses can be formed and informed in better and worse ways. If parents make the effort, say, to respond in affectively nuanced ways to situations in which things go wrong, children will have an easier time to pick up the difference between actions that call for shame and others than do not. Similarly, children can have more or less of a chance to learn how to affectively deal with contingency, depending in part on their educators. That is, affective learning is real learning; it is a process that can go better or worse, first steps being stepping-stones to more complex "lessons", and so on. That is, we can think of the emotional responses as formed, even educated kinds of bodily responses, and all this still without thinking of them as being cognitive or belief-like.

Hence, Jaggar and I disagree about the nature of emotions while we partially ascribe to them a similar role in normative guidance: a breaking through given understandings, a going beyond alleged facts.[93] Let us look more closely at what she describes as a positivist account of emotions:

---

92 Another way how the accusation of positivism against an account like mine could be spelled out is to accuse it of being *atomistic.* That is, one could argue that my notion of feeling states, and my notion of spontaneous aversions and attractions, is atomistic in the sense that I think of them almost like in terms of a sense-datum, or of providing the subject with raw sense-data. A lot depends on how exactly one thinks of sense-data, of course, in order to see what this accusation would amount to. When I argued in Chapter 1 that I take emotional responses to pick up on *general* properties of a situation, I took myself to argue that emotional responses are more than just a way of providing the subject with raw sense-data. Hence, emotional responses can provide the subject with complex content too, in the sense of content that is interconnected with other contents. That is why I would not describe the notion of emotional responses I presented as atomistic, and thus not positivist in this sense either.

93 Another disanalogy between Jaggar's and my account is that *her reason* to take emotions to uniquely be able to play this normative role is different. In her account, we find the view that there is a given power structure in place between people, and this power structure can be equal or unequal. Emotions, then, can play the role of striving toward equality in the power structure (while reason, presumably, often reproduces the unequal power structure that is in place). For that reason, outlaw emotions have the potential to correct reason, according to her, because they can operate "outside" the current power structure and ideology (that is what makes them *outlaw* emotions).

Just as positivist accounts of sense perception attempted to distinguish the supposedly raw data of sensation from their cognitive interpretations, so positivist accounts of emotion tried to separate emotion conceptually from both reason and sense perception. As part of their sharpening of these distinctions, positivist con[s]truals of emotion tended to identify emotions with the physical feelings or involuntary bodily movements that typically accompany them, such as pangs or qualms, flushes or tremors; emotions were also assimilated to the subduing of physiological function or movement, as in the case of sadness, depression or boredom. (Jaggar, 1989, 154–155)

As a result of rejecting such a positivist account of emotions, she then argues that emotions cannot be defined as *feelings*, which is again in direct contrast to what I have argued so far:

The continuing influence of such supposedly scientific [positivist] conceptions of emotion can be seen in the fact that "feeling" is often used colloquially as a synonym for emotion, even though the more central meaning of "feeling" is physiological sensation. On such accounts,

---

There are several questions one could ask about Jaggar's account: why can reason not see beyond the given power structure? And why do some people have these helpful outlaw emotions, and others do not (or others have kinds of emotions such that they rather preserve the given power structure)? And even if one has outlaw emotions—are they always good because they go beyond the given power structure, or can they nevertheless also sometimes be misguided, despite being "outlaw"?

To the last question, she responds:

"I suggest that emotions are appropriate if they are characteristic of a society in which all humans (and perhaps some non-human life too) thrive, or if they are conducive to establishing such a society" (Jaggar 1989, 168).

And her response to why some people experience such helpful outlaw emotions and others do not is along the following lines: only subordinated people experience outlaw emotions; hence, one needs to listen to them in order to be able to make the power structure equal, as this is the epistemic privilege to see power inequality that subordinated people possess. In her own words:

"(...) the perspective on reality that is available from the standpoint of the subordinated, which in part at least is the standpoint of women, is a perspective that offers a less partial and distorted and therefore more reliable view. Subordinated people have a kind of epistemological privilege in so far as they have easier access to this standpoint and therefore a better chance of ascertaining the possible beginnings of a society in which all could thrive" (Jaggar 1989, 168).

One question that remains unclear is why this is uniquely the role of outlaw *emotions* and why there would not also be a corresponding notion of "outlaw thoughts" in her account.

To make a long story short, a great disanalogy between her and my account is her assumption of a power structure that explains the unique helpfulness of (outlaw) emotions, and that explains, according to her, why some people's emotions are helpful in this way and others' are not. I, in contrast, do not assume such a power structure, and therefore had to explain why emotional responses are uniquely helpful (which cannot be done by reason) in another way; and just as much, I had to explain in another way why some emotional responses are helpful and others are not (I cannot refer to providence from a subordinated viewpoint/person for that purpose).

emotions were not seen as being *about* anything: instead, they were contrasted with and seen as potential disruptions of other phenomena that *are* about something, phenomena such as rational judgments, thoughts, and observations. (Jaggar, 1989, 155)

Here, we find an interesting combination of topics we have investigated earlier. If I understand Jaggar correctly, she argues that because the positivist notion of emotions had some influence, people now often take "feeling" and "emotion" to be synonymous. And this, she says, is wrong because "feeling" is a physiological sensation rather than an emotion. And because physiological sensation or feeling is not *about* something, the thought goes, now emotions in this positivist (and colloquialized) view are falsely taken to not be about anything (and thus quite "dumb"). And as such "dumb physiological reactions", the emotions can only play a role as potential *disruptions* of other mental phenomena, which *are* about something.

I have argued in the first chapter that not being cognitive does not preclude emotional responses from being object-directed, hence from being *about* something. Even if that response to Jaggar were not successful, we would now have another route to respond to her charge that *non-cognitive* emotions (like in the positivist view) must be merely physiological reactions and thus dumb: *there is* a kind of education and training of emotions that is *not* an imparting of a cognitive structure onto them. Hence, so-trained emotions can still be partially a physiological sensation, in which the *felt, affective* aspect itself is educated and informed. This does not mean, as she seems to imply, that we *identify* emotions with feelings. Nevertheless, we should register the fact that emotions have a crucial feeling aspect to them, even one that is partially based on physiological responses. The point is that this feeling aspect *itself* is not necessarily an uneducated, dumb kind of response, just because it is partially based on physiological sensation. And all of this we can now argue because we have the notion of affective learning available.[94]

Let us take a closer look, however, at the type of position Jaggar targets, for instance, theories that explain emotions as "knee-jerk responses" in evolutionary terms. Jesse Prinz (2004)[95] suggests that emotions are *learned bodily responses* in this sense. The emotional responses we then have are, according to him, *embodied*

---

94 And to make my response to the above quotation complete: it is a bit odd that Jaggar would look at the role of "disrupting other phenomena that *are* about something" as something small or inferior, as it seems implied in the above quotation. These disruptions are, after all, the main role she takes the emotions to play in her own account.

95 Where he also develops a notion of "basic emotions", albeit a different one from mine.

appraisals.[96] Let us look what kind of "learning" is involved in the learned bodily responses Prinz suggests:

> Evolution has undoubtedly endowed us with distinctive physiological responses to various situations that our ancestors encountered. The heart is predisposed to race (along with several other physiological responses) when we see looming objects, snakes, crawling insects, or large moving shadows at night; or when we hear loud noises or the screams of conspecifics; or when we smell the odor of a predator. The racing heart and the other physiological changes that occur under these conditions collectively serve as a danger detector. They occur under these situations because of how we are wired. Perceptual experiences of dangerous situations are wired to cause appropriate physiological changes to occur. Some of this wiring is innate, and some is learned. Learned fear responses capitalize on phylogenetically primitive machinery. (Prinz, 2004, 69)

At first glance, it might seem that only one notion of learning is involved in Prinz' account. However, I propose that we should understand his position to include two kinds of learning. On the one hand, there is the learning explicitly described here, which is learning that takes its starting point from how "we are wired", in his words, and from what he calls "phylogenetically primitive machinery", and which *expands* this "machinery". And on the other hand, there is the *implied* learning in his account, namely, the learning that happened over millions of years and generations through the course of evolution, which built the "phylogenetically primitive machinery" in the first place. I will focus on the role of this second kind of learning that is implied in Prinz' account. I am interested in this implied kind of learning through the course of evolution because it seems that the only other accounts that have tried to give a non-cognitive notion of emotions a crucial role to play in normative guidance are accounts that rely on this kind of implied evolutionary learning.[97] And arguably, this is the closest one could get to a positivist account of emotions, where emotions still play a role in normative guidance: even though here the emotions are learned responses, from the perspective of the individual, they are often mere knee-jerk responses. So, I take Jaggar's accusation of positivism to target accounts like these, and I would like to show how mine is different. In addition, one could argue that evolutionary learning accounts like Prinz' also portray a kind of learning of the emotions that is not cognitive. Here too, I would like to show how my suggestion is different.

---

96 Here is Prinz' gloss on Appraisal Theories: "Appraisal theories claim that emotions necessarily comprise representations of organism-environment relations with respect to well-being. An embodied appraisal theory says that such representations can be inextricably bound up with states that are involved in the detection of bodily changes" (Prinz, 2004, 52).

97 Besides Prinz, see de Sousa (1987, 2002) and Kitcher (2005, 2006, 2011).

There are two similarities between an evolutionary learning account like Prinz' and my view. First, similar to what I have proposed in my account of affective learning, such an evolutionary learning account relies on the crucial role that *chance* plays in the learning process (random mutations that are then weeded out through trial and error) and the resulting diminished role of *control* in the learning process. Second, such an evolutionary learning account tries to explain the shape of our emotions in a way that does not rely on *cognitive* shaping.

And all this, it is argued in evolutionary learning accounts, ends up with emotions as functional guides in our lives. Indeed, unlike in my account, the result of such evolutionary learning is often taken to be superior to other possible guides in our lives, as it is that which most stood the test of time through many generations of human beings, and that which is most "natural" for our species.

Three things are crucially different in my account. First, I deliberately do not invoke *evolution* to explain why emotions play a crucial role in normative guidance. Though evolutionary theorists disagree on any number of questions relevant to ethics and morality, they tend to share the following feature: ethical learning is not primarily studied on the level of the individual, but insofar as human beings qua species have acquired evaluative tendencies. Accordingly, the questions I pose about individual ethical learning need to be asked *in addition* by the accounts that start out from evolution. That is, whatever normative tendencies we *as a species* have acquired, operates as a *given* on the level of the individual. If my responses as an individual are (evolutionarily) *predisposed* in one way rather than another and I am simply "wired" this way, then it seems that this is exactly something I *cannot learn* to do differently.[98] It seems an unfortunate or fortunate fact about myself, without strong options to improve upon.[99] Thus, insofar as we are talking about individual people here and now, "evolutionarily learned" responses are

---

[98] Even if one contends that evolutionary inheritance can itself be plastic rather than rigid, in the sense that the predisposition one inherited is malleable, the point still stands. What is inherited, then, is a certain *frame* within which this plasticity can be expressed. So, in that case, I still cannot learn to do things in a way that is outside this frame because of the way I am "wired". The limiting case would be a predisposition that is, as it were, completely plastic; so, this would be a predisposition that could develop itself in *any* direction. But I think we would not take this to be a predisposition anymore, in any interesting sense of the term.

[99] I hope these considerations help understand why I stated above that it does not matter for the thought experiment whether we imagine a child who is about to learn to have a *completely unformed* character (like a tabula rasa) or whether it is already born with some tendencies. Ultimately, I think, if there were already tendencies at the beginning, they should not matter ethically. All that matters is what the child learns afterwards, affectively but also cognitively, whether or not there are some "inborn tendencies" and whether or not these "inborn tendencies" were evolutionarily advantageous.

like knee-jerk responses. And I have tried to show how my notion of affective learning prevents emotional responses from being knee-jerk responses.

Second, it is unclear whether evolutionary accounts of ethical learning commit the Naturalistic Fallacy. In an evolutionary account of learning like Prinz', we can ask the same questions on the level of the species that one otherwise would ask on the level of the individual: is it *good* that emotions and physiological reactions are shaped in this way? This is a version of Moore's Open Question argument (Moore, 1903). Whenever we observe that such-and-such is a tendency to respond that has been acquired in evolutionary ways, we can ask "but is it good?". And the question is open. Just because some trait or tendency to respond was functional for past generations to survive and procreate, the trait or tendency is not morally good.[100] I am not claiming here that evolutionary accounts must run into this problem, or are unaware of the challenge it poses. Nevertheless, evolutionary accounts often start out from descriptive claims about attitudes we have acquired; in other words, they start out from a causal story. They accordingly face a challenge that my approach does not face: what grounds the transition from a descriptive, causal theory to a normative theory?

Third, the way chance and control enter the picture is crucially different in my account. I do not *only* tell a story about chance and what behavior stands the test of time according to some external circumstances (as the story of evolutionary learning does). Importantly, in my account, *another capacity* besides the cognitive one plays a crucial role in figuring out what to learn, and in solidifying one's responses. This other capacity does not allow as much control over the learning process as the cognitive one. But it is not, in contrast to the evolutionary story, just a function of external circumstances and adaptive reactions to it either. There is *some* control in affective learning, through the affective capacities. By showing the responses of pain or anger to a certain action, for instance, and so eliciting a feeling of shame in the other, we as *individual* human beings have some control over the shaping of each others' emotional responses. Hence, it can still be a *human* practice, sensitive to current needs, to shape our emotional responses.

---

100 The issue of the (possible) tension between our evaluative judgments as a result of evolution and our evaluative judgments as tracking some form of real value is, of course, much more complicated and beyond the scope of this short book. Street (2006) argues that the value realist runs into a dilemma between either claiming that there is no relation between evolution and the truth of evaluative judgments at all, or claiming that the evolutionary grown evaluative judgments do (fully) track the truth. Both seem implausible according to Street, and thus she sees the value realist forced to give up realism. In contrast to that, I would not hesitate to bite the bullet and accept the first horn of the dilemma, namely, to say that there is no relation between evolution and the truth of evaluative judgments (except occasionally by accident).

We have, in this way, indirect control over each others' emotional responses. Emotional responses, as we saw, can be shaped in better or worse ways. One's emotional responses can be better or worse at picking up differences between types of situations; they can be better or worse at engaging with contingency; etc. In the evolutionary story, presumably, the way emotional responses were formed was due mostly to external circumstances, such as whether it was functional to experience fear in a certain situation.[101] And even if other humans influenced the emotional learning back then, it being hard-wired now would make it insensitive to our current human (indirect) control. So, the way chance and control play a role in the evolutionary account is different from mine, even though we both emphasize that the shaping of the emotions is less under our direct control than what a cognitivist learning account would suggest.

This is how the proposed account in this book goes against an identification of normativity with rationality, while being different to similar proposals like Jaggar's and Prinz'. The most central notion for our argument is the concept of affective learning. As a final step to sharpen the proposal made here, let us ask in what sense the proposal is a version of sentimentalism before we can move on to Chapter 4.

3.4 Sentimentalism

I had already mentioned sentimentalist accounts as kindred but slightly different accounts of the role of emotions in §§ 2.2 and 3.1, but only in footnotes. I now want to give the comparison to sentimentalism a more prominent space, adding more explicit thoughts on the relation to my proposal. This will also make clear the importance of Chapter 4 for the argument of this book.

---

101 It is important to note that I only consider Darwinian (or biological) evolution when making the claim that it is mainly external circumstances that determine the shaping of emotional responses according to evolutionary accounts. Cultural evolution, by contrast, as put forward, for instance, in Heyes (2018), tells a very different story. In Heyes' account, cognitive gadgets, like literacy, are passed on to subsequent generations through social learning rather than through biological replication: "people with a new cognitive mechanism pass it on to others through social interaction" (Heyes, 2018, 1). This kind of evolution, cultural evolution, is arguably just as much under the control of the humans currently alive as affective learning is according to my account. Interestingly, Heyes only mentions the cultural evolution of *thinking* in this context. My account of affective learning would be fully coherent with an account of cultural evolution of this kind, and would add another aspect to it: there might also be a cultural evolution of our *affective* capacities, through affective learning over many generations. Hence, besides cognitive gadgets, we would in this combined account also have "affective gadgets" as some of the gains of cultural evolution.

In his *Treatise of Human Nature*, David Hume makes a very similar claim to ours, namely, that reason alone cannot move us to act. He says reason alone "can never immediately prevent or produce any action by contradicting or approving of it" (T 458). He maintains that it is impossible "from reason alone (...) to distinguish betwixt moral good and evil" (T 457). Hume thinks this proves that "actions do not derive their merit from a conformity to reason, nor their blame from a contrariety to it" (T 458). In conclusion from this, Hume holds that "moral judgments or evaluations are not the products of reason alone" (Cohon 2018). More generally, Hume's position in ethics is known for four theses: "(1) Reason alone cannot be a motive to the will, but rather is the "slave of the passions", (2) Moral distinctions are not derived from reason. (3) Moral distinctions are derived from the moral sentiments: feelings of approval (esteem, praise), and disapproval (blame) felt by spectators who contemplate a character trait or action. (4) While some virtues and vices are natural, others, including justice, are artificial" (Cohon 2018).

The first three out of the four theses seem to be directly relevant to our position, while we can ignore 4 for the present purposes. For a version of (1), that reason alone cannot be a motive to the will, and (3), that moral distinctions are derived from the moral sentiments such as feelings of approval and disapproval, we have argued ourselves, albeit in different terms, throughout the book. One of the main differences between our account and sentimentalist accounts will turn out to be a different perspective on (2), that moral distinctions are not derived from reason.

Before I offer a response, however, let me point out that this way of putting it is not only Hume's, but is in some version shared among all of the important sentimentalists and moral sense schools of moral judgement. Adam Smith, in his *Theory of Moral Sentiments*, offers an analysis congruent with Hume's as described above, with the interesting (but for our purposes not significant) difference in how he thinks of sympathy (the most important sentiment with which we evaluate things normatively). Sympathy, according to Smith, arises when we *imagine* how we would feel in someone else's circumstances. Hume, by contrast, thought of sympathy as feeling how others *actually* feel in a certain circumstance. That is why Smith's is sometimes called a "projective" account of sympathy, while Hume's is called a "contagion" account. That is, Smith and Hume disagree on the moral psychology involved in *how* we evaluate morally with our sentiments, while they both give the sentiments the primary role to play (over reason). The difference between Hume and Smith can become significant, however, because Smith's account seems to accommodate the idea of fallibility (of our sentiments) more easily than Hume's. To allow a certain level of fallibility in our emotional responses, while still arguing for the normative role they can play, was an important point in our argument in § 3.1.

Compare to this, finally, Hutcheson's moral sense school of moral judgment. Hutcheson argues for the existence of many kinds of internal senses (as opposed to external ones like seeing, hearing, etc.): there is not just a moral sense but also a sense of honor, a sense of taste (that is, an aesthetic sense), and so on. What unifies them as (internal) senses is that they generate "pleasures and ideas *immediately*, without intervening cognitive work—the sense of taste "strikes us at first with the Idea of Beauty" (*Inquiry*), along with its accompanying pleasure" (Dorsey 2021). Normative guidance comes from such senses, according to Hutcheson: "(...) aesthetic goodness will be determined (...) by the operation of the sense of imagination. Honorable actions will be determined by the operation of the sense of honor. Morally good actions will be determined by the operation of the moral sense, and so on" (Dorsey 2021). Hence, here too, we find the idea that it is a *sense* (something felt) rather than reason that does the moral evaluation for us. It is slightly distinct from sentimentalist accounts like Hume's and Smith's, as the moral sense here is understood as a specifically *moral* sense, to be fully distinguished from other sentiments (or emotions). But let us leave these fine-grained distinctions aside, as for our purposes, it only matters that it is a certain kind of sense, as opposed to reason, that does the evaluative work.

I have focused here on the traditional figures in the history of philosophy who defended a sentimentalist view. This should not obscure the fact that these kinds of positions have also been seriously defended afterwards and are also well alive in contemporary moral philosophy. For instance, neo-sentimentalist views have been popular from the 1970s on in the literature on *pro-attitudes* (cf. Williamson (1970), Blackburn (1988), and Schueler (1991)), and continue today (cf. Rabinowicz and Rønnow-Rasmussen (2004)). Pro-attitudes are non-cognitive in the sense that they do not have propositional or truth-apt content, but they are still directed at options (they are motivations for or against their objects). Other current neo-sentimentalist positions are to be found, for instance, in Barlassina and Hayward (2019), Hayward (2018), and Hayward (ms). In the empirical psychology literature, some well-known views are also neo-sentimentalist, such as Haidt's (2011, 2008, 2005, 2003, 1999) and Damasio's (2003, 2000, 1994, 1985).

Why is our account, thus, not just a version of (neo-)sentimentalism? We said that we share with sentimentalist views that reason alone cannot be a motive to the will, and that moral distinctions are derived from the moral sentiments such as feelings of approval and disapproval. The response to the "why not sentimentalism"-question is exactly along the lines of how we contrasted our account from mere non-cognitivism about emotions and from the feeling-toward-value theory: we are only sentimentalist about *one kind* of mental state, the emotional responses. Not about morality (or emotions) *tout court.* Thus, against Hume (and other sentimentalists), we disagree with the thesis that 'moral distinctions are not derived from reason'. While we agree that *some* normative guidance derives from moral sentiments such as feelings of approval and disapproval, we uphold the idea that also *some* normative guidance comes from reason, and from cognitive (sophisticated) emotions. That is, our account is somewhere between a cognitivist and non-cognitivist account of emotions, and, as we can see now, somewhere between a sentimentalist and rationalist moral theory. Again, that reason plays *some* role in normative guidance (in some circumstances, but not others), seems importantly true. To defend this here in this book, would go beyond its scope. This book is about exactly those kinds of emotions (basic emotional responses) that do *not* fit into the rationalist account of morality, hence those mental states that put in question the identification of normativity with rationality. Of those kinds of emotions, I want to give an appropriate account, and show that also they play a crucial normative role in our lives. So, rationalism cannot be right *tout court.* But, on the other hand, sentimentalism cannot be true *tout court,* either. Non-cognitive emotions and rational capacities play important, albeit different, normative roles in our lives. Again, if one has such a (prima facie) non-unified account of normative guidance, one needs to say something about the relation of the two capacities in normative guidance. Chapter 4 will be concerned with exactly that question. It approaches that question by asking how we can think of the unity between emotional responses and our rational capacities – that is, how they need to cooperatively work together for fully virtuous normative guidance. This is a first start of how to think of the unity of non-cognitive and cognitive mental states (at least in the realm of normative guidance), and thus by extension, also a start in how to think of a position between sentimentalism and rationalism.

Conclusion of this Chapter

The challenge that emotional responses are fallible, I argued, does not refute my proposal. It does not show that we do not need the emotional responses for our moral decisions in certain situations. Similarly, the claim that the emotional responses are nothing more than a "habituated form of reason" is not compelling. According to this claim, emotional responses can only play a normative role because a *cognitive* structure has been imparted onto them. I argued that this challenge is not successful because we have to think of the training and educating of our emotional responses in a way that does not fully depend on the imbuement of a cognitive structure onto them. This is what I have called *affective learning.* This led to a core insight: the emotional responses are *educated,* without being *cogni-*

tive. In the third section, I then considered two positions in which emotions play a crucial normative role, to the effect that they might appear close to my own position. I argued that both accounts are importantly different to mine because they fail to accommodate *affective learning* as a way of improving our (individual) emotional responses over time.

Chapter 4: The Virtue of Flexibility and the Unity of Feeling and Cognitive Capacities

In this chapter, I take up strands of argument from the previous three chapters and show how they collectively support a revised conception of virtue. Traditionally, philosophers have argued that virtue is a stable state. We want the virtuous person to be reliable, to act in predictable and consistent ways, reflective of a settled psychological state. If my arguments are compelling, however, we want more. We also want the virtuous person to be inventive and responsive to change. In other words, flexibility, as I call these attitudes and dispositions, is a virtue.

In Chapter 1, I developed the notion of basic emotional responses, which are emotional responses that are non-cognitive, but nevertheless object-directed. I argued that they play a unique role in normative guidance, namely, by giving us negative reasons to reconsider and potentially revise established beliefs and habits. I briefly argued that the disrupting of established beliefs and habits plays an important role in ethics; I discussed this in terms of "the importance of the capacity to reconsider." In this concluding chapter, I start by elaborating on this idea (§ 4.1).

In the second chapter, I then argued that on a basic level and in rough terms, all mental states can be classified, in a fundamental fashion, either as feeling states or cognitive states. I argued that each of these two kinds of mental states has a unique feature that essentially characterizes all instances of it. Namely, what essentially characterizes feeling states is their phenomenology, while what unites cognitive states is their impetus toward coherence. While the second chapter was thus engaged with showing the *difference* between these two kinds of mental states, it did not touch on the question of how we can then understand a mental *unity* between them. Any virtue, however, if it is a character trait, is a total state of mind. We are not kind on account of our emotions and just on account of our cognition. We are kind, and just, or virtuous in any other way on account of how emotion and cognition *work together.* I will respond to that lack of my account in explaining this unity by introducing an Aristotle-inspired "table of characters" in the second section of this chapter (§ 4.2).[102]

In Chapter 3, I argued against three challenges. None of them, I concluded, refutes the idea that we need the emotional responses for our moral decisions in at

---

102 In this chapter, it will become obvious that my approach is inspired by Ancient philosophy and, broadly speaking, Aristotelian. While I will only mention Aristotle explicitly in this chapter, my approach is also indebted to the moral psychology of Plato's *Republic* (Plato, 1997b). In particular, Barney (2016) and Lorenz (2006) have an interpretation of the moral psychology of the *Republic* that fits well with my approach.

https://doi.org/10.1515/9783110780932-007

least some situations. But what would it mean to fail to act according to our emotional responses? In response to this question, I now develop a table of characters. Two of the three non-virtuous characters developed in this table, as we will see, are not virtuous because they do not or cannot act according to their emotional responses. The goal of the last section of this chapter will be to show that the rigid character, the character in which the cognitive capacities always overrule the feeling capacities, is in no way better than the fickle character, that is, than the character in which the feeling capacities always overrule the cognitive capacities. This last point will highlight what I have tried to argue throughout the book: Even though we tend to assume that when it comes down to it, it is usually better to go with our cognitive judgment than to go with our feelings, this assumption betrays a cognitivist bias. Instead, it is no more virtuous to overrule one's feelings than it is to overrule one's cognitive states. Rather, if one wants to get closer to virtue, one needs to *stop* overruling one's feelings, so that both kinds of mental capacities can become a cooperative unity in one's decision-making.

4.1 The Virtue of Flexibility

First, let me introduce some terminology. The capacity to disrupt established beliefs and habits, which I have called the capacity to reconsider, gives rise, I argue, to the need to introduce a virtue that has not been considered so far in virtue ethics: the virtue of flexibility of character. Let me be more precise. Aristotle, who is uniquely influential in contemporary virtue theory, does not consider the stability of character, the corresponding term from which I develop the virtue of flexibility, *itself* a virtue. Rather, he says, for any virtue to really be a virtue, the agent needs to act from it *stably*.[103] As this is commonly translated, a virtue is a stable disposition. The agent's stable way of acting is part of what makes her way of acting *good*. Stability of character is a feature of all the virtues in Aristotle's

---

103 This adverbial way of translating the relevant passage is the most literal translation, I argue, in contrast to translating it as "acting from a stable disposition", as is more common. The notion of a disposition (hexis) does not appear in the relevant passage at all. And I would argue that it does make a difference how we think of the role of stability in virtue, depending on whether we translate it adverbially or as a modifier of "disposition". This debate, however, would go beyond the scope of this book. The relevant passage in the *Nicomachean Ethics* is the following:

"Tas aretas ginomena (...) ean kai bebaiōs kai ametakinētōs echōn prattêi". *NE* II.4 1105a32–33.

And it is commonly translated as: "if he does them [the things that come about in accordance with the excellences] from a firm and unchanging disposition" (translation by Sarah Broadie; Broadie and Rowe (2002)).

ethics, and it is thereby a kind of meta-virtue. Somewhat loosely speaking, however, we may say that according to Aristotle-inspired views, stability, as long as it is the stability of virtues, is itself a virtue. It is one of the good-makers of virtue that it is stable, and in that sense, stability is a virtue of virtue.

Correspondingly, I submit, the flexibility of character should be thought of as a meta-virtue in this way. Strictly speaking and spelling out what this means, flexibility is not a virtue on par with the other virtues; it is not one of the virtues. Analogously to the meta-virtue of stability, there is a meta-virtue of flexibility. In other words, flexibility is a good-making feature of all the virtues. That is, the flexibility of character also pertains to all specific virtues: while the agent needs to act from the virtues stably, she also needs the capacity to reconsider in regard to them, whenever she is acting from them in specific situations. This is a novel suggestion I make, which has no equivalent or correlate in Aristotle's ethics. It is, in fact, what I take to be the most significant omission in Aristotle's ethics.[104]

Note that we do not have to understand stability and flexibility as notions that stand in tension with each other. I argue that stability is essentially constituted by an internal flexibility, an internal ability for change. Take the example of a bike. What distinguishes a stable from a less stable bike is that it has the flexibility to hold up under all sorts of circumstances: one can ride it uphill, downhill, with lots of stuff on it, over sticks and stones, and so on. That is, its flexibility in terms of how it can react to its environment actually enables it to stay stable over time. If the bike were rigid (that is, if it lacked some internal springs and joints that ensure internal flexibility), it would break in some of these situations. Instead, it is built in a way so that it can flexibly move with the forces coming from

---

104 Aristotle has a different way in which he introduces a form of flexibility into the virtues: the doctrine of the mean (*NE* II.1 – 6). The doctrine of the mean says that, for instance, the virtue of courage requires different kinds of responses in different situations. Thus, the virtue of courage might require not to experience too much fear in one situation, but it might require experiencing more fear in another, so that it is just enough to act in the right way. The "ability to find the mean" is instilled in the character of the subject via habituation. According to Aristotle, reason—initially the reason of teachers and parents, eventually one's own reason—is the guide of this process. My account of flexibility of character as a meta-virtue departs from Aristotle's picture by not considering reason as the sole guide.

Burnyeat (1980) was first to note that the question "what is virtue?" is answered in an Aristotelian account, to a significant extent, by asking "how does one become virtuous?". Burnyeat (1997 and 2000) also shows that while Aristotle's account of habituation and education of the emotions is reason-guided, it otherwise shares many of the subtle points about habituation and virtue that I make in this chapter. And Lawrence (2011) argues that while it would certainly be wrong to attribute a non-rationalism to Aristotle's account of habituation, it would be equally wrong to describe it as a rationalist account of habituation—hence, the contrast to my account that emphasizes the role of affective learning is perhaps less significant than it might first seem.

the environment. Hence, the bike is stable partially thanks to being internally flexible.[105]

In the following, I will talk about stable and flexible *characters*, respectively. That means that the agent's character exhibits the meta-virtues of stability and flexibility, respectively (leaving open whether she has acquired all or some of the specific virtues or not). Before I proceed, hence, let me briefly clarify how the notions of a capacity, a virtue, and a character are distinguished and how they are related in my account. I said that the *capacity* to reconsider our beliefs and habits gives rise to the need for a *virtue* of flexibility. That is, I take a capacity to be something that we *can* do due to our psychological set-up. A virtue, then, is that which specifies how we use this capacity *well*. That is why recognizing a hitherto unrecognized capacity gives rise to the need to formulate a corresponding virtue. A virtue, however, does not *just in any way* specify how we use a capacity well. Rather, a virtue specifies *how one's character needs to be shaped* if we want to have this virtue. Hence, "having a virtue" is shorthand for "having one's character shaped in a certain (good) way". Having a meta-virtue, one might then add, is how this shape of character is being held: stably and flexibly, in contrast to rigidly or in a fickle way. For instance, having the meta-virtue of flexibility in having the virtue of courage means not making courage an all-overriding, absolute principle while still being able to be courageous to the degree that is needed in the situations one encounters.

I will also talk about rigid and fickle characters, as kinds of character that only exhibit one or the other meta-virtue: a stable character that is not also flexible is an overly stable character, hence rigid. A flexible character that is not also stable is an overly flexible character, hence, fickle. The idea is that there is a good and bad form both for stability and for flexibility of character, and having the good form of both, being stable and flexible, prevents the bad forms. If you have a stable character that is not rigid, your habits and beliefs exhibit a certain form of continuity over time without being impenetrable by new inputs and situations. If you have a rigid character, your habits and beliefs are impenetrable in this way, hence they exhibit a bad form of continuity. If you have a flexible character that is not fickle, your habits and beliefs exhibit a certain form of discontinuity over time, due to their ability to change according to new input and situations. If you have a fickle character, this discontinuity takes on a bad form. It is not just a discontinuity in the form of "change over time", as change over time implies that there is still *some-*

---

105 Some metaphysicians (e.g., Galton and Mizoguchi, 2009) hold that an object is the interface between its internal and external processes. One could correspondingly say that a virtuous character is something like the interface between its internal processes, which keep it flexible for change, and its external processes, which keep it stable over time.

thing that unites the states that change. Rather, it is a discontinuity in the form of radical difference, where the agent leaps from here to there without exhibiting any relevant kind of unity. The kind of unity we are looking for here, I will argue, is narrative. Namely, I will suggest, the minimal unity one needs in order to have a flexible rather than fickle character entails that the different states, beliefs, former and current habits add up to a biographical story that makes sense to the agent herself. This unity, I concede, is relative to the agent's perspective; it is a unity by her lights. But we will see that, though this is a minimal kind of unity, it provides us with a standard that virtuous states of character must meet.

To illustrate the idea of a narrative unity, imagine someone who lives a very different life from yours, to the extent that it is difficult for you to see where the unity in her decisions is. Imagine, for example, that you have a childhood friend who did not finish high school because she unexpectedly had a baby in her teenage years, with someone with whom she did not have a relationship. Later on, you learn that she and the father of her baby got married two years after the baby was born, and then had another child. However, when you visit her again two years after that, you learn that they got divorced and live separate lives. To you, this might look very disunified. First, there was the radical and unplanned change of quitting high school and having the baby. Then, there was another radical change of plans by committing to a relationship with the father of her baby two years later and having another baby with him. And yet another two years after that, there is again a radical change of plans by divorcing the father of her two children and living without him. So, this might look disunified to you in a way that makes her character look fickle. However, on your visit you get to talk with her about the past few years of her life. She tells you how she made her decisions. It turns out that she already had a crush on the father of her children during high school, even before they got intimate. When she decided to keep the baby, she was hoping that this would lead to a relationship with him down the line. When this actually happened, they seemed to lead a happy life together, and so they got married and decided to have another baby together. However, when their second child was about one year old, the father developed mental health issues that had not been foreseeable. His mental health issues eventually led to their divorce. But she has never stopped loving him and is still happy she had a relationship and family with him.

Now that you know the narrative behind your friend's decisions, you see that there is actually great unity over time. She has loved the same person for many years. She has always done what she thought was best in the light of that narrative. She wanted to be with him, and she wanted him to be well. Eventually, this also required her to be flexible: when his mental health issues became too severe, she had to divorce him, despite her love for him. None of the changes in her life, however, now seem radical and disunified. Her character is not fickle at all. On the contrary. Her character is stable at the same time as it is flexible. The point is that the very same actions, as you saw them before you knew her narrative, could indeed have been a sign of a fickle character. It could equally well have been that there is no such unifying narrative as in the case of your friend. But my claim is that as soon as there is such a narrative from the first-person perspective, this is enough to say that the subject achieves some coherence in her life over time, and thus does not have a fickle character.

How does the terminology of fickle and rigid characters fit into our previous claims, that is, into the distinction between feeling states and cognitive states? The thesis I want to defend in this chapter is that if we merely listened to our cognitive states when making decisions, we would have rigid characters. Likewise, if we merely listened to our feeling states when making decisions, we would have fickle characters. I argue that this follows from the different unique natures of the two kinds of mental states. Only the cognitive capacities strive toward coherence. But they do so "absolutely", in the sense that coherence trumps all other considerations. This would lead, if not held in check by our feeling states, to an overly coherentist character, to the extent that this character would be rigid. Equally, the unique nature of the feeling states can lead us astray if they are not held in check by the cognitive states. The modus operandi of the feeling states, we have said, is their phenomenology. They give each situation and experience a certain kind of quality, a certain way it feels to be in that situation. This can be instructive in deciding what to do. But *only* relying on the way a situation feels when making decisions would likely lead to a bad form of discontinuity over time, because feelings can jump from here to there without an impetus toward coherence. That is, it would likely lead to a form of discontinuity that is a mere jumping from one thing to the next, without even a minimal form of narrative unity.

If we want to avoid either of these problems, we have to give *as much* weight to our coherentist mental states as we do to our non-coherentist ones.[106] This is not supposed to be understood numerically. "Equal weight" here should only mean that from the outset, before anything is decided, both capacities are to be

---

[106] Dreyfus (1992) proposes that there is a more sophisticated type of human cognition than the kind of cognitive capacities that I consider here. This more sophisticated type of cognition is action guiding, he maintains, in a non-rule-governed but still regular way, implying that being rule-governed would be rigid, while this more sophisticated form of cognition would not be rigid. I agree with him that the goal is to find a non-rigid but still informed capacity for action guidance, but I disagree with him that we should look for this kind of mental capacity in *cognitive* capacities only. Rather, I argue, for this we need to include the crucial contribution of feeling states into our conception of decision-making.

taken equally seriously. Of course, it can turn out that as a matter of fact, one needed to rely on one capacity more often than on the other. This is likely dependent,
among other things, on what kind of situations one encounters in one's life. We
can imagine that someone who lives in a tumultuous environment, where econom-
ic and other basic life necessities are not a given, struggles to achieve continuity in
her life. In such an environment, it seems likely that achieving continuity is such a
struggle that the agent most often needs to rely on her coherentist, cognitive states
when making decisions in order to get by. Her life already provides her with more
than enough irregularities. That differs from the typical situations a middle-class
subject in the western affluent part of the world encounters. For such a subject,
life itself does not provide as many irregularities, that is, as many occasions to reconsider her beliefs and habits. This subject is on the one hand less in danger of
having a badly discontinuous life. But on the other hand, this subject is in greater
danger than the first one of becoming rigid in her ways of thinking and acting.
Thus, it is likely that for a subject in the second kind of situation, it is more important to rely on her feeling states once in a while than for the first one. But let me be
clear that for both of these subjects, it is still true that in general, they should give
equal weight to both capacities. That is, from the outset, before anything is decided,
they should take both capacities equally seriously.

It follows, thus, against a common (cognitivist) bias, that it is sometimes best to
go with our feeling and *against* our beliefs (even if we do not know *why* that would
be good), because our beliefs tend to have an overly coherentist tendency. Going
with our feeling states once in a while allows us to get to a different viewpoint outside the "coherent picture" suggested by our beliefs, from which we can reconsider
our beliefs and habits.[107] But it also follows that it is not always right to go with
what our feelings suggest. Sometimes, our feeling states are indeed too fickle, as
they do not operate according to any coherentist principle at all, and so it is important to be able to rely on one's cognitive capacities.

Now that we see how our feeling and cognitive states contribute to flexibility
and stability of character, we are in a position to ask how they can be unified, in
the sense that they are both aspects of the mental life of *one* subject, contributing
to the beliefs and habits of *one* agent.

---

107 Betzler (2007) argues something similar when she says that actions expressing emotions serve
the function of helping the agent re-adapt to the environment within his evaluative perspective
after pressure to revise or re-affirm his ongoing evaluative perspective in light of changes in his
environment that call that very perspective into question.

4.2 The Unity of Feeling and Cognitive Capacities and Three Ways of Failing to Achieve Unity

In the philosophy of mind, theorists at times distinguish between mental states that can be described on a sub-personal level, which are often associated with some particular region, organ, or activity of the person, on the one hand, and mental states than can only be described on the personal level, on the other hand. Teroni and Deonna (2020), for example, argue that for the study of emotions it must be the phenomenology *on the personal level* that matters, rather than thinking that there could be such a thing as sub-personal entities that have their own experiences.

Let me borrow this terminology and say that virtues are properties on the *personal* level, rather than on any sub-personal level. One is not courageous or generous on account of some subset of one's dispositions. Though some mental states may be more prominently involved than others in a given virtue, it is the person as a whole who is courageous or generous. Accordingly, a plausible account of virtue cannot situate virtue either in feeling or in cognition. For a person to be genuinely virtuous, both her feelings and her cognition need to cooperate. In other words, there needs to be unity between the two kinds of mental states in order to attain virtue. But how can we think of this unity? How can cognitive and feeling states be unified in a way that results in a flexible yet stable character?

Here, an Aristotle-inspired "table of characters" is helpful. For this, let us first say a bit more about the sense in which each kind of mental state can be in a better or worse shape. The table of characters, then, lists characters with various combinations of feeling and cognitive states in their good and bad forms. Both feeling and cognition, I argued, can be trained, educated, and improved. Let us call the good, trained form of each capacity *strong* and the bad form *weak*. That is, we can have *strong or weak* cognitive capacities, and *strong or weak* feeling capacities. For each of them, being strong or weak means something different, because their unique nature is different.

Strong feeling capacities:
Strong feeling capacities *clearly show* what one is attracted to or aversive from; they clearly show how one feels in regard to an action or situation. They have a *strong phenomenology*, in the sense that they are *strongly and clearly felt.*[108]

---

108 This bears a resemblance to Descartes' notion of "clear and distinct representations". A clear representation is, according to him, the *conscious recognition* of a representation. A distinct rep-

Weak feeling capacities:

Weak feeling capacities do not clearly show what one is attracted to or aversive from, so they do not clearly show how one feels in regard to an action or situation. They have a weak phenomenology, in the sense that they are weakly and unclearly (unspecifically) felt. It is thus not clear to the subject how she feels in regard to the actions available and to the situations at hand.

Strong cognitive capacities:

Strong cognitive capacities are *maximally coherent.* They make no mistakes in terms of coherence when making inferences, they represent objects' logical properties correctly, and they can take very complex inferential structures as their object.

---

resentation, by contrast, is the case when the subject is conscious of *all properties* of a representation. Together, Descartes says, they are sufficient criteria for truth beyond any doubt:

"And having observed that there was nothing in this proposition, *I am thinking therefore I exist*, which makes me sure that I am telling the truth, except that I can see very clearly that, in order to think, one has to exist, *I concluded that I could take it to be a general rule that things we conceive of very clearly and distinctly are all true*, but that there is some difficulty in being able to identify those which we conceive of distinctly" (Descartes, translation by Maclean, 2006, 29).

This is how Descartes puts it in the original French:

"Et ayant remarqué qu'il n'y a rien du tout en ceci: *je pense, donc je suis*, qui m'assure que je dis la vérité, sinon que je vois très clairement que pour penser il faut être, *je jugeai que je pouvais prendre pour règle générale que les choses que nous concevons fort clairement et fort distinctement sont toutes vraies*, mais qu'il y a seulement quelque difficulté à bien remarquer quelles sont celles que nous concevons distinctement" (Descartes, 1925).

Applying Descartes' notions, I could rephrase my characterization of strong feeling states as feeling states that achieve a clear representation, but that still cannot achieve a distinct representation (the subject is not conscious of *all properties* of a representation through her strong feeling states). And this would be another way to make my point that emotional responses, as feeling states, can be object-directed without being representational. Despite the fact that the notion "representation" shows up here, we should be aware that this notion does not appear in Descartes' treatise. He talks about "the things we see clearly and distinctly". This adverbial way of putting it exactly avoids that we need to think in terms of representations in order for a mental state to be object-directed. In other words, applying Descartes' original notions, I could say that strong feeling states are those feeling states that give their indications to the subject *clearly,* in the sense that the subject's conscious recognition of her feelings is easy. By contrast, strong feeling states, exactly because they are not representational or cognitive, do *not* give their indications to the subject *distinctly* in Descartes' sense of the word, as this would require of the feeling states to represent (all) the properties of the object at hand.

Weak cognitive capacities:
Weak cognitive capacities are not fully coherent. They often make mistakes in terms of coherence when making inferences, they have trouble representing objects' relevant logical properties, and so they have trouble taking complex inferential structures as their object. So, they are not fully able to make cognitive states coherent among each other and coherent with other attitudes.

This distinction between strong and weak versions of each kind of mental state extends my response in Chapter 3 about the *training* of the emotional responses. In addition to what I have argued there in favor of the notion of affective learning, we can now additionally see that something different is involved in the training of feeling states than in the training of the cognitive states. The affective learning and the training of feeling states is (partially) about forming them in a way so that they are *strongly and clearly felt*. By contrast, the training of cognitive capacities must (partially) be about training them to be *as coherent as possible*.[109]

With these distinctions in mind, we can now propose a table of characters that includes four kinds of characters. The overall good (virtuous) character, the flexible yet stable character, needs to have a strong version of *both* capacities. For any combination of capacities where one or both of the capacities are weak, there arise *specific problematic forms of character.*

Tab. 1: Forms of Character

Strong Cognitive Capacities, Strong Feeling Capacities	Strong Cognitive Capacities, Weak Feeling Capacities	Weak Cognitive Capacities, Strong Feeling Capacities	Weak Cognitive Capacities, Weak Feeling Capacities
Virtuous Character Has the virtues of stability and flexibility.	**Rigid Character** Has some version of the virtue of stability, without the virtue of flexibility. Self-controlled character	**Fickle Character** Has some version of the virtue of flexibility, without the virtue of stability. Akratic character	**Inert Character** Lacks both kinds of guidance. Does not have virtue of flexibility, nor of stability.

---

109 I qualify these statements about the training of each kind of mental state with "partially" because for both mental states the training must also involve other aspects. Crucially, for both mental states, the training involves a training to track the truth or true value, which we might call "normative training". The point about not identifying normativity with rationality was exactly that *both* capacities can be trained to track the truth or true value. However, *how* they track this, and correspondingly how they are *trained* to track this, differs significantly, as I argue here.

If a subject has strong cognitive capacities but weak feeling capacities, this results in a character that strongly strives toward coherence, but that has no capacity to reconsider her habits and beliefs. Thus, this leads to a *rigid* character. I argue that this character shares important features with what Aristotle calls the self-controlled character. By contrast, if a subject has strong feeling capacities but weak cognitive capacities, she jumps from here to there, but has no sufficient capacity to seek a satisfying form of coherence. This results in a *fickle* character. This character, I argue, shares important features with what Aristotle calls the akratic character.

We can also imagine a kind of character in which *both* capacities are weak. By contrast, in the two previously mentioned characters, while one capacity is weak, the other one is strong. This means that the problem with these characters is that one capacity can reign without being held in check by the other. These characters do not, however, have the more serious problem that there is no guidance at all, as in the character where both capacities are weak. It might be a rigid or fickle kind of guidance, but a subject with one of these characters will always have at least one capacity that guides her in her actions and beliefs. By contrast, in the character where both capacities are weak, the subject lacks *any* kind of guidance at all. I call this the *inert* character. There is no straightforward correlate in Aristotle's ethics for this character.

Let me first examine each character separately, as I think that each of them clarifies some issues at hand. That is, the virtuous character illustrates the way in which we have to understand the unity between cognitive and feeling capacities. The rigid character illustrates what happens if we cannot rely on our feeling states in normative guidance. The fickle character illustrates what goes wrong if we *only* have the feeling states as normative guide. The inert character illustrates what it means when both capacities are weak.

4.2.1 Virtuous Character: The Unity of Cognitive and Feeling Capacities

The virtuous character illustrates the way in which we can have a unity between cognitive and feeling states. In the virtuous character, there is a unity of the two kinds of mental states, in the sense that they *freely* inform each other and hold each other's influence in check. This is not mere coexistence, and there is no systemic tension and fight between the two kinds of mental states. The cognitive capacities' impetus toward coherence is strong, but freely makes space if a feeling strongly goes against a certain coherent belief or action. Equally, the phenomenology of the feelings is strong and clearly shows the subject's aversions and attractions. At the same time, these strong feelings freely make space for other beliefs or actions if they are needed to make a coherent decision or commitment.

Let me say a bit more about the difference between a unity and a mere coexistence of the two kinds of mental states. A unity of two kinds of mental states, in contrast to a mere coexistence, entails that the two kinds of mental states do not just act "in addition" to each other,[110] taking the other as a contingent external factor. Instead, the subject's mind exhibits a functional internal structure that entails both kinds of mental states. This structure allows that the two kinds of mental states influence each other and that they hold each other in check, even before the subject would notice any kind of tension in their "recommendations". For the virtuous subject, the two kinds of mental states do not usually appear separately on the level of experience, except in situations when a change is needed. If it were not like that, that is, if the two kinds of mental states were rather added to each other in a mere coexistence, we would have to ask whether it makes sense to think of their coexistence as a *single* mental state at all or whether we rather need to think of them as an aggregate of several mental states.

This suggests that we need to think of the unity of the two kinds of mental states in terms of a blend rather than an aggregate. The difference is that in a blend, the two ingredients are related in such a way that they cannot be disentangled. An aggregate, by contrast, would be reducible into its divisible components, the two separate kinds of mental states. Note that while we can always *conceptually* analyze things into components, this does not have to be the case on the level of experience by the subject. That is, even if I can conceptually identify different aspects of a unity or a blend, these aspects are not separable from each other on the level of experience. Hence, we should not conceive of them as separable components of experience.

---

110 To reject such an "additive" view about mental capacities is in agreement with Boyle (2016). Similarly, Fiecconi (2019) suggests that human rational and non-rational capacities are intrinsically built to coexist and cooperate.

By contrast, some philosophers working on emotions explicitly argue for a disunified view on how the affective and cognitive aspects come together in (sophisticated) emotions. Ben-Ze'ev (2000), for example, describes emotions as a complex of many disparate things, while it is unclear what unifies them as an entity. And he argues that an account of them as a unified entity is not necessary. This is in agreement with a tendency in contemporary psychology, where it is customary to describe and analyze many different aspects of emotions without making any claims about how all these different aspects then amount to one entity, the emotion.

One danger of not seeking an account that shows the unity between feeling and cognitive states is that it becomes unclear whether we can still conceive of the subject of these mental states as having "one mind". That is, if we think of the mental states as separate, we might have to attribute to each of them a mind of their own. See Davidson (1982) for a version of the two-minds worry.

It is important to note that while I claim that this kind of mental unity is needed for a *virtuous* character, I do not claim that it is *in principle* impossible to experience several disunified mental states at the same time. As a contrast to that, Brentano (1874), for instance, famously claimed that *any* psychological phenomenon must be a unity and that a subject can only experience *one* psychological phenomenon at a time. He called this the necessary unity of consciousness (Brentano, 1874, Chapter 4). Hence in his view, there could not even in principle ever arise a disunity between feeling and cognitive states as we discussed it, not even in moments of change or in the problematic forms of character. This makes it clear that his claim is about the *nature* of mental states or psychological phenomena, while my claim is a *normative* one on what is a good (or virtuous) mental setup on the whole. In my account, such disunity is possible, but it is either a sign that a change is needed, or that the subject has a problematic form of character.

Now, we can imagine several different kinds of mental unities between cognitive states and feeling states. One such unity that we have encountered so far pertains to the sophisticated emotions. We said about them in Chapter 2 that they might be equally well characterized by both dimensions I have discussed, namely, how it feels to experience them, and having an impetus toward coherence. This is precisely one criterion for a unity between cognitive and feeling states: on the level of experience by the subject, there does not appear to be a separation between the feeling and cognitive aspects at all. Hence, we can conclude that the sophisticated emotions are a good candidate for a mental unity between the two kinds of mental state. And it is plausible that there are other such mental unities of the two kinds of mental state, each playing various different roles in motivation, action, and decision.

But this is not yet the kind of unity we are addressing when we talk about virtue. Instead, when we talk about virtue, we are interested in the unity of the subject's mental life *as a whole,* in regard to *all* potential cognitive and feeling states. That is, the mere fact that someone can experience some mental unities between cognitive and feeling states (such as sophisticated emotions) does not yet guarantee that *her mental life* is unified in regard to all its cognitive and feeling states. These are two different questions, as we could imagine a subject who experiences several mental unities of cognitive and feeling states, such as a sophisticated emotion and others, but these respective mental unities are not unified *with each other.*[111] Imag-

---

111 And there is yet another distinction to be noted between two kinds of unity we have been considering so far, namely, a distinction between achieving unity between feeling and cognitive states on the one hand, and achieving a narrative unity over time, on the other.

   That means that achieving unity between feeling and cognitive states is a separate endeavor from achieving (narrative) unity over time, that is, from achieving coherence over time. I have arine, for example, that for a subject, a sophisticated emotion makes her want to eat vegan today (so she experiences a mental unity of a feeling state with a respective cognitive state, a belief, that she wants to eat vegan). However, she also experiences the mood of nostalgia (a different kind of feeling state) today, which is unified with a (cognitive) belief that for old times' sake, she should eat turkey with her family tonight. Even though each of the two mental units successfully unifies a cognitive and a feeling state, her mind *as a whole* is disunified in regard to all the cognitive and feeling states involved. In short, there is still a disunity between her sophisticated emotion that tells her to eat vegan and her mood-cum-belief state (the nostalgia) that tells her to eat turkey even though each of these is a mental unity between cognitive and feeling states. So, if we want unity between feeling and cognitive states *in general* for virtue, it is not enough to point out that there can be mental states that are a unity between these two kinds of mental states.

For a subject for whom the feeling and cognitive states are unified *in general*, and that is the point about virtue, this initial incongruence between her sophisticated emotion and her mood-cum-belief state is not necessarily a problem. For her, what happens (before any of this comes to the level of experience) after such an incongruence is detected, is that the various feeling and cognitive states can freely inform each other. None of the involved states are impenetrable to the input of the others. Ultimately, what comes to the level of experience will already be the result of this unifying process, an all-things-considered motivation to act in one way.

As a contrast, a non-virtuous subject might experience a mental unity, such as the sophisticated emotion and the mood-cum-belief unity we just considered. But for this subject, the feeling and cognitive states involved cannot inform each other freely. There will be no unifying process that results in an all-things-considered motivation that then comes to the level of experience. Instead, the various unreconciled feeling and cognitive states will come to the level of experience themselves, being incongruent and in tension. Hence, in the non-virtuous subject the feeling and cognitive states are too impenetrable for each other in order to inform each other properly and in order to hold each other in check. Each kind of mental state operates on its own terms without regard for the other.

It might now seem that on my account, having somewhat weak cognitive capacities is actually better than having strong (maximally coherent) ones because the weaker ones do exactly what I end up arguing is important for the virtue of

---

gued that to achieve a narrative unity or narrative coherence over time is obtained by having strong cognitive capacities, while the feeling capacities do not play a role in this. That is in clear contrast to the achievement of unity between feeling and cognitive states: here, both capacities are involved in the endeavor of achieving unity, as both need to be strong and cooperative.

flexibility: they allow that the subject does not always act according to maximal coherence. It seems that with weak cognitive capacities, it is easier to achieve this than with strong ones. However, to attain a state of incomplete coherence by having weak cognitive capacities is one thing, and it is another thing to attain such a state by having strong feeling capacities. One reason is practical: weak cognitive capacities *always* have trouble achieving the coherence they are supposed to achieve, no matter whether this is a situation where they would need to be interrupted or changed by the feeling capacities or not. Hence, their incomplete coherence is too general and unspecific. Another reason is conceptual: generally speaking, it is not the same to arrive at a certain state of mind because of an incapacity or a weakness, or to arrive at that state of mind due to the strength of another capacity. In other words: conceptually, it is not good to "achieve" flexibility if it is just the result of a weakness in terms of coherence. This goes to the heart of my proposal: being flexible is *an actual achievement*, something that is the result of the *strength* of certain capacities, and not, as cognitivist accounts might suggest, a lack or a weakness of coherence. Flexibility, then, must be achieved through the strength of the feeling capacities, rather than through the weakness of the cognitive capacities. We will encounter two kinds of character that result from having weak cognitive capacities, namely, the fickle and the inert characters. There, it will become clearer why this is not the same as having flexibility of character.

4.2.2 The Non-Virtuous Characters: Three Ways of Failing to Achieve Unity

The problem that all three following forms of character share is that in them, the feeling and cognitive states, as it were, run merely side-by-side instead of forming a unity. They are, at least to some degree, impenetrable to each other's influence. They only take each other as a contingent external factor to be dealt with. The way in which this disunity manifests itself is different in each form of character, however, and will be discussed for each separately.

Rigid Character: Weak Feeling Capacities

The rigid character illustrates what happens if we cannot rely on our feeling capacities in normative guidance. If a subject has strong cognitive capacities but weak feeling capacities, this results in a character that strongly strives toward coherence, but has no capacity to reconsider her habits and beliefs. Thus, the claim is, this leads to a *rigid* character that can only act according to maximal coherence.

In a rigid character, hence, the mere coexistence or disunity of the two mental capacities comes about because the feeling capacities are weak. In other words, they are so weak that they cannot play their part in the functional internal structure in which they are supposed to be unified with the cognitive capacities. As a reminder, weak feeling states do not give much of an indication how the subject should act, as they only provide the subject with an unclear, unspecific phenomenology. That is why, eventually, the cognitive capacities have to take over the decision-making alone, and so the functional internal structure, the unity, disintegrates over time.[112] As a result, a subject with such a character can only make decisions rigidly, as she can only rely on her cognitive capacities, which strive toward maximal coherence.

I am aware that this description of what causes the disunity between feeling and cognitive capacities in the rigid subject is to some degree circular: I claim that because of the weak feeling states, over time the unity disintegrates, while I also claim that because there is such a disunity, the subject keeps having weak feeling states (as she never gets to exercise them properly). This circular formulation is intended. This is an Aristotelian idea. Aristotle says that if one wants to become good, one has to start by performing good actions. But for that, one might say, one already needs to be good. This circularity, however, is not vicious, and it is not, in the end, a circularity at all. Namely, in performing X-actions one does not yet necessarily have an X-character. One becomes courageous, say, by performing courageous actions; and it is possible to perform courageous actions by following a teacher's guidance (cf. *NE* II.4, Aristotle, 2002). I imagine scenarios of improvement and decline as either upward or downward spirals. Hence, it is always a bit unclear how one gets out of the problematic circle into an upward spiral, and it is a separate question altogether how one got into the problematic circle

---

112 When the cognitive capacities have to take over the decision-making alone, all decisions have to be made through thinking rather than through a cooperation of feeling and thinking. It is plausible to say that this results in what Williams called the phenomenon of "one thought too many". Williams observes that if one is in a situation in which one can only save one out of two people, one of which is one's wife and the other a stranger, and decides to save one's wife instead of the other person, it would be "one thought too many" (Williams, 1981, 18) if one were to give an explanation of this choice purely based on thinking processes. Surely, Williams' point is, our feelings and our relationship to this person must be part of our explanation of why we chose to save her rather than the other person.

Similarly, Wolf (2012) argues that certain kinds of relationships (such as love) might even prohibit the agent from being unconditionally committed to acting according to morality, construed in purely cognitive terms. Thus, some situations lie beyond cognitive justification, so that we must acknowledge that (cognitively construed) morality is limited in its ability to guide our lives (Wolf, 1992). Hence, we might say that the rigid subject struggles particularly in those cases when special relationships are involved, as those require of us even more than other situations that we make our decisions with the cooperation of feeling and cognitive capacities, rather than with cognitive capacities alone.

in the first place (here: how one got to have weak feeling states). However, I think we can meaningfully describe the circle—in this case, the circle of disunity and weak feeling states—without knowing the cause of how this circle started.

It might seem that I have so far equivocated two different ways of how the feeling and cognitive capacities can be disunified, while these two ways would have different consequences for my account. The first way is to describe the disunity or the mere coexistence of the two mental capacities by emphasizing their inability to inform or penetrate each other. This emphasis suggests that both kinds of mental states have an impetus to guide the subject, while they are *in tension* with each other and "recommend" different actions and beliefs. The second way to describe the disunity emphasizes the *weakness* of one of the mental capacities, and so suggests that this capacity lets the other capacity take over the lead in guidance because it is just too weak to interfere. While these two may seem like two incompatible ways of thinking of the disunity of the two mental capacities, I argue that they are one and the same. Both the tension and the weakness model of disunity are just two aspects of the same problem. This is so because even a weak mental capacity can be in tension with the other mental capacity. That is, even when one mental capacity is weak, it can still go against the recommendations of the other if it is not unified with it. That is, the disunified weak capacity still tries to interfere with and interrupt the other one, even if it always loses because it is too weak. In the example of a rigid character, then, the model of disunity is this: the cognitive and feeling capacities are often in tension with each other because they are not unified. That is, they are not unified in a functional internal structure, and thus give uncoordinated recommendations as to how to act and what to believe. And in the case of a rigid character, because of the weakness of the feeling capacities, it is always the recommendation of the cognitive capacities that ends up leading to the action or belief. Hence, the fact that the feeling capacities are weak still allows for the two capacities to be *in tension* with each other. And that tension can come up in each decision, even if it is, in the case of the rigid character, clear from the beginning that it is the cognitive capacities that will end up leading to the action or belief.

Granting all that I have said so far about the rigid character and disunity, one might now say that this does not yet show that being rigid—or, simply, being mainly led by cognitive capacities—is bad. In other words, one could say that even if being rigid betrays a kind of disunity in the mind and a tension with the feeling capacities, this does not give us independent reasons against being a cognitivist. That is, someone could say: "What is so bad about pushing against one's feelings if one has one's cognitive capacities to follow, and what is so bad about the resulting mental disunity?". I want to say something in response to this briefly, as I will later claim that being rigid is just as bad as being fickle because both of these characters essentially have the same problems.

I have three responses to the above question. I hope to have established that making decisions based on cognitive capacities alone makes the subject rigid, in the sense that she acts and believes according to maximal coherence, trumping all other considerations. Hence, the remaining challenge of the objection is to show that being rigid in one's habits and beliefs in this way is bad. That is, the challenge of the objection is now that someone could say: "I accept that making decisions with cognitive capacities alone makes me rigid, but what is so bad about being a bit rigid?". As a first response, rather than giving a conclusive answer to this question, I want to point out that I am not alone in supposing that being rigid or cognitively controlled is bad. For instance, Sosa (2014) is concerned with the fact that our beliefs become stale and rigid over time. He argues that over time, we forget *the reasons why* we came to certain conclusions and beliefs and that this makes those beliefs rigid. This leads him to the conclusion that we have good reason to always reconsider the available evidence anew even if we have formed accurate beliefs or attained secure knowledge about the same matters before. This seems to assume, as I have, that to have rigid beliefs is bad in itself, and something to be avoided. That Sosa operates with this assumption is also corroborated by an earlier work of his. In Sosa (2007), he implies that we can improve our beliefs if we intentionally alternate the media outlets we subject ourselves to, in order to encounter different points of view.[113] Arguably, we improve our beliefs by this practice because this *reduces the rigidity* of our beliefs.

As a second response to why being rigid would be bad, I want to remind the reader that I argued in Chapter 1 and in the first section of this chapter that the capacity to reconsider—and thus the virtue of flexibility—is by most people considered to be important for a good character. Rigid beliefs prevent one from having this capacity to reconsider, and thus it is bad to have rigid beliefs.

---

113 This same point is also made by Vogt (2012). The reason why Sosa (2014) is concerned with arguing for the practice of newly considering the available evidence is because he takes this to be a response to Kripke's Dogmatism Paradox (cf. Kripke, 2011). Kripke pointed out that while we take knowledge to be a good thing, it seems that if you *know* something, you are entitled to disregard future evidence against it. However, disregarding evidence can never be rational. Hence, this leads to a paradox, namely to the paradox that knowing something makes one irrational.

In a way, the very fact that Kripke takes this to be a paradox suggests that we usually assume that it is bad to have rigid beliefs. That is, the second horn of Kripke's paradox, that it can never be rational to disregard evidence, seems to be a way of saying that having rigid beliefs can never be good.

My third response to the objection does not assume that relying on cognitive capacities alone makes one rigid. Rather, in this last response, I want to hint at the larger hypothesis within which I take the book to make a first step. I take the argument of this book to be a first step for the hypothesis that, in general, how an action *feels* can itself be an ethically justifying reason to do it or not to do it. The idea is that there is something to be lost in our lives if we do not allow feelings to play this role in our moral decision-making. While a defense of this claim would require a debate about the nature of ethics, I want to point out that if this larger hypothesis can be defended, then it is clear that a rigid and cognitively controlled character is bad. That is, if this hypothesis can be defended, then making decisions purely with one's cognitive capacities betrays a lack of a significant ethical capacity.

To corroborate this, one could argue that feelings and emotions are in some way *more intimately related to the self* (or to one's "character") than cognitive capacities. Williams (1966) seems to suggest this when he investigates the relationship between morality and the emotions. If one can substantiate the claim that feelings and emotions are in some way more intimately related to the self than other mental states, then it seems clear that only being led by cognitive capacities is bad. That is, if such a more intimate relationship exists, then not acting on the basis of feelings is in some sense not fully acting as oneself.[114]

While this last response only serves as a hint to show how one could respond to the objection within the frame of the larger hypothesis, I hope that the first two responses serve as an independent reason why being rigid or overly cognitively controlled would be bad.

Let us now go back to the question of what kind of disunity between the cognitive and feeling capacities is involved in the remaining non-virtuous characters.

Fickle Character: Weak Cognitive Capacities

In the fickle character, the disunity between the cognitive and feeling capacities arises because the cognitive capacities are too weak. That is, they are so weak so that they cannot play their part in the functional internal structure in which they are supposed to be unified with the feeling capacities. As a reminder, weak cognitive capacities are not fully able to strive toward coherence. That is why, eventually, the feeling capacities have to take over the decision-making alone,[115] and so

---

114 See Teroni (2016) for another perspective on the question of how intimately the emotions and the self are related.

115 This might seem to be an odd possibility from the perspective of the standard model of action explanation. The standard model of action explanation has it that an agent's desires *together with*

the functional internal structure, the unity, disintegrates over time, and the result is a fickle character.

The fickle character illustrates what goes wrong if we only have the feeling capacities as normative guide. If a subject has strong feeling capacities but weak cognitive capacities, this results in a character that is strongly and clearly pulled in one direction or another at any given point but that has no capacity to create coherence in these actions and beliefs over time. Thus, the claim is, this leads to a fickle character that jumps from here to there. This is so because feeling states lead the subject by providing her with a certain phenomenology or quality of the situation, which then makes her go one or the other way, but there is nothing in such a phenomenological quality that would provide coherence over time.

One could object that a subject being fully led by her feeling states is actually a rigid subject, not a fickle one. That is, it might look like the fickle subject actually has rigid guidance from her feeling states because her feelings always *strongly* pull her in one rather than another direction. However, I argue that *over time*, this subject likely alternates between courses of action without continuity, because the different feelings she experiences over time are not (necessarily) coherent with each other. That is, no matter how *strongly* her feelings pull her, this does not create continuity or coherence in their guidance over time, let alone rigidity. That is, she is incoherent in beliefs and actions over time, even though she is always strongly affectively pulled in one direction or another.

An extreme form of being guided by feeling capacities and of not being able to penetrate the feelings' pull by any kind of cognitive control, one might say, is illustrated by the phenomenon of addiction. And as a similar objection to that mentioned above, one could say that addiction rather looks like a *rigid* way of being guided by one's feelings (as addiction makes one rigidly doing the same again and again). However, if you consider the *internal struggle* a subject goes through

---

her beliefs explain her actions. That is, for the standard model of action explanation, we always need a conative *and* a cognitive mental state in order for an action to be performed. However, there have been other accounts of action explanation that challenged the need for a cognitive state. Betzler (2009), for example, holds that actions like sighing do not entail beliefs, but the action still seems to be under the agent's control and thus intentional. Thus, no cognitive mental state is needed for an explanation of this action. Betzler emphasizes in her account that instead of a belief, an *unreflective valuing stance* can represent reasons for actions in such situations.

Similarly, Gendler (2010) introduces a new mental state that is non-rational or not fully rational, which can nevertheless take over the role of belief in action explanation. She calls this new mental state "alief", which is an automatic and habitual attitude that is belief-like, but less rational.

In a similar vein as these two accounts, I take it to be possible for an action to be based on feeling states alone, perhaps together with other less-than-fully-rational mental states.

when she is addicted, you realize that addiction is not a rigid condition at all. The subject goes back and forth between wanting the object of her addiction, and wanting to be free of it. And these two maxims will make her perform different and mutually incoherent actions over time. Hence, this is a fickle rather than rigid kind of character.

One could perhaps counter this by saying that if the addicted subject gives up the struggle against the addiction and simply "accepts" her compulsion to get a certain substance or to pursue a certain activity, she indeed has a rigid or at least a coherent character. That is, we might say, using Harry Frankfurt's terminology,[116] that this is a subject who not only has a desire for the substance or activity, but also a second-order desire or volition that she have this desire. The challenge from this subject for my account is this: what if a subject *always feels the same way*, namely, always feels like she wants the substance or activity she is addicted to? She has no feelings of regret, no feelings of wanting to be free of the substance, no struggle of back and forth or internal tension, etc. Then she has coherence over time while only following her feeling capacities, perhaps even to the degree of being rigid. Against that, I argue that her coherence can only be a contingent one. Always feeling pulled toward a substance or activity does not lead to a unifying personal narrative. It is contingent that she feels like that about this substance or activity. There is nothing in the substance or activity and nothing in the nature of feeling states that would give her something like a substantive coherence over time, a coherence that could not fall apart if the contingent factors change.

Inert Character: Weak Feeling and Weak Cognitive Capacities

In an inert character, both capacities—feeling and cognitive—are weak. As a contrast, while it may be complicated and exhausting to have one *strong* and disunified feeling or cognitive capacity, the resulting internal tension can be productive. It propels the subject *to be motivated to change* something about her character. And this is precisely what the inert character lacks.

On the one hand, the inert character has weak feeling capacities. The agent's feeling capacities only give her unspecific and weak recommendations because their phenomenology is weak. On the other, her cognitive capacities are weak, in that they do not fully strive toward coherence. Hence, none of her mental capacities make her motivated or convinced to believe something or to act in a certain way.

---

116 Frankfurt (1971) introduced the notion of second-order desires and volitions, that is, desires and volitions to have certain desires, in order to investigate the structure of the will. His claim is that, in contrast to non-persons, persons have the capacity to want to be different or not, that is, the capacity to have second-order volitions.

Any kind of action or belief seems under-motivated for a subject of this kind. Technically, then, it might sound off to speak of a *failure of unity* of the two mental capacities in this case. Both of them are weak, and so there cannot be much of a tension between their recommendations on what to do or to believe in the first place, one might say. That is, it seems that in the inert character the precondition for a failure of unity is not met, namely, that there *could* be a unity of two things.

However, though there is no inner struggle such as that between strong-but-disunified mental states, there is a failure of unity. As a reminder, we said that even in the rigid and fickle subject, where one capacity is so weak that it is constantly overruled, this weak capacity still does (often) go against the recommendation of the other capacity, and thus is in tension with it. Hence, we still considered the rigid and fickle characters to come with internal tension, even though this tension always gets decided in favor of one of the capacities. In the same way, there *would* be the potential for a tension between the capacities in the inert character, if only her capacities were strong enough for the subject to experience the tension. That is, there is no reason to think that the weak recommendations of the feeling and cognitive capacities in an inert character would be cooperative and unified if they were strong enough. To be sure, there is no tension *on the level of experience* for the inert subject, because both capacities are too weak for this tension to come up in experience. But her capacities are nonetheless disunified and *would* (often) give different recommendations. Hence, the inert character is also a way of failing to achieve unity between the two mental capacities.

To conceptualize the inert character in this way opens up conceptual room for another character that does not appear in my table of characters: a character in which both capacities are strong, but not unified. We could call her the *torn* subject. She painfully goes back and forth between her options, as both of her capacities pull her strongly in their respective directions but without being cooperative. Interestingly, this torn subject may act in quite the same way as the inert one, even though she does this because of strong rather than weak capacities: she just cannot decide between her options, and so perhaps ends up doing nothing. To compare her to the other characters: she experiences the same kind of internal tension as the rigid and fickle subjects, just that for her, it is not the case that it is always one of the two capacities that ends up leading to an action or belief. So, we can summarize that there is more to the unity of feeling and cognitive capacities than just having two strong capacities.

I argue that the torn subject is a temporary and fleeting kind of character, in contrast to the ones I include in the table of characters. This character repeatedly has to go through forced decisions, as agents cannot stand still and not do anything. Hence, both capacities being strong, they have to negotiate a lot in these forced decisions and have to cooperate in order to get to an action or belief, even though they are not yet cooperative in nature. Eventually, through repeated forced coordination, they can become cooperative. By contrast, this upward spiral is not the case for the inert subject. Even though the inert subject too has to make forced decisions as an agent, her capacities are weak, and so they lack the capacity to "teach" each other how to cooperate, as it were. This is because, in contrast to the torn subject, her cognitive capacities do not fully strive toward coherence, and her feeling capacities do not provide her with a clear phenomenology in how she feels about the situations at hand. Hence, there is no (forced) cooperation between these capacities in the inert character, even when she makes forced decisions. Rather, she will plausibly merely go with the flow of contingent factors in the situations involved.

The inert character illustrates what happens if none of the capacities strive toward a particular action or belief. That is, it shows that it is even more problematic not to have any aspirations than to have one capacity constantly be overruled by another because this results in a standstill rather than a motivation to unify one's capacities. So, we can see that the inert character is even more problematic than having at least the fickle kind of guidance that strong feelings can give, for example. A character in which both capacities are weak seems to lead to a cynical outlook, and in extreme cases perhaps to a depressed one. Any kind of action or belief seems under-motivated for a subject of this kind. This must lead to difficulties in deciding on any course of action at all, and similarly, in difficulties to believe anything at all.[117] Even more, commitments and plans, which necessarily range

---

117 This leads to the paradox of Buridan's Ass: a donkey is equally close to two identical piles of hay. Because it cannot make up its mind as to eat one or the other (because none of them is in any way better than the other), it starves to death.

(There is already a version of the paradox to be found in Aristotle, and the Arabic philosopher Al-Ghazali is thought to have taken it up from him. Averroes then developed it further. The name stems from an even later uptake of the paradox by the 14th century French philosopher Jean Buridan.)

Note that the paradox of Buridan's Ass sounds similar to a problem that I addressed in Chapter 2. There, I said that the cognitive capacities *alone* would not be motivated to go one way or the other if several coherent options were available. But the difference (and the reason why this did not lead to the paradox of Buridan's Ass) is that in such a case, the two coherent options are still not *identical*. They are both *coherent*, and so the cognitive capacities have nothing to decide between them. But they are not necessarily equally good. Hence, there will be something that makes the subject go one way or the other as long as there are some minimally strong feeling states that can pick up the difference between the two coherent options and break the tie in an otherwise deadlock situation. In the inert subject, by contrast, it is not only the case that the cognitive capacities cannot break the tie (because they are weak and thus not sufficiently striving toward coherence), but neither can the feeling states (because they are felt too weakly). In this latter

over an extended period of time, seem almost impossible with this kind of character. While commitments and plans are difficult for the fickle character too, this is
for a different reason. The fickle character is at least motivated in the moment, on
a feeling basis, to pursue something (even over time). She is then too unsteady to
follow through on it over an extended period of time. In contrast to that, the inert
subject cannot motivate herself to pursue anything, even in the moment itself, let
alone over an extended amount of time. So, the difference between these two subjects lies in the fact that such things as plans and commitments can have a genuine
(affective) pull for the fickle subject, which might lead to a short-term pursuit of it.
For the inert subject, there does not arise such a pull at all in the first place. According to the inert subject, nothing ever seems worth doing or believing, not on a
feeling basis, nor on the basis of being cognitively coherent.

The reason why not-ever-being-compelled is worse than being momentarily
compelled and then not being able to follow through is that in the latter case,
there is a chance that the subject might learn to follow through "while on the
task", as it were. In other words, because the fickle subject still does have (only
feeling-based) aspirations, she always encounters new chances again to learn to
follow through, and to start an upward spiral, as it were. The inert character, by
contrast, is quite literally in a deadlock. Aspirations, whether cognitive or affective
ones, which would make her reach out to new chances, are themselves lacking.
Hence, her character is self-reinforcing its inertness. While the fickle subject experiences a constant tension between what she aspires to and what she follows
through on, the inert subject does not experience such a tension (while there is
a *potential* tension if the capacities were stronger). The very lack of experiencing
this tension leads to it being a deadlock.

What the inert character shows us, then, is that while it may be complicated
and exhausting to experience a tension between feeling and cognitive states, as is
the case in the rigid and fickle characters, this is actually productive, because it
propels the subject to change something about her character. The subject that experiences a tension can be motivated to learn.[118] The subject that does not experience such a tension is not motivated to learn, and is thus, ethically speaking, in a

---

situation, there is not enough for the subject to go one way or the other either in terms of coherence *or* in terms of affective pull.

There have been various attempts to solve the paradox. Chislenko (2016), for example, argues
that a decision to act non-intentionally allows us to resolve these cases.

118 This seems to be a similar point as Burnyeat's (1980) when he says that shame (feeling tension
about what one has done) is the semi-virtue of the learner.

direr situation than the subjects who constantly experience a form of tension between their capacities.

4.2.3 Being Rigid Is Just as Bad as Being Fickle

While it is important to see how the inert character is worse off than the rigid and fickle characters and how the rigid and fickle characters are worse off than the virtuous character, a crucial point for my account is that there is *no* difference in goodness between the rigid and the fickle character (that is why the line between them is drawn less bold in the table).[119] In fact, introducing such a difference in goodness between these two characters would reintroduce a hierarchy between cognitive and feeling capacities. That is, if I were to say that the rigid character is not as bad as the fickle character, I would in fact say that not having enough guidance from one's feeling capacities would be less bad than not having enough guidance from one's cognitive capacities. In other words, my thesis that we have to give equal weight to both capacities when we make decisions can be rephrased into the thesis that a rigid character is just as bad as a fickle character. In contrast to that, most people would probably assume that it is better to be a bit rigid than to be fickle. This shows, from a new angle, that my proposal is quite radical, at least in terms of how much it contrasts with our usual (cognitivist) assumptions.

In regard to one aspect, Aristotle would agree that self-control (rigid character) is just as bad as akrasia (fickle character). Namely, he says that both are not fully virtuous but also not vicious and that both are characterized by an internal tension between affective and intellectual guidance. But in regard to another aspect, Aristotle would strongly disagree that they are ethically of equal value, because exercising self-control over time can lead to virtue, he says, while acting akratically

---

119 And as there is no difference in goodness in my account between an only-reason-guided and an only-emotion-guided subject, my approach to virtue does not presuppose Aristotle's Function Argument, as presented in Barney (2008). Aristotle's Function Argument is often taken to aim at a determinate specification of the *highest achievable human good.* As I dissolve the hierarchy between rational and non-rational human goods in my account, such a specification would be impossible, and thus this seems to be an important disanalogy to Aristotle's ethics.

However, Lawrence (2001, 2006) argues that it is actually not so clear whether Aristotle's Function Argument aims at such a specification at all. Hence, if the Function Argument plays a different role in Aristotle's ethics, it is still an open question whether my account would be compatible with Aristotle's on this matter or not.

over time can lead to vice.[120] In my account, however, self-control is not closer to virtue than akrasia, and further exercising self-control would not get one closer to virtue, but instead, it would keep one away from virtue as long as one does not take the feeling capacities as normative guides too. Equally, akrasia is not closer to the inert or to the vicious character than self-control, in my account.

The virtuous, rigid, and fickle characters in my account fit well with what Aristotle says about virtue, self-control, and akrasia. However, as mentioned before, he does not say anything about a character like the inert one. At the same time, Aristotle also considers vice a form of character, and this form of character has not appeared in my account. And interestingly, there is at least one feature that Aristotle's conception of vice and the inert character share: both of them are not motivated to change their character. Neither of them experiences an inner tension between feeling and cognitive capacities. According to Aristotle, then, it seems that no matter how tumultuous and difficult the relation between feeling and cognitive states might be in the other characters, the inert character might be the worst of all, ethically speaking. There is nothing in my account that would contradict that judgment.

Conclusion of this Chapter

In this chapter, I started out with the observation that the capacity for reconsideration, which we already discussed in Chapter 1, gives rise to the need to introduce a virtue that has not been considered so far in virtue ethics, namely, the virtue of flexibility. Like the virtue of stability, this is a meta-virtue, a good-maker of all virtues. As a holder of the meta-virtues of flexibility and stability, I introduced the notion of a flexible and stable *character*, which is the virtuous character. But we still needed to connect the talk of flexibility and stability to our earlier distinction between feeling and cognitive capacities. I argued that it follows from the respective natures of feeling and cognitive capacities that if the cognitive capacities were to take over the decision-making alone, we would arrive at a rigid character, lacking the virtue of flexibility, as this character would strive toward maximal coherence and disregard all other concerns. On the other hand, if the feeling capacities were to take over the decision-making alone, we would arrive at a fickle character,

---

120 Another aspect that is quite different between Aristotle's account of characters and mine is that my account does not assume that there are *natural* differences (in goodness) between human beings' characters when they are born. That is, while Aristotle assumed that different individuals by nature are born with various kinds of characters in terms of goodness, I do not think so. See Leunissen (2013) for more details about Aristotle's notion of natural character.

lacking the virtue of stability, as this character would be fully led by how things qualitatively appear to her in any given moment, without any strife toward coherence over time.

After having connected the virtues of flexibility and stability with the distinction between feeling and cognitive capacities, we needed to address the topic of the unity between these two capacities, in order to avoid worries of a dualistic mental life. The notion of virtue helped us see how the unity between feeling and cognitive capacities is possible: in a cooperative way of holding each other in check, the two capacities can be thought of as an internal functional structure of one mind. The three kinds of non-virtuous characters, then, are three ways of failing to achieve that unity.

One of the important outcomes of this chapter was that the rigid character, the character in which the cognitive capacities always overrule the feeling capacities, is in no way better than the fickle character, that is, than the character in which the feeling capacities always overrule the cognitive capacities. This last point highlighted what I have tried to argue throughout the book: even though we tend to assume that when it comes down to it, it is usually better to go with our cognitive judgment than to go with our feelings, this is a cognitivist bias we have. Instead, there is nothing more virtuous in overruling one's feelings than in overruling one's cognitive states. Rather, if one wants to get closer to virtue, one needs to *stop* overruling one's feelings, so that both kinds of mental capacities can become a cooperative unity in one's decision-making.

Chapter 5: Spontaneous Aversion and Attraction in "Good Thinking"

So far, I have argued in this book that spontaneous emotional responses, in the form of an aversion or attraction, have been a neglected kind of mental state in our philosophy of mind. I then argued that feeling states, of which these emotional responses are paradigmatic cases, play the important role of keeping our character flexible by disrupting engrained habits and beliefs. This gives rise to a hitherto neglected (meta-)virtue, the virtue of flexibility. That is, discovering the important role these feeling capacities play in our ethical and moral decision-making also made us discover that we neglected the virtue of being able to reconsider our ways.

Now, is flexibility only a virtue in the practical sphere, in deciding what to do? In Aristotle's terms: is it only a character virtue, or is it also an intellectual virtue? The answer seems obvious: being flexible is also a virtue of our thinking and believing, not only of our acting. Hence, the (meta-)virtue of flexibility is also a virtue in the theoretical sphere. However, so far, we have only considered examples in practical decision-making (although we have always called its role "disrupting engrained habits *and beliefs*"). Hence, let me complete the picture in this last chapter by showing how we can think of the role of the feeling capacities in thinking and believing, i.e., in the theoretical sphere.

When we considered the role of basic emotional responses in ethical decision-making, I argued that we need to distinguish between the notion of *rationality* and *normativity.* That is, I argued that "what is the best to do" is not (always) the same as "what is the most rational to do". I argued that we have to distinguish two senses of "rationality" that are all too often conflated. Rationality as a good-maker term appears in sentences such as "it is the most rational thing to do". Rationality as a term that distinguishes intellectual from non-intellectual forms of deciding appears in sentences such as "rationally, I should not eat the cake, but I really desire to do so". The fact that these two senses of rationality are often conflated without even noticing reveals a common assumption that the intellectual "recommendation" in deciding what to do is the better recommendation (than the one from desire, affections, emotions, etc.). In other words, the fact that the identification of these two senses of rationality is often not called into question is a symptom of the cognitivism I argue against in this book.

Now, extending my argument to the theoretical sphere might go too far for some. I now argue that "what is best to believe" is not (always) the same as "what is the most rational to believe". That is, even when it comes to *believing*, I argue, the intellectual "recommendation" might not always be better than what

https://doi.org/10.1515/9783110780932-008

our feeling states recommend us to believe. The response might be: but believing *is* an intellectual endeavor, so at least here, our intellectual processes need to be the ones that determine what we believe. I will indeed show that this is not (always) so.

When we distinguished cognitive states from feeling states, I suggested that what is most characteristic about cognitive states is their impetus toward coherence. The better trained our cognitive capacities are, the more our cognitive states tend toward coherence. That is, a purely cognitive way of making decisions would tend to maximal coherence (between the various beliefs, but also between beliefs and other attitudes). By contrast, about feeling states, I said that what best captures their nature is a description of the phenomenology or quality of each feeling state. We can individuate and characterize the core features of a feeling state by "merely" referring to how it feels to experience it. That is, we can determine by a phenomenological method alone what essential characteristics a feeling state has. The better trained our feeling capacities are, the more clearly and more strongly a feeling state appears to us.

With this distinction in mind, we can foreshadow the argument I am going to give in this chapter. If we took "the best way of thinking" to be only done by our cognitive capacities, it would amount to the claim that the best way of thinking is "maximally coherent thinking". However, as I will argue, the norms of good thinking are not exhausted by maximally coherent thinking. Other norms, even such that go *against* coherence, are just as required for good thinking. And for some of them, we need our (well-trained, strong) feeling states to get there. Hence, the normativity of "the best way of thinking" will not be identical with rationality in thinking either.

In the first section, I will ask what it means to think well. Broadly speaking, there have been two sets of positions on this question, that is, coherence-theories of good thinking on the one hand and evidence-theories on the other. As it turns out, already with these traditional approaches to good thinking, the requirements can come in conflict—not all coherent beliefs correspond to evidence, and not all evidence-based beliefs are coherent with each other. This leads us to adopt a pluralism about epistemic standards of goodness from the outset. What will follow will show that we will have to extend the norms for good thinking by at least one more standard. In the second section, I bring to mind again the most important characteristics of feeling states, the kind of mental state we said has not been considered enough in theories of ethical decision-making and good thinking so far. This prepares the ground to then ask in the third section what role these feeling states play in good thinking. I consider the situation in which one is confronted with a claim and just feels like "there is something wrong with this", despite the fact that the argumentation for the claim seems completely coherent and based on evidence. I will argue that this is an occurrence of the directional feeling state of spontaneous aversion to a claim. In a nutshell, I will argue that one ought to follow this feeling state in such a situation, and that it would be epistemically wrong not to do so. Having argued for this, I will in the fourth section consider what this means for our list of epistemic standards of goodness. It will turn out that we need to add to considerations of coherence and evidence the standard of goodness of creativity—the ability to have such (well-trained, strong and clear) feeling responses to claims, and to follow them by going against evidence and coherence-considerations. This newly introduced standard of goodness will turn out to be the *epistemic aspect* of the more general virtue of flexibility that we have already encountered in Chapter 4. In the fifth and last section, I will consider a potential objection to the view presented. One could say that while it might be right that, for a good thinker more generally, it is important to be creative in these ways, for "good thinking" itself, strictly speaking, coherence and evidence play a more fundamental role than creativity. That is, for good thinking itself, the norm of creativity might be supererogatory. I will argue that it does not make sense to separate the notion of (good) thinking from the (virtues of the) subject of thinking and that more generally, taking the norm of creativity to be supererogatory while coherence as fundamental would simply betray the same bias toward stability and against flexibility that we already encountered in the practical sphere.

5.1 What Is "Good Thinking"?

"Good thinking" has generally tried to be captured by two competing theories. One can broadly be called coherence-theory of good thinking, the other evidence- or correspondence-theory.[121] This is how Alex Worsnip puts it:

> For many epistemologists, and for many philosophers more broadly, it is axiomatic that rationality[122] requires you to take the doxastic attitudes that your evidence supports. (...) Yet there is also another current in our talk about rationality. On this usage, rationality is a matter of the right kind of *coherence* between one's mental attitudes. So, rationality requires one not to combine attitudes in various ways. (3, 2018b)

Worsnip then goes on to show how these two requirements can come into conflict with each other. To put it succinctly: Just because a set of beliefs is coherent does

---

121 For other ways of characterizing the two competing sets of positions, cf. Olsson, 2021.
122 Obviously, Worsnip here uses the term "rationality" differently than how we do, that is, as a good-maker term, where it is identical with normativity for thinking.

not mean that each of its beliefs corresponds with evidence. And just because several beliefs each correspond with evidence, does not mean that they are coherent with each other. We have thus, at a minimum, a problem of (occasional) incompatibility of two strong norms of good thinking.[123] This is a problem we already have in epistemology, independently of what I am about to argue. What I argue in this chapter, hence, adds *another* consideration to the wider issue that our norms for good thinking cannot (always) all be compatible. Hence, I will not spend any time here trying to resolve this greater issue of what we could call "value pluralism[124] about good thinking". I am operating on the basis of the idea that there are several not-always-compatible norms of good thinking, so that it is not in all cases unambiguously determinable what is the "right" thing to believe.[125] That is, there are already independent reasons to believe that (maximal) coherence cannot be the (only) norm of good thinking. Starting from that, I want to show that we actually do and ought to apply *yet other* norms when we evaluate the goodness of thinking, some of which depend on our feeling capacities. I will come back to this topic in § 5, when I argue why the norms we "get" from the feeling capacities are not supererogatory. But first, let us consider again what we said what feeling states are and what we get out of this picture about the question of good thinking.

---

123 Moreover, we also have the problem that coherence apparently does not come in an all-or-nothing format. As Worsnip (2018a) shows, there are certain forms of incoherence that seem to trouble us more than others. Hence, (in-) coherence comes in degrees, and in different forms (instrumental, conceptual, etc.), and it is not clear which forms and which degrees are important to what degree in our assessment of the goodness of thinking.

124 This is a term usually used in the context of *moral* value pluralism—roughly, it is the view that we cannot have one overarching value from which all others derive, or a set of (always) mutually coherent moral values. Rather, the reason why there can be (real) moral dilemmas in the first place is that there simply are *several* (foundational) moral values, which do not always cohere, and thus there can be situations where no clear overarching "right" (moral) decision can be made.

For moral value pluralism, see, for example, Mason, 2018.

125 Some might argue that the notion of an absolutely right or correct belief—that I am showing to be problematic here—is awkward anyway. The best we can get, they would maintain, is the notion of a right belief *with respect to* some norm of believing. While I agree with this in its general form, I think it is noteworthy to realize that we do not have a convincing notion of an absolutely correct belief available. We thus arrive at a position that does not consider any of those norms of good thinking as more fundamental. Or, more cautiously, that there is no norm for good thinking whose application is more appropriate than any other purely based on the nature of belief.

5.2 What Are Feeling States, Again?

We said that we can individuate and characterize the core features of feeling states by "merely" referring to how it feels to experience them. What best captures their nature is a description of their phenomenology or quality. Among the feeling states, there are (at least) two that are *essentially directional* because they either draw us to the object or pull us away from it: spontaneous attraction and spontaneous aversion.[126] There are also other feeling states which *can* be directional but are not essentially so: being angry, fearful, joyful, or sad, for instance.

We argued in Chapter 2 that emotional responses, either as spontaneous aversion or attraction, are object-directed, but in a less-demanding way than cognitive states. This is so because, as we said, they have no representational structure. As such, they cannot take complex entities as their objects, such as propositions or inferential structures.

We maintained that due to their nature as described here, feeling states cannot—in a strict sense—be more or less coherent with each other. Each feeling state just brings a certain quality with it—sometimes directional, sometimes not—and qualities cannot be incoherent with each other. There might be sets of feeling states that are more likely to co-occur, but in principle, there is nothing incoherent in feeling, for instance, joy and sadness as a response to the same event.[127]

---

126 The notion "spontaneous" here should not be understood as "independently of habits or skill", as in "completely contingent from the subject's training". Rather, "spontaneous" denotes here the aspects of being episodic (rather than ongoing), occurring (rather than habitual), and to some degree non-voluntary.

127 Perhaps, at the most problematic, one could construct a situation in which we have two *directional* feeling states, each pulling in the opposite direction, which would amount to something like incoherence. I tend to think of these situations as Plato did of the case of Leontius, (in *Republic* 439e–440a), when Leontius at the same time felt disgust (a pull away) about the dead bodies but also felt a desire to look at them, even finding them a "lovely sight" (a push toward them). Plato argued that desire and aversion will not co-occur *for the same object, at the same time, in the same place, about the same part/aspect of the object*, etc.

But my deeper point here is exactly *not* that they *cannot co-occur* but that it *is not a problem* if we are in any two feeling states at the same time, even if they seem to pull us in different directions. Except, perhaps, for problematic forms of feeling capacities, which can result in a constant going back and forth on something, which we discussed in Chapter 4 when we considered the "fickle character".

This seems to show a clear difference to cognitive states, where it seems to be *inconceivable* that we hold two mutually incoherent beliefs at the same time (e.g., to believe A and not-A).

Feeling states do not only have no representational structure; they do not have any "inner" structure at all, as it were.[128] Their quality, we said, "extends over the whole state". That is, when we experience a feeling state, we experience the same quality over the whole time we are in this state—we are not going through steps or distinguishable parts of that state or quality. A feeling state, then, is an undifferentiated whole in this sense.

In a way, then, a feeling state—in the moment of experiencing one—is a brute fact about ourselves. This is not inconsistent with the idea that feeling states can be well-trained feelings. No matter what processes of affective learning have gone on in the past that now result in the kind of feeling one has in a specific moment, in the moment itself, the feeling state is just what it is, a fact about oneself, something to deal with. To some degree, this is true about cognitive states, such as beliefs too. No matter what processes occurred to get me to believe something right now, at that specific moment it is a fact about myself that I so believe it. However, it seems that there is a difference between beliefs and feeling states in such a moment. If someone were then to give me an argument to not believe something anymore, I would be able to consider it in that very moment, and change my belief if necessary. There is no equivalent for feelings.[129] No matter what you say or

---

128 Perhaps the same intuition about the nature of feeling states could have been captured by Bertrand Russell's distinction between *presentation* and *judgment* when he explains what he means by "knowledge by acquaintance". I have been saying that feeling states do not have a representational structure, but nevertheless a minimal psychological content. In Russell's vocabulary, this would have meant a mental state that is capable of *presentation* (my minimal psychological content), but does not have an inner structure (propositional or otherwise), and thus cannot represent an object in this more sophisticated way—and therefore is not akin to judgment ("cognitive", in my sense).

Here is how Russell contrasts presentation from judgment: "I say that I am *acquainted* with an object when I have a direct cognitive relation to that object, i.e., when I am directly aware of the object itself. When I speak of a cognitive relation here, I do not mean the sort of relation which constitutes judgment, but *the sort which constitutes presentation.* [my emphasis] (...) That is, to say that S has acquaintance with O is essentially the same thing as to say *that O is presented to S*" (Russell, 1917, 152).

129 Of course, there is talking about feelings, as, for instance, in psychotherapy, which changes them in certain ways over time. But I would say there are at least two differences. First, usually, a feeling state does not change immediately or while still in the situation that triggered it, no matter how much one says in such a moment. Feeling states seem to have to pass "just the way they are" for the moment being, and any kind of talking could only have an influence on them on a more long-term perspective. And second, it is not clear that these "techniques" of changing a feeling state are based on talking or reasoning in any way. They might, again, be less cognitive forms of changing feeling states, akin to the concept of affective learning I introduced in Chapter 3. And the concept of affective learning, again, would predict that it is not single feeling states in the moment

do in an attempt to change my feeling in a certain moment, it will not change my feeling *just now* (even if I understand and agree with you). Feelings have their own timespan, as it were, immune to influence during that moment.[130] They are raw or brute facts about us (at a specific moment) in that stronger sense than beliefs.[131]

Before we can move on to the question of how thus-described feeling states can contribute to good thinking, we have to face a potential worry. The worry is that this is a form of atomism about feeling states. We just said that they do not have an inner structure, as their quality extends over the whole state. They are an undifferentiated whole. For that reason, they are immune to influence in the moment itself, and therefore a brute fact about ourselves in the moment of experiencing them. It now seems that feelings are something like *impenetrable atoms of qualities.* The worry is that all they can do, then, is to provide the subject with something akin to raw sense-data. That is, they can only provide the subject with content that is not and cannot be interconnected with any other content.[132] In that way, they cannot possibly guide the subject in any meaningful way—there are just these raw qualities the subject experiences when being in the feeling state, but as these qualities cannot be interconnected with other content, this does not and cannot *mean* anything for the subject.

---

itself that can change (through learning by trial and error, for example) but rather the more general feeling capacity in how one feelingly responds the next time in a similar situation.

130 This might be related to the fact that they do not have a representational structure, or indeed any "internal structure" at all. I said in Chapter 2 that I think it is relevant that beliefs have an (internal) propositional structure, in order for them to be able to be coherent or incoherent. As in: they must represent things *in parts and in their relations to each other*, in order to be able to be brought into comparison with each other, so in order for their components to be evaluated. If we imagine a feeling state, by contrast, as simply "extending in the same quality over the whole state", with no internal structure, then it seems that this is one reason why they cannot be coherent or incoherent with anything else. There are no components or structures to be brought into comparison. And this also seems to be a reason why they are immune, in the moment itself, to any kind of influence. There is nothing "within" them—no structure, no parts, no relations between parts—for any influence to latch onto, to change them. So, in that sense, they are more of a brute fact about ourselves in the moment than beliefs.

131 See, for a comparable thought, Baier (1990), where she builds on Hume's notion of the inertia of emotions.

132 It is noteworthy, however, that Bertrand Russell thought that sense-data (at least the ones of which we have knowledge by acquaintance) are usually complex, that is, containing parts: "The sense-datum with which I am acquainted in these cases is generally, if not always, complex. This is particularly obvious in the case of sight. I do not mean, of course, merely that the supposed physical object is complex, but that the direct sensible object is complex and contains parts with spatial relations" (Russell, 1917, 153).

This worry is closely related to the position we considered in Chapter 3, when we responded to Jaggar's view that non-cognitive feeling states necessarily are "mere products of nature", and hence something like "mere knee-jerk responses". We said that this view assumes a false dichotomy—between feeling states being uneducated, mere knee-jerk reactions on the one hand, and them having to be cognitive (that is, we might now want to add, internally structured) responses on the other. With our concept of affective learning, we showed how our feeling capacities can be trained (and thus educated, not mere products of nature) without becoming cognitively penetrated or imbued with reason. Hence, our concept of affective learning broke open this wrong dichotomy.

With our concept of affective learning, thus, we can see how a feeling state might be like an impenetrable atom of quality in the moment of experiencing it, but nevertheless can still be a trained (and thus meaningful, guiding) response. That is, even if it is a brute fact about ourselves in the moment, it is an educated response (in a non-cognitive way).

But this does not yet fully address the worry that all these responses can do is to provide the subject with something akin to raw sense-data, that is, content that cannot be interconnected with other content. It addresses the worry insofar that we can see that it would not be a problem if all that feeling states can provide us with are raw sense-data. That is, why would it be a problem that the kind of experience I have when I am in a feeling state is experiencing something akin to a raw sense-datum, if I can trust that my feeling capacities have "picked out" the right kind of feeling response in this situation due to being well-trained?

The worry that might remain is that this kind of response cannot be guiding if its content cannot be interconnected with other content. But we already addressed this worry when we showed in Chapter 1 how emotional responses can be object-directed, in the less-demanding way. In virtue of being directional, they pull us toward or away from the object, even if they do not have the capacity to represent the object. (And they do this in an educated way if they are well-trained due to affective learning, as described above.) There was a further worry that the object emotional responses can be directed at in this way can always only be a particular (e.g., the particular piece of meat in front of me), that is, something that will not give the subject general guidance on how to act. I responded by saying that I do not see a problem in being Humean about this. That is, we can think of particulars as bundles of general properties. Emotional responses can be a response to one or more general properties in a particular. In that case, an emotional response is a move toward or a pull away from a general property. This means that the response *does* give the subject general guidance on how to act—it says how to act in relation to the general property it takes as its object, and this general property is repeatable (in virtue of being a general property).

So, a feeling state is an impenetrable atom of quality and a brute fact about ourselves in the moment. It does not have an internal structure, and therefore cannot be coherent or incoherent with other states, and therefore cannot represent its object. Despite all of this, it can be an *educated* response, and it can be directed at objects, and its object (and therefore it itself, as a response) can be interconnected with other content.

The point I am making could perhaps be summarized like this: while the feeling state is an impenetrable atom of quality in the moment of experiencing it, its object and its capacity are nevertheless sophisticated in some sense. The feeling capacity, the capacity with which we "pick out" the feeling states we are in in a given situation, is educated (through affective learning). The object of the feeling capacity, a (Humean) general property, is interconnected with other content.[133]

Having now brought to the fore our conception of feeling states and of their paradigmatic members, spontaneous aversion and attraction, once again, we can finally ask what role they play in good thinking.

---

[133] The dichotomy between feeling state and feeling capacity that I suggest here should not be taken too strictly. For reasons of scope, I can only hint at the more complex picture here. It might seem that I am suggesting a simplistic picture in which there are distinct, given feeling states, and a malleable, "teachable" feeling capacity, and all we can do in affective learning is to train the feeling capacity to pick out the right (already circumscribed) feeling states. The more complex picture does not assume this dichotomy. Conceptually we can distinguish between the capacity with which we feel, and the feeling states we are in, in a given moment. The third element in the picture is the object a given feeling state is directed at. If we are realists, we assume that the object is a given, and the quality of the feeling state is a response to it. If we are transcendentalists, we say that our feeling capacity has a certain form, and this preconfigures what kind of feeling states we can experience in relation to an object. At the same time, this also preconfigures what kind of objects we can have feelings about at all—under which aspects something can become an object for our feeling capacity.

My position is the latter, the transcendental one. The form of the feeling capacity (which changes with affective learning) does not just preconfigure our feeling states in the sense that, for instance, in one form it mainly tends to pick out feeling states of type 1, and in another form, it rather tends to pick out feeling states of type 2. Rather, by changing (training) our feeling capacity, we change, expand, or transform the kinds of feeling states we can experience in the first place. And with this, of course, again, the kinds of objects we can have feelings about (what aspects can become an object for our feeling states). In other words, there are not any feeling states independently of the form of our feeling capacity. Feeling states are the kind of experience we can be in, given the form of our feeling capacity.

5.3 What Is the Feeling States' Role in "Good Thinking"?

There are various ways in which feeling states can be thought to play a role in good thinking. Two are especially pertinent to the framework I have suggested in this book. The first is focused on the virtue of flexibility we introduced in Chapter 4. The second is focused on the directional nature of feeling states, specifically of their paradigmatic members spontaneous aversion and attraction, which are *necessarily* directional. It will be the latter aspect that leads to the main point of the chapter. But first, let us consider the role of feeling states in regard to the virtue of flexibility in good thinking.

A) Feeling states determine how the subject holds her beliefs (dogmatically or non-dogmatically)

Whether we dogmatically (rigidly) hold our beliefs or whether we can easily reconsider them is a matter of feeling. Do we *feel threatened* by the idea that we might have to reconsider our beliefs? Are we fearful of the process of reconsidering? It is not surprising or out of the ordinary if we dislike to have to reconsider our beliefs. It is quite to be expected. To believe something seems to have a *stabilizing, calming* effect on us. We have *settled* a certain issue (for now). Jane Friedman calls beliefs a closed or closing state of mind. In contrast to that, having an open question, an inquiry in mind, is an open state of mind, and is to some degree literally unsettling. Friedman calls these "interrogative attitudes".[134]

Hence, to *reopen* a question for which we hitherto thought we had settled on a belief is associated with heightened insecurity, less orientation, new open questions. In other words, it is to be expected to dislike this, to feel threatened by it, and to try to avoid having to do it.[135] But there are different habits or attitudes

---

134 cf. "(...) to think of the attitude at the centre of inquiry as much like this—as a questioning or "asking" attitude, one directed at the question itself. Inquirers have questions open in thought" (Friedman, 2019, 299).

135 Perhaps this is stated too generally. We can have beliefs which we would very much like to revise, if only an opportunity were offered to us to do so. In such a case, one might say, having the belief does not have a calming effect on us, and to reopen the question on the matter would not be associated with unsettling feelings, but with excitement and hope.

But I think we need to differentiate between the general settling effect of believing something, no matter its content, and the settling effect of believing something that one also *likes* to be true. That is, even if I believe something of which I wish it were not true, the fact that the question is closed for now still has a calming effect on me—it means that for now, at least, I do not have to put any effort of inquiry into the matter. Even though things might be dire, at least they are settled, as it were.

we can cultivate toward situations which present us with the affordance of having to reconsider our beliefs. In other words, we can train our feeling capacity in just how threatened, how fearful and unsettled we get in the situation in which we are called to reconsider our beliefs. The idea is that the more unsettled and fearful we tend to respond to new open (and reopened) questions, the less we are inclined to reconsider our beliefs (i.e., the more rigid or dogmatic we are). The virtue of flexibility, then, consists in cultivating the right kind of feeling habits in relation to open states of mind or interrogative attitudes.

So, this seems to be a straightforward way in which feeling states play a role in good thinking, once we give the virtue of flexibility its due place, now not only in ethics but also in epistemology. Good thinking consists, among other things, in non-rigid, non-dogmatic thinking. If we want to be good thinkers, we need to achieve the virtue of flexibility. For that, we have to train our feeling capacities in a way so that it is easy for us to reconsider our beliefs when necessary. This is a quite clear example that shows that good thinking does not only consist in conditions such as holding justified or true (or both) beliefs, but also in *how* one holds one's beliefs: rigidly or not.

This is a straightforward result from the account I put forward in this book. It is only once we acknowledge the importance of the virtue of flexibility that we can see this important role of the feeling states in good thinking. But it does not yet address the role in good thinking of the *specific type of mental state* I argued has so far not been attended to in the debate on whether we should be guided by our feeling states. The mental state I posited and said has not yet been sufficiently attended to consists in basic emotional responses—non-cognitive feeling states, which are nevertheless object-directed, and which are directional. I called them spontaneous aversion and attraction. I see a specific role of that kind of mental state in good thinking, and it is parallel to their role in decision-making about what to do. In decision-making on what to do this kind of emotional response may disrupt engrained habits and beliefs by being spontaneously attracted to or averted from an object, and thus recommend a different action. In thinking (going through the process of what to believe), this kind of emotional response may make us feel like "there is something wrong with this", even when a claim or argument seems completely coherent and evidence-based, or conversely, "there is something fundamentally right/worthwhile about this", even when a claim or argument seems incoherent or not in good evidential standing. I will

---

This might best be put in terms of the idea that, generally, we are continually engaged in various epistemic projects. Within such a project, it is better to attain knowledge and worse to remain in doubt, even if the content of the beliefs we have achieved is unsettling in some other sense.

argue that, in order to be a good thinker, it is important to follow these emotional responses in the form of spontaneous aversion and attraction in such a situation.[136]

B) Spontaneous Aversion and Attraction in "Good Thinking"

Imagine going to a public talk, and the speaker puts forward a nice new take on a current issue. They make a lot of sense. Their claims are all mutually coherent, and the speaker brings forward a lot of good evidence for their claims. After the talk at the reception, you have a casual conversation with another audience member about it. They ask you: are you convinced? You find every step of the argument convincing, in the sense that it is sound. You have seen the evidence. However, your response to the person opposite the table is: "I do not know, there just seems something wrong with this". You cannot go any further to explain your feeling. You cannot give the person opposite you any reasons for your feeling. I claim that it is important, *as* a good thinker, to stick to that feeling, despite the evidence and coherence that speak against it. It would be *epistemically wrong* for you to dismiss this feeling. And I claim that this is a spontaneous aversion to a claim just in the same way as we have described spontaneous aversion in decision-making cases about what to do in Chapters 1 through 4. To make space for this, we will have to expand our list of epistemic standards of goodness beyond coherence and evidence-responsiveness.

I argue, analogously to the decision-making cases, that what the spontaneous aversion does here for us is two things. First, it breaks up our usual habits of thinking (these habits make every step of the argument seem convincing). And second, it does not just break up a set of beliefs (the claim); it also gives us an indication *in which direction* our thoughts should go (that there is something wrong with the claim). To understand the contrast between this "directional" breaking up and a non-directional one, consider the following. Anything can stop our current consideration of a claim. For instance, while we are considering the claim p, a bird flies against our window, we are startled, and abandon the consideration. This event broke up the process of considering the set of beliefs of claim p.[137] But it did

---

[136] Throughout this chapter, I will only use examples of spontaneous aversion, not of spontaneous attraction, against considerations of coherence. I do this for reasons of simplicity. I take it to be unproblematically mirrored in the case of spontaneous attraction.

[137] I obviously make no distinction here between "breaking up a set of beliefs" and "breaking up the process of considering a set of beliefs". This is intentional. I take the "process of considering a set of beliefs" to be the process of "being about to assent to this set of beliefs". Thus, if this process is broken up, it is similar enough to breaking up a set of beliefs someone has already assented to. This way of talking has the advantage that we do not have to distinguish between cases where

not give us any indication in which direction our thoughts should go. It was a non-directional breaking up of the process. If we do not return to the process of thinking through these considerations, we will end up with a suspension of judgment on the matter. The directional case of spontaneous aversion is different. In that case, we do not just break up the current process of considering certain beliefs. The very movement of breaking up the current set of beliefs already pulls us in a certain direction—away from the claim, thinking there is something wrong with it. Let us say we do not return to the considerations after the breaking up due to the spontaneous aversion. In such a case, I think it would be wrong to say that we would end up with a suspension of judgment on the matter. The very move of the spontaneous aversion is already something like a pre-judgment on the matter, that the claim is wrong (in a sense to be specified).

So, a spontaneous aversion is more than just a (well-trained, feeling-based) interruption of a habitual thinking process. The feeling state of spontaneous aversion is directional, we said—which exactly means that its impact on our mental processes moves us in a certain direction. And what I argue here is that, in order to be a good thinker, we should follow the direction that these feeling state pulls us toward.[138]

What exactly does that amount to? My suggestion is this. If we are confronted with such a (strong and clear)[139] directional feeling state in the moment of considering a claim, which goes against considerations of coherence and evidence, it means that we should *investigate the matter in that direction*. Two important aspects need to be noticed here. First, I do not suggest to take the feeling state as a reason *to believe* (or disbelieve) the claim. That is, if I experience a spontaneous aversion to a claim, it is not my suggestion to then believe that the claim is false.[140] This would be too strong a version of my claim. But my claim could also be understood in a weaker sense than I intend it. That is, I do not only contend that when experiencing a spontaneous aversion to a claim, we should investigate the matter further. I contend that we should then further investigate the claim *in that direc-*

---

someone is considering a claim they have just heard the first time and cases where someone is reconsidering a claim they already hold but have been triggered to reconsider.

138 I am now always operating on the assumption that we have fairly well-trained feeling capacities in these examples, through affective learning as described in Chapter 3.

139 Remember that we clarified in Chapter 4 what distinguishes strong from weak feeling capacities: "Strong feeling capacities *clearly show* what one is attracted to or aversive from; they clearly show how one feels in regard to an action or situation. They have a *strong phenomenology*, in the sense that they are *strongly and clearly felt*".

140 Whether we *could* believe something on the basis of such a feeling is a different question, of course—similar to the question of whether doxastic voluntarism is possible.

tion, that is, in the direction the feeling state suggests to us. This means, more specifically, that we should pursue the investigation in a way that assumes that what the feeling state indicates to us *is true*, and it is a matter of finding out in what sense or why it is true. So, in the example above, where you feel that there is something wrong about the claim the speaker made, you should investigate the matter further under the assumption that there indeed is something wrong about the claim, and you just have to find out what exactly that is.

So, what I suggest amounts to the following. If you are confronted with a set of beliefs (a claim) that seem coherent and evidence-based, but you have a strong and clear spontaneous aversion against the claim—the feeling "there is something wrong with this"—you should investigate the matter further under the assumption that your feeling about this is right (you just have to find out in what sense it is right). Hence, I say, the feeling state should make you investigate the claim in a direction contrary to "common practice", as it were—against what considerations of coherence and evidence-responsiveness would suggest in such a situation.

Let us briefly compare this to the practical cases of Chapters 1 through 4. In the practical sphere we had the example of a habitual vegetarian who, now in this specific moment, has a spontaneous attraction to the meat in front of her. We said that in such a case, she should eat the meat. Hence, in the practical case, experiencing this directional feeling state (strongly and clearly, and under the assumption of well-trained feeling capacities) means one should *act* in the direction the feeling state suggests. The theoretical case is thus not fully analogical. When you experience this directional feeling state (strongly and clearly, etc.), it does not mean you should *believe* what the feeling state suggests. It means you should *investigate while assuming* that there is something right about that direction.[141]

Now, the claim that "if we have a feeling that something must be right or wrong, then we should investigate in that direction" might seem trivial. Let me show why it is not. First, we say this is so in cases where either our evidence, or coherence-considerations (or other epistemic considerations) would tell us to

---

[141] My suggestion here bears some important resemblances to Sosa (1991)'s point that an epistemically virtuous subject is not just a subject who believes what evidence commands her to believe, but who also looks for the kind of evidence that is most relevant for the epistemic project she is embarked on. For instance, if one is interested in finding out which food is healthy, neglecting evidence that concerns cancer hazards would not be epistemically virtuous.

Considered in the terminology of this framework, thus, what I am suggesting here for the directional feeling states is that they play an important role in directing the subject toward the most relevant kind of evidence and considerations for the subject. They do this not by cognitively getting there, but by pushing or pulling the subject in the right direction, against considerations of coherence and other kinds of evidence. If the feeling capacities are well-trained, we can think of this pushing and pulling of the feeling capacities as truth-tracking.

go *in a different direction*, or at least explicitly not in *that* direction. That is, there seems to be something irrational, or idiosyncratic, or ignorant about going in the direction of the feeling state in these situations. Second, we do not only say we should investigate in that direction "somehow", leaving it at a 50/50 chance whether there is something about what the feeling state suggests or not. We say that the feeling state alone is enough to take it to be true (in a to be specified sense), and that is quite a strong claim. The then following investigation is a pursuit in trying to find out *in what sense* or *why* it is true. That is, this investigation is, in some sense, not fully open-minded anymore, due to our following of the feeling state. It is an investigation that follows a certain already given "hunch", an investigation that already has a commitment toward a certain direction. And third, we can think of some quite problematic forms of "sticking to one's feeling about this" in the epistemic process, and we need to be careful to distinguish our claim here from these problematic forms.

Let us consider an example that might show a problematic form of "sticking to one's feeling about this" in the epistemic process, and see whether we can distinguish this problematic form from our claim. So, let us say that we live in a society where there are implicit biases against one gender, women, that are not there against other genders.[142] Let us say that this results in a common habit of referring to women—even when they are referred to in their function as experts—as "girls", while this habit is not common at all when referring to men. Imagine further that in a specific instance of this—a student referred to her professor as "girl"—someone points out to her that doing so reinforces biases against women experts. Let us say that this claim is then followed up by a coherent theory about the impact of language-use on reinforcing implicit biases in society and that it is further backed up with credible evidence. Imagine now the student responding to this with "I just got a feeling that there is something wrong about revising our language in these feminist ways".

---

142 Let me be clear that the way I have chosen the topics for the various following examples should not suggest that in one topic (e.g., gender, as in the first example), one is doomed when following one's feeling states from the start, while in another topic (e.g., utilitarianism, as in the following example), one seems to always be right in following one's feeling states because the theory is broken anyway. That is, I could have constructed the examples the other way around too, where a gender-example would show how it was right to go against the gender-theory and with one's feelings, and a utilitarianism-example would show how it would be problematic to follow one's feeling states in this instance, and the theory would be right. I chose the examples the way I did because I think these are common, familiar ways in which these debates are currently happening in our cultural environment.

My account would suggest, it might seem, that the student should now investigate the matter in that direction, that is, she should assume that it is true that there is something wrong about revising our language in this way, and she now only has to investigate why this is so. But this seems to be too quick. What is potentially problematic about this is that in this example, this kind of "sticking to one's feeling about it" can be in the service of a defensive response, rather than an unbiased feeling that there might be something wrong with the claim at hand. A defensive response is the case if confronting a claim is too uncomfortable so that one instead finds ways to defend one's position. In this imagined case, for example, the student might say this in order to avoid confronting her own implicit biases about women. Confronting one's own implicit biases is uncomfortable much in the same way as having to revise one's beliefs.[143]

So, how can we explain that in some cases, following one's feeling of "there is something wrong with this" is an indication of a defensive response, and in other cases it is a requirement for good thinking?

One aspect that is different in the problematic case (defensive response) as opposed to the cases in which we should follow the feeling, is that, like in the example above, the "sticking to one's feeling" is obviously *in the service of the already existing habits and beliefs.* That is, methodologically speaking, we should be skeptical about the normative guidance of our feelings in cases where they obviously support something that is (practically, or personally) much easier for us to support than the rivaling suggestion. If I am not a vegetarian and it would require of me to change quite a few habits in my daily life if someone convinced me that I should be a vegetarian, then responding with a feeling of "there is something wrong with this" does not have a great epistemic standing. It does not, exactly because the suspicion (or likelihood) is strong (high) that this is not my well-trained feeling states that lead me to feel "there is something wrong with this" but rather a defensive response that indicates how uncomfortable it would be for me to revise my beliefs about this.

So, let us look at an example where the "there is something wrong with this" feeling is not an unconscious defensive response to the claim but rather a hunch that should be followed. Peter Singer, in *Famine, Affluence, and Morality,* makes a coherent and evidence-based argument to the effect that "we ought to give money

---

143 We are reminded here of the other role of feeling states in thinking, that is, trying to achieve the virtue of flexibility in *how we hold* our beliefs (non-rigidly). The goal, we said, is having the feeling capacity cultivated in a way that prevents us from having too much fear about revising one's beliefs, when confronted with a situation that requires belief-revision. So, here we could say analogously, that we would want to cultivate our feeling capacity in a way that prevents us from having too much fear about confronting our own implicit biases.

away, rather than spend it on clothes which we do not need to keep us warm. (...) we ought to give the money away, and it is wrong not to do so" (Singer, 1972, 235). He starts from the seemingly trivial principle that "(...) if it is in our power to prevent something very bad from happening, without thereby sacrificing anything else morally significant, we ought, morally, to do it" (Singer, 1972, 235), and he arrives, through coherent and evidence-based arguing, at the quite stark conclusion that we should not buy any more clothes than what we need to keep us warm and give all the remaining money away.

While this claim has been brought up by a philosopher, it could also happen in everyday life. Imagine watching the news together with someone, and there is a report about how in a certain area of the world children are hungry because of the effects of a recent war intervention. You could have just that kind of conversation. Your interlocutor could say, coherently and evidence-based, "generally, if it is possible for us to prevent something bad without giving away anything that is morally important, then we should do it. Now, if we have money that we would like to spend on new clothes, but we already have clothes that keep us warm, then it follows that we should not buy those close but rather give the money to these children."

You see that your interlocutor's argument is coherent. You see that the evidence shows that these children are hungry. But you just have a feeling that there is something wrong with the argument. My account now says that you should follow this hunch (i.e., this directional feeling state), and investigate it under the assumption that there really is something wrong with the argument, you just have to find out what.

Let us imagine that it then turns out that there are all kinds of problems with utilitarian thinking and that it does not at all follow that you should not buy any new clothes anymore. For example, it turns out that in this particular instance, there seems to be a very narrow conception of "things with moral significance" at play, such that only things that are needed for bare survival count as significant enough to be pursued. However, no one wants a life that only consists in bare survival—so that the utilitarian thinking in this instance does not give us the right answer on where our money should go.[144]

---

144 Of course, this is not a proper refutation of Singer's points. To do this here would lead us too far astray from the main line of argument of the book. I do think the main problem of Singer's claim in this article is the narrow view on "admissible values". And I do think that it would be *morally wrong* to tell someone who is not living an excessive lifestyle that they are not supposed to buy new clothes again. And to get to that resistance against Singer's claims, we do first need to listen to our spontaneous aversion against this kind of claim, even if his argument is coherent and evidence-based, to then figure out where the problem with his argument lies.

I chose this example exactly because it would be all too easy now to say that here too, we seem to have a strong self-interest (rather than an honest hunch that there is a problem with the argument) in disagreeing with Singer's claim. Of course, so the idea goes, it is in our interest to find something wrong with an argument that shows that we should give most of our money away. So, we could not trust any feeling of "there is something wrong with this" in such an instance either.

I find this too easy. Notice the difference to what I called "the problematic case". There, it was *unconscious biases* that led to the feeling that revising our language would be wrong. There, it could be argued that something *in the very feeling* of aversion against the argument is an effect of an unconscious bias. In the Singer example, by contrast, everything is in the open. Of course, we do not want to give our money away. We do not need to claim that we have a feeling that "there is something wrong with this" for that. The fact that we do not want to give our money away is also transparent to ourselves, so there is no danger in being unconsciously led by biases and habits in our consideration of the claim. If anything, we feel *consciously* defensive about the claim, in the full knowledge that this is simply because we do not want to give away our money. So, it seems difficult to see how we could *deceive ourselves* in this example. Being deceived about our own feeling states, however, is exactly what made the problematic case problematic.

The question, then, is how we can know about ourselves, whenever we have this feeling of "there is something wrong with this" in relation to a claim, whether we are led by unconscious biases (deceiving ourselves, being defensive), or whether we have an honest hunch that there is something wrong with it. It is one thing, however, to say that it is difficult to determine which is the case in a particular instance, and it would be another thing to show that there is no difference in these cases at all. That is, to show that all instances of feeling "there is something wrong with this" are cases of unconscious biases, defensive responses under self-deception. We *can* describe the difference between the one type of case and the other, even if it is difficult to always determine which is the case in a particular instance.

The feeling of spontaneous aversion I put forward is not a defensive feeling about a claim or its consequences. It is a hunch that there is something wrong *with the argument*. It is a specifically *epistemic* feeling, as it were, about the validity of the argument, not a feeling about the consequences of a certain claim.[145] It is

---

145 That is, I argue that well-trained directional feeling states act (and we ought to let them act) *on the process of belief formation*, in a way that is immune to what some have called "practical encroachment".

an aversion to the argument, not to the outcome. I grant that this might be difficult to be kept apart by the subject experiencing the feeling. But I think there is a way for the subject to "feel out" the difference. That is, a subject who has a spontaneous aversion against an argument can honestly ask herself: is my feeling response directed at the potential consequences if this claim turns out to be right, or is it a response that is directed at the argument itself, that there is something *theoretically* wrong going on here? Of course, whether or not a subject engages in this honest self-examination depends on how much she wants to get it right.[146] All that matters for my account is that it is *possible* for the subject to feel out the difference between being defensive against the claim, and having a feeling that there is something theoretically wrong with the argument.

We can, to illustrate, expand the utilitarian example in a way so that it would not be in our self-interest to find the argument wrong. We said that it might turn out that one of the main weaknesses of the utilitarian argument in this instance is that it operates on a very narrow conception of "things with moral significance", that is, only things that are needed for bare survival count as significant enough to be pursued. However, no one wants a life that only consists in bare survival. Let us say this is what we find out as a result of following our spontaneous aversion to Singer's argument. As a result, however, we have to conclude that if there are more needs than those for bare survival that deserve inclusion in the calculus, then that means that in the long run, we have to give away *even more* than just the extra money we could save from not buying new clothes. So, in the long run, having the aversive response "there is something wrong with this" to Singer's claim leads us to conclude that we have to give away even more than what Singer claimed. I find it plausible that we would still have the same aversive response to Singer's argument in such a case, even though this response would be *against* our self-interest. This is so because, as I said, it is a hunch that there is something wrong *with the argument*, independently of how advantageous the consequences of the argument would be for us (as long as we do not have to suspect implicit biases skewing our feeling states about the argument).

---

146 For her to "feel out" the difference, to do that kind of self-examination, depends on how much she wants to get it right, and on having her feeling capacities trained to notice the difference (through a process of trial and error). It is important here, again, to emphasize that this kind of self-examination, and the training of the feeling capacities, do not need to be thought of as processes of imbuement of reason, or of cognitive penetration, as we have already argued at length in Chapter 3. That is, this kind of self-examination, just like the process of training of the feeling capacities, can be thought of differently than the standard cognitivist suggestion that we somehow take a cognitive, critical distance to our feelings and examine them "from the perspective of reason" or similar.

Let us look at one more example of a spontaneous aversion against a coherent claim, this time from the natural sciences, before we move on to address a potential worry. There are a bunch of diseases or other deteriorations of our body we take to be irreversible. For example, we have all learned that once one has a cavity in one's tooth, all one can do is to extract the matter that is affected and fill the cavity with synthetic material so that the decay does not expand any further. There is a huge amount of evidence for this, and it is not incoherent with anything else we believe. Imagine now that there is a dentist who just gets the feeling that "this cannot be right". He just cannot shake the feeling that there must be a way to make tooth decay reversible, to build up tooth matter again once it has deteriorated. My account says he should follow this hunch, take this to be true on the basis of his feeling state, and pursue the question of how or in what sense it is right. If he is not a researcher himself, he can push for people he knows in research to follow on this hunch, for example. For someone as experienced as him to have a hunch like that is an indication that there must be something true about it. In contrast to the two examples above, there is not even potentially any self-interest or implicit bias involved here. We can imagine such a case, thus, purely on the basis that this is something that actually happens to people sometimes. All that my account says is that *if* this happens, it is epistemically right to follow the feeling state, and it would be epistemically wrong not to follow it. (And indeed, recently, some researchers have found out that there might be a way to grow back dentine, the main "ingredient" in healthy teeth, after all.[147])

Hoping these examples have made my proposal of the role of directional feeling states in good thinking plausible, let me briefly address a potential worry that could come up at this point. I said in Chapter 1 that emotional responses of this kind can be object-directed, but only in a less demanding way. This is so because they cannot represent their object, and so they cannot be directed at more sophisticated objects, such as propositions and inferential structures. Now, however, I have been talking about a spontaneous aversion *to a claim (or argu-*

---

147 Cf. Neves, Babb, Chandrasekaran, and Sharpe (2017): "The restoration of dentine lost in deep caries lesions in teeth is a routine and common treatment that involves the use of inorganic cements based on calcium or silicon-based mineral aggregates. Such cements remain in the tooth and fail to degrade and thus normal mineral volume is never completely restored. Here we describe a novel, biological approach to dentine restoration that stimulates the natural formation of reparative dentine via the mobilisation of resident stem cells in the tooth pulp. Biodegradable, clinically-approved collagen sponges are used to deliver low doses of small molecule glycogen synthase kinase (GSK–3) antagonists that promote the natural processes of reparative dentine formation to completely restore dentine. Since the carrier sponge is degraded over time, dentine replaces the degraded sponge leading to a complete, effective natural repair. This simple, rapid natural tooth repair process could thus potentially provide a new approach to clinical tooth restoration."

ment), that is, a spontaneous aversion to a (set of) proposition(s). How can I now give this role to emotional responses, if I said they cannot be directed at more sophisticated objects, such as propositions?

The point here is that even if they are directed at propositions (e.g., in a claim), they are so in this less demanding or less sophisticated manner. That is, feeling states are directed at propositions just in the same way as they are directed at the meat in front of me. They do not represent the proposition, they do not distinguish between parts of the object and their interrelations, and so on. All they are, as it were, is an (affectively) educated directional response to the proposition. Even though there would be more "in" the object to be potentially directed at— parts, interrelations, meanings—their way of being directed at it is either a push away from it (aversion) or a pull toward it (attraction). That is, feeling states take a proposition as their object "as an undifferentiated whole", congruent with their own nature.

That is the reason why this way of being directed at the proposition does not give me *reasons* for or against the claim. It is an educated, feeling-based indication that there is something right or wrong about it *as a whole.* So, if I have a (clear and strong, well-trained) spontaneous aversion to a claim, I then know I should investigate what is wrong about the claim. But I will not, under any circumstances, be able to derive a counterargument against the claim from this feeling state. This would require that the feeling state could latch onto parts, interrelations between the parts, the propositional structure of the beliefs involved. Equally, if I have a (clear and strong, well-trained) spontaneous attraction to a claim, I know I should investigate what is right about the claim. But I will not, under any circumstances, be able to derive the reasons why the claim is right from this feeling state.[148]

Now, understanding the role of these directional feeling states in good thinking, we need to ask what extra standard of goodness we have introduced into the concept of "good thinking" by arguing for this role.

5.4 Extending Our List of Epistemic Standards of Goodness

We have said in the first section of the chapter that the commonly accepted standards of goodness—coherence and evidence-responsiveness— already yield a pluralist picture of good thinking (we called it "value pluralism about good thinking").

---

148 This is why, in Chapter 1, I argued that we can only see a *negative* role for emotional responses in decision-making—breaking up engrained habits and beliefs in a directional way. The positive role would consist in "making suggestions" of what to do or believe instead, which is not something that can be provided by a mental state of this kind.

Our considerations of the feeling states' role in good thinking will lead us to acknowledging that we have even more standards of goodness for thinking, besides coherence and evidence-responsiveness. But having adopted value pluralism about good thinking already, this should not pose a deep problem. Even if not a deep problem, the principle of parsimony might still put pressure on us against introducing another standard of goodness for good thinking, and lead us to ask: "is this really necessary?". I will address this worry in the next section, where I argue that the standard of goodness introduced by considering the feeling states' role in good thinking is not supererogatory. But let us first see what epistemic standard of goodness is newly introduced at all by considering the feeling states' role.

So, what is it that leads us to think that "a really good thinker" is not one who is "merely" coherent and evidence-responsive but one that has the right kind of feeling-based hunches about a claim?

Let us reconsider our examples from the last section. We had someone disagreeing with Singer's coherent and evidence-based utilitarian argument on the basis of the feeling "there is something wrong with this". And we had someone insist that it must be possible to grow back tooth matter on the basis of such a feeling state, despite the common evidence-based conception that this is not so. In both cases, we imagined that the following of the direction suggested by the feeling state, *against* the coherent and evidence-based claims, ultimately leads to a better position (a non-utilitarian or more sophisticated utilitarian position or the discovery of dentine-growing matter). But even if it occasionally would not lead to a better position, I argue, we would take this kind of thinking to be better thinking than if the subjects had ignored their feeling states about the claims (or if they were subjects who never experienced such strong and clear hunches). It seems to be easy to come up with various more imagined and real examples where people would value this kind of feeling-based thinking more than one where this is not the case. But it is not easy to determine what standard of goodness it is that we are tracking with this value judgment about thinking.

Let us sample some things that are commonly said about such kind of thinking. Familiar attributes of such thinking seem to be: it is a deeper kind of thinking, more provocative, more revisionary, less dogmatic, more original, more creative, more idiosyncratic, more authentic, and more flexible.[149] The term that seems

---

149 There is also the positive value judgment about feeling-based thinking that simply states as the reason why it is better: "because it is more feeling-based". That is, the judgment is that the fact of being feeling-based *itself* already makes it a better kind of thinking. As it is the demonstrandum of my considerations here to say that a more feeling-based thinking is a better kind of thinking, I cannot take the value judgment that "feeling-based itself is better" to help me argue for it.

to be most expansive of all these attributes seems to be "creative". The term "creative" seems to include most of the connotations and intuitions of the above attributes.[150] So let us, for purposes of simplicity, call the newly introduced epistemic standard of goodness "creativity". Hence, a result of considering the feeling states' role in good thinking is that, besides coherence and evidence-responsiveness, we think that (a certain form of) creativity is required for good thinking.

Consider the parallel to the practical sphere again. Having considered the role of feeling states in decision-making about what to do led us to realize that the virtue of flexibility—the ability to reconsider our ways—has not yet been given due notice besides the virtue of stability. Equally in the theoretical sphere, now, considering the role of feeling states in good thinking leads us to realize that the standard of goodness of creativity has not been given due notice, besides the standard of goodness of coherence. Just as we argued in the practical sphere that stability of character without flexibility of character would lead to a rigid kind of character, we can now see that aiming for maximal coherence in thinking without also aiming for creativity would lead to a rigid and perhaps sort of empty kind of thinking.

However, there is an important parallel to the practical sphere, here. I said in the introduction of the book that I take "the argument of this book to be a first step for the larger hypothesis that, in general, how an action *feels* can itself be an ethically justifying reason to do it or not to do it". That is, ultimately the larger hypothesis is that there is something good about making feeling-based ethical decisions, independently of what other standards of goodness (such as flexibility) it promotes. But, I said, I cannot argue for this larger hypothesis in this book, as this would require a debate about the nature of ethics. Analogously, we can think of the argument in the last chapter of this book as a first step for the larger hypothesis that, in general, a feeling-based kind of *thinking* is better than one where no such feeling-states are involved, no matter what other standards of goodness it promotes. But again, I cannot argue for this larger hypothesis in this book, as this would require a debate about the nature of epistemology.

150 The notion of creativity is, of course, itself a contested one. One line of disagreement is about whether creativity consists in producing a creative outcome, or whether it is all about the process (the thinking or acting) with which something is brought about. Hajek (together with popular views in psychology) is of the former view, saying that a product is creative if it is at the same time novel and valuable. (cf. Hajek, 2014, 288). Nanay, in his experiential account of creativity, is of the latter view; saying that the process of thinking still counts as creative if it is a novel way of doing things for the subject, while historically speaking, such a product has already existed. (cf. Nanay, 2014, 19). Another open question in this debate is whether a creative product or process necessarily also needs to be original, or whether these are two separate concepts.

I do not mean to enter the debate on what creativity is with my use of the concept, here. "Creativity" is the name I give to this cluster of attributes of a "deeper kind of thinking, more provocative, more revisionary, less dogmatic, more original, more creative, more idiosyncratic, more authentic, and more flexible", which I take to be a result of having and following (strong, clear, and well-trained) directional feeling states.

I am not now introducing yet another virtue—a virtue of creativity—besides the virtue of flexibility. I take it that creativity, as a standard of goodness for thinking, is a form or aspect of the virtue of flexibility. Creativity, again, is having one's feeling capacities trained in a way so that one has these directional feeling-based hunches about a claim or argument in a clear way, and that one follows them. It is thus the epistemic side of the virtue of flexibility—thus of the same virtue that allows one to reconsider one's ways in the practical sphere.

Remember that we said, in the practical sphere, that *the right kind* of stability is different from rigidity. That is, in the practical sphere we said that if we understand stability of character as *including* some form of flexibility of character, then we get stability without rigidity. We illustrated this idea with a metaphor about a bike. What distinguishes a stable from a less stable bike, we said, is exactly that it has *the flexibility to hold up under all sorts of circumstances:* one can ride it uphill, downhill, with lots of stuff on it, over sticks and stones, and so on. That is, its flexibility in terms of how it can react to its environment indeed enables it to stay stable over time. If the bike were rigid (that is, if it lacked some internal springs and joints that ensure internal flexibility), it would break in some of these situations. Instead, it is built in a way so that it can flexibly move with the forces coming from the environment. Hence, the bike is stable partially *thanks to* being internally flexible.

So, the right kind of stability of character is not opposed to flexibility of character, but rather on the contrary, depends on it. Is there an analogous point to be made in the theoretical sphere? Does the right kind of coherence in thinking perhaps *depend on* a form of creativity (even though creativity in our sense always disrupts coherent claims again)? At least the following could be plausible. The creative thinker, in our terms, is a thinker who allows herself to follow her (clear and strong, and well-trained) spontaneous aversion, her feeling of "there is something wrong with this" about any claim. So, it seems likely that she is the kind of thinker who is continually on track of the *necessary deep revisions* we need in our thinking about a subject matter—the deep revisions one might miss if one is too concerned with coherence in the moment itself, dismissing one's feeling of aversion to the claims at hand. That is, it is possible that such a creative thinker is *more coherent in the long run,* exactly because she allows herself to go against the current "surface level coherences" of the claims she considers. This would be an analogous argument to the one in the practical sphere. While it is not possible to argue conclusively for such a speculative view, let me try to make it at least plausible with the following thoughts.

Creative thinking—thinking that includes having and following feeling-based hunches—might be more coherent in the long term because, plausibly, deeper insights "survive" longer. By considering directions that seem a bit "out of the way" in the current circumstances, one might track an insight that turns out to be more tenable in the long run, when considered *independently* of the current circumstances. That is, while considerations of coherence would always favor coherence with "the things we currently take to be true", more revisionary and deeper insights might seem incoherent with the current states of affairs but turn out to be more coherent with the bigger picture that emerges over the long run.

Methodologically speaking, if we are thinkers that are always to some degree on the look-out for the deeper necessary changes in our conceptual frameworks, we will be less distracted by superficial coherence-considerations. If my account is right, by following our directional feeling states, we do exactly that. That is, *if* such a (strong and clear) directional feeling appears, and if we have well-trained feeling capacities, we will, by following it, be able to rethink our current conceptual framework by not letting us be too distracted by coherence-considerations. And that will, in the long run, help us track the deeper revisions necessary in our thinking, making our thinking more coherent in the long run. This would, then, allow us to say that there is a good and a bad form of coherence in thinking, the latter leading to rigidity, just like there is a good and bad form of stability of character. It is the internal flexibility provided by the feeling states that makes the good forms of coherence and stability of character different from the bad forms.

Being thinkers who are always to some degree on the look-out for the deeper necessary changes in our conceptual frameworks makes us revise our frameworks *continually*, rather than keeping them until external pressure overthrows them. That is, if we follow our directional feeling states in thinking, we might achieve a kind of progress in our thinking along the lines of Neurath's boat[151]—always replacing the parts in our conceptual framework that need (deep) revision, without ever throwing out the entire boat altogether. Again, this would give us a kind of coherence in the long run thanks to going *against* coherence-considerations in the moments when we follow our feeling states.

It seems that we often implicitly already think of good thinking in these terms, even though explicitly, we take ourselves to be cognitivists about thinking. We often encounter phrases such as "thinker A discovered 'a philosophical gem'"[152], or "this consideration helped us achieve important 'leaps of thought'"[153]. These gems and leaps are the product of creative thinking in our sense—thinking done by a thinker who allows herself to go against current considerations of coherence,

---

151 Neurath's boat is a metaphor introduced by Otto Neurath and popularized by Willard Van Orman Quine in *Word and Object* (1960).
152 Hajek, 2014, 289.
153 Hajek, 2014, 289.

following a feeling-based hunch that there might be a deeper insight to be found here. And I have argued in this final chapter that emotional responses in the form of spontaneous aversion and attraction are what we need for such directional, counter-coherence and counter-evidence thinking.

5.5 An Objection: The Difference between "Good Thinking" and "a Good Thinker"

An objection to the introduction of new epistemic standards of goodness besides coherence might be: "Well, it might be true that 'a good thinker'—a subject who is good at thinking—is being assessed under more norms than just coherence, namely, also under the norm of evidence-responsiveness, and now also under the norm of creativity that I introduced. But 'good thinking' *itself*", so the objection goes, "the very act of thinking, just needs to be maximally coherent, and that is what it means for it to be good. That is, *full coherence* is the ultimate goal of good thinking *itself*, and hence a fully and purely cognitive endeavor. Whatever other norms might be considered for 'a good thinker' are norms that are external to 'good thinking', as it were, because they are about *the subject* of thinking, not about the process of thinking *itself*".

In a way, this seems then to be a debate on whether we are concerned with truth-theories (what are the markers of truth), traditional epistemology (what are the markers of the best epistemic justification), or virtue epistemology (what are the virtues of good thinking), and whether these questions can be considered separately from each other.

The objection seems to assume that we can talk about good thinking independently or as separated from the (virtues of the) subject of thinking. And this seems to be an acceptable assumption in many truth-theories and in traditional epistemology. The move one makes with virtue epistemology, I think, is to say that we *cannot* talk about good thinking *itself* without considering (the habits or virtues of) the thinker. That is, it does not make sense to imagine a kind of thinking that is not always done *in a certain way by a certain subject*—because this subject always already has certain habits and skills that pertain to her way of going through thoughts and her way of holding her beliefs.

The objection, coming from a non-virtue-epistemological angle, would thus go: For good thinking *itself*, it is only maximal coherence that is relevant as an epistemic norm. Hence, for good thinking, any of the other norms would be supererogatory.[154] Of course, the objection would clarify, these other norms might become essential when we talk about "the good thinker", the subject of good thinking. But for good thinking *itself*, they remain just "nice to haves" that do not make the thinking worse if they are lacking.

Let me be clear that the kind of epistemology I do here is operating on the level of virtue epistemology. That is, I am not concerned with any thinking that can be characterized separately from the (habits, skills, and virtues of the) subject of thinking. But I operate on this level because I think it does not make sense at all to talk about the process of thinking independently of the subject or agent of the process. That is, I do not think we can come up with convincing truth-theories and justifications of belief without already doing virtue epistemology.

So, when I argue that a good thinker is not only governed by the norm of coherence (but equally by the norms of evidence-responsiveness and of creativity), I take this to also apply to "good thinking itself", if it makes sense at all to talk about that. What would it be to characterize *thinking well* if we did not include all the humanly possible virtues that have an impact on our thinking?[155] This might just be a version of saying that intellectual virtues are not separable from character virtues.

Now, even if the objector accepts that it thus does not make sense to separate good thinking from the (virtues of the) subject of thinking, the larger issue is still at stake. That is, does not the principle of parsimony put pressure on us to say that the newly introduced standard of goodness for thinking—a certain form of crea-

---

154 "Supererogation is the technical term for the class of actions that go 'beyond the call of duty.' Roughly speaking, supererogatory acts are morally good although not (strictly) required" (Heyd, 2019).

I would argue that in an Aristotelian framework of goodness, there cannot be any supererogation. That is, whatever is the *best* (among the humanly possible) habit to have is what we call virtue. So, there cannot be anything beyond human virtue that still applies to humans. What is beyond human virtue is unattainable. But what is unattainable cannot be part of virtue (it is superhuman, "hyper hemas", beyond us). Hence, there cannot be any supererogation—something that would be good to have but that is not part of virtue.

155 The objector could put her point also with the thought experiment of a "cognitive zombie". That is, she could ask what would be wrong with an epistemically faultless believer who does not feel anything with respect to the truth or plausibility of a claim. Her point would be that there is nothing *epistemically* defective about such a thinker. My point in this section was that such a subject is inconceivable. It is not possible to be an epistemically faultless believer if one does not (ever) feel anything with respect to the claims one encounters. This is so because a thinker without feeling capacities lacks the directional pull of the feeling states, which leads her to go beyond considerations of superficial coherence in the moment. A cognitive zombie would not be able to get to deeper revisions in her conceptual framework, and such a subject cannot be called an epistemically faultless believer.

tivity by going against considerations of coherence and evidence if our feeling pulls us in a different direction—is supererogatory? One could say: "Of course, it is nice to attempt to be creative in one's thinking, but somehow this does not seem as fundamentally important as being coherent and evidence-responsive."

I think this is another version of the common bias we have toward stability and against flexibility (of thinking and acting). Implicit in this distinction between the allegedly more fundamental norms of coherence and the allegedly supererogatory norm for creativity is the idea that it would somehow be worse to be an unstable (but creative) than to be a stable (but uncreative) thinker. Just like I argued that being rigid in one's actions is just as bad as being fickle, I argue here that it would be just as bad to be uncreative (in our specified sense) as to be incoherent in thinking. There simply is no good argument in sight as to why being (maximally) coherent would in some sense be a privileged norm for thinking over the norm of being creative (in our specified sense). Again, a thinker who is always maximally coherent, but who does not have any good (feeling-based) hunches about in which direction to go with an argument seems to be a defective thinker. That is, that kind of thinker is just as defective as one who does not take considerations of coherence into account.

Conclusion of this Chapter

In this final chapter, I extended my account of non-cognitive emotional responses and the virtue of flexibility to the theoretical sphere. I asked what it means to think well. It turned out that already with the traditional approaches to good thinking, considerations of coherence and evidence, the requirements can come into conflict. This led us to adopt a pluralism about epistemic standards of goodness. Considering the nature of feeling states, I then asked what role these feeling states play in good thinking. I considered the situation in which one is confronted with a claim and just feels like "there is something wrong with this", despite the fact that the argumentation for the claim seems completely coherent and based on evidence. I argued that one ought to follow this feeling state in such a situation, and that it would be epistemically wrong not to do so. On the basis of this, I then showed that we need to add to the considerations of coherence and evidence the standard of goodness of creativity—the ability to have such (well-trained, strong and clear) feeling responses to claims, and to follow them by going against evidence and coherence-considerations. This newly introduced standard of goodness turned out to be the *epistemic aspect* of the more general virtue of flexibility that we have already encountered in Chapter 4. I then argued that the standard of goodness of creativity is not supererogatory for good thinking. Taking creativity to be supererogatory while coherence as fundamental would simply betray the same bias toward stability and against flexibility that we already encountered in the practical sphere.

I would like to point out at the end of this chapter that these results also have an effect on what we take to be good philosophy. Showing that certain feeling states play an important role in good thinking also means that they play a role in being a good philosopher. In a nutshell, good thinking, and thus good philosophy, is not only done with our cognitive capacities but also with our feeling capacities. That means, in turn, that in order to be good philosophers, we not only have to train our cognitive capacities, but also our feeling capacities.[156] This does not seem to be an exaggerated demand. I think it is what is often implicitly already taken to be the best kind of philosophical thinking. It does stand in some tension with the common *explicit* belief that what we do in philosophy is a purely (or predominantly) cognitive activity. But this only shows that there is a need to bring in line our implicit and explicit beliefs about good philosophical thinking. In order to do that, consider the following.

We all know the stereotype of the annoying philosopher who, against all other sciences (and humanities and social sciences), says: "I do not care what they have shown; it just does not seem right to me". Many people's response to this is something along the lines of: "Ugh, what an arrogant attitude this is". Except for fellow philosophers—they seem to understand that this does not (have to) come from a place of arrogance.

And indeed, I hope to have shown with this final chapter that this attitude can be justified. This is what makes us good philosophers (good thinkers). This is what makes us go beyond dogma and the already known, and what makes us see deeper points about the issues involved. And that is our job.

But of course, this is also what makes us (as philosophers, as thinkers) more prone to self-deception in the specific sense of "covering up our own attachments to beliefs (biases, habits, etc.)" with this feeling-based methodology. So, we have to be careful in distinguishing the good form of this (our philosophical well-trained

---

156 This bears some resemblance to the pragmatist idea found, for example, in Dewey's writings, that in order to be a good thinker and philosopher, we need to have experiences in life that form us in some ways. (cf., for example, Dewey (1933, 1997)).

It is also similar to Aristotle's idea that one cannot (even intellectually) understand the *Nicomachean Ethics* before having gone through virtuous habituation (and thus before having a certain age).

Both of these examples, however, just make the quite general point that some (life) experience is required for a good thinker. It is a stronger and narrower claim to say that we need to habituate our feeling capacities (through affective learning) in order to be good thinkers.

feeling states) from the bad forms (i.e., sticking to it as a defensive response, a feeling that defends our old ways of thinking and our habits).

In order to learn to distinguish well between the good and bad forms of going with the feeling "there is something wrong with this", we first have to make explicit that *there is* indeed a good form of this and that we have already accepted it as a methodology for good thinking in philosophy. That is, we first have to admit to ourselves *that we are not cognitivists* in what we take to be "really good thinking" (or really good philosophy) even if we tend to have this self-image otherwise.

Only once this is made explicit, i.e., once we admit to ourselves that it is not the exclusively cognitivist, but a more feeling-based thinking that we value the most, only then can we start making more fine grained distinctions and learn to distinguish well between cases in which we fall prey to the defensive form and cases in which we are about to do really good thinking.

In this book, I have moved from the practical sphere (the role of feeling states in ethical decision-making) to the theoretical sphere (their role in thinking). I have argued that in both spheres, a specific kind of mental state has not yet received enough attention, that is, the non-cognitive, directional feeling states that I called spontaneous aversion and attraction. And in both spheres, paying more attention to the role of these feeling states led us to the introduction of new norms: the virtue of flexibility, and creativity in thinking as an aspect of flexibility.

In the introduction, I alluded to a larger hypothesis within which I argue for the role of the feeling capacities. I took the argument of this book in the practical sphere to be a first step for the larger hypothesis that, in general, how an action *feels* can itself be an ethically justifying reason to do it or not to do it. Likewise, in the theoretical sphere, I take what I said to be a first step for the larger hypothesis that, in general, a feeling-based thinking is better than one where no such feeling-states are involved, no matter what other standards of goodness this promotes. But I restricted myself not to argue for these larger hypotheses, which would require debates about the nature of ethics and epistemology, respectively. Rather, I argued for the importance of the virtue of flexibility and creativity, as a first step. The most important aspect of this first step consisted in showing that feeling states need not be cognitively penetrated (or "imbued by reason") in order to play their important role in action-guidance and in thinking. The next step would be to show that it is not only by making us more flexible in acting and more creative in thinking that they play an important role. The broader idea would be that cognitive states are, fundamentally, not in a privileged position to guide our actions or thinking. No matter what difference we can make out between the cognitive and feeling capacities, the idea is, it will be a further argument to say that this difference would put the cognitive capacities in a privileged position to guide our actions or thinking. This further argument has traditionally been "stability" in the case of ethics, and "coherence" in the case of epistemology. I have shown that contra stability and coherence, flexibility and creativity are just as important.

And I think any such further argument that would use a difference between the cognitive and feeling capacities to argue for the privileged position of the cognitive capacities must fail. It must fail because it has to assume that this special feature about the cognitive capacities (whatever it is) is somehow superiorly important for either acting or thinking. And that will always be a claim about the nature of ethics or epistemology, respectively, more than an argument about acting or thinking.

Conclusion

I started out in Chapter 1 with the proposal that there is a kind of mental state that has not been considered so far in the literature: a kind of emotion that is not cognitive but nevertheless object-directed. I call this kind of emotion a basic emotion, or an emotional response. A basic emotion is directed at something, but it is "basic" in the sense that it does not have the complexity and sophistication of emotions that are plausibly construed in cognitivist terms. If there is such a mental state, I argued, it can play an independent role in normative guidance. This proposal is novel insofar as emotions, if they are taken to figure in normative guidance at all, tend to be theorized as linked to or penetrated by cognition. This does not apply to basic emotions. They are neither cognitive nor relevantly tied to cognitive states. In other words, these are not rationally informed or reasoned emotions; they are not emotions we as reasoners shape such that they are reason-responsive. They are genuinely non-cognitive.

My next task was to argue that this non-cognitive emotion can play an independent role in normative guidance, namely, by taking on the negative role of disrupting engrained beliefs and habits when needed. I say "can play" rather than "does play" because, even though in my account feeling states are not habituated to conform with reasoning, they can be in better or worse shape. They can be improved by ways of growing up and ways of engaging with the world, improving our ability to affectively process situation-responsive input. The mental state called "basic emotion" plays its normative role by way of showing up either as a spontaneous aversion or a spontaneous attraction. I argued that while these kinds of emotional responses cannot play the positive role of coming up with new options for acting or believing, their educated way of disrupting engrained beliefs and habits is itself an important contribution to normative guidance. After having considered various potential objections to this view, I concluded that the capacity to reconsider is something that we value normatively. When we assess others as moral and ethical agents, this is one dimension we attend to: we expect others to be able to reconsider, in ways that are responsive to the ways in which life changes and situations unfold. Hence, I argued, the negative role of emotional responses gives them a crucial role in normative guidance.

In Chapter 2, I then took a step back in order to offer a framework in the philosophy of mind that corroborates an important distinction that was implicitly introduced in the first chapter: the distinction between feeling and cognitive states. In the second chapter, I then argued that this distinction is fundamental, in the sense that all mental states can be divided into these two classes. I argued that each of these two kinds of mental state has a unique feature that essentially char-

https://doi.org/10.1515/9783110780932-009

acterizes all instances of its kind. Feeling states, I argued, are essentially characterized by how they feel or, in other words, by their phenomenology, while cognitive states are essentially characterized by their impetus toward coherence.

This fundamental difference between cognitive and feeling states strengthened my claim that the contribution of emotional responses to normative guidance cannot be replaced by cognitive capacities. In other words, because feeling states in general and emotional responses in particular are a way to provide the subject with a phenomenology of how the situations at hand feel, and because the cognitive capacities cannot provide this input to the subject, I argued that we need feeling states when we make moral and ethical decisions.

It is in Chapter 3, then, that I turned explicitly to competing accounts, according to which the emotions can be normative guides, though only because they are shaped by reason. I address the objection that even if feeling states are phenomenologically salient prompts to assess situations one way or another, the way we make sure that they make us move in the right direction is by reason. To some extent, the objection goes, we should have shaped them through cognitive education or training beforehand; in addition, we may rationally assess our emotional responses on the spot, dismissing some and validating others. I argued against this and some related objections to my approach. The defense of my approach led me to an important background issue, namely, how we understand the normativity involved when making moral and ethical decisions. I argued that philosophers often identify normativity with rationality, which leads to the cognitivist bias that I wish to dispel. I tried to show that the identification of normativity with rationality is neither necessary nor plausible. I argued that feeling states not only make their own contribution in ethical decisions; they also have their own role to play in moral education, and they do not depend on an imbuement with cognitive structures in order to play these roles. I showed that we do not have to think of the emotional responses as brute forces or dumb responses just because they are not cognitive. Emotional responses can be educated in their own, non-cognitive ways.

If we do not have to identify normativity with rationality, the conceptual space for my second proposal opens up, which I presented in Chapter 4. I defended the view that we need to recognize a virtue that has not been considered so far, namely, the virtue of flexibility. For this, Chapter 4 first needed to look back to earlier chapters and unify several lines of argument. Picking up the idea from Chapter 1 that the capacity to reconsider one's ways, which is achieved by the disruption by emotional responses, is a necessary capacity for ethical and moral agency, I argued that disruption and reconsideration need their own virtue. That is why we need to introduce a virtue that has not been considered so far, the virtue of flexibility. Like the virtue of stability in Aristotle, I argued, the virtue of flexibility is a meta-virtue, a good-maker of all virtues.

To have a virtue is to have one's character shaped in a certain way. This is a minimal premise. Based on it, I introduced the notion of a flexible and stable character. I argued that flexibility and stability of character can fail by either being fickle (flexible without being stable) or by being rigid (stable without being flexible). In order to explain how we can understand the difference between a flexible and a fickle character, I introduced the notion of a narrative unity. I said that as long as the subject has a personal narrative that unites her actions and beliefs for her over time, she fulfills a minimal standard of coherence. And this minimal standard of coherence is enough for her character to not be fickle, but rather flexible.

I then connected the framework of flexible and stable characters to the claims I made in the philosophy of mind, namely, to the distinction between feeling and cognitive states. I argued that it follows from their respective unique natures that "only being led by cognitive capacities" leads to a rigid character, while "only being led by feeling capacities" leads to a fickle character. Hence, for a virtuous character, one that is at once stable and flexible, we need to be able to be normatively led by both of our capacities—feelings and cognition.

This opened up the question how these two capacities can be unified, that is, how they can both be a capacity of a *single* mind. In other words, we needed to say more in order to avoid a dualist picture of the human mind. I argued that if the feeling and cognitive capacities are both strong, that is, well-trained and clear in their expression, they are able to interact as two cooperative parts of an internal functional structure within one mind. In that case, they can freely inform each other and hold each other's influence in check. Hence, in the case of a virtuous character, the two capacities are unified. On the level of experience, the *virtuous* subject thus only experiences one of the two capacities separately in the special case when change is needed. In contrast to the virtuous character, there are three ways of failing to achieve such a unity of the two capacities, and in these three characters, the two capacities' "recommendations" do regularly show up separately in the experience of the subject, creating tension. These three characters, the rigid, fickle, and inert character, together with the virtuous character then formed the material for the Aristotle-inspired table of characters I presented.

The most important point in presenting and comparing these three non-virtuous characters was to show that a person of rigid character (the character that is only led by cognitive capacities) is, speaking both morally and prudentially, in no way better than a subject who lets her feeling capacities rule most of the time. With this, I was able to formulate the main contention of this book from a new angle: that, contrary to common cognitivist assumptions, it is not better to have a character that exerts too much cognitive control over one's feelings than to have a character that regularly has strong feelings overrule the cognitive capacities.

The important takeaway of this part of the book was thus that the rigid character is not better than the fickle character. The only good, that is, virtuous character is the one that lets her feeling capacities determine her actions and beliefs *just as much* as she lets her cognitive capacities do so (and here I specified that "just as much" is not an arithmetic notion). And importantly, one does not get any closer to virtue by overly exercising one's cognitive capacities. Rather, if one wants to get closer to virtue, one needs to *stop* overruling one's feelings so that both kinds of mental capacities can become a cooperative unity in one's decision-making.

Having completed my account with that chapter, I then asked in the fifth and last chapter whether this account can also be extended to the theoretical sphere of what it is to think well, beyond ethical decision-making. I argued that the virtue of flexibility is also a virtue in the theoretical sphere. I hence completed the picture in this last chapter, by showing how we can think of the role of the feeling states in thinking and believing. With the distinctions in mind that I introduced in Chapters 1–4, I argued that if we took "the best way of thinking" to be only done by our cognitive capacities, it would amount to the claim that the best way of thinking was "maximally coherent thinking". However, as I argued, the norms of good thinking are not exhausted by maximally coherent thinking. Other norms, even such that go *against* coherence, are just as required for good thinking. And for some of them, I argued, we need our (well-trained, strong) feeling states to get there. I considered the situation in which one is confronted with a coherent and evidence-based claim, but in the moment of hearing it has the feeling that "there is something wrong with this". I said that this is a spontaneous aversion to a claim and that we ought to follow this feeling state in order to be good thinkers. I showed that if we are confronted with such a (strong and clear) directional feeling state in the moment of considering a claim which goes against considerations of coherence and evidence, it means that we should *investigate the matter in that direction*. I argued that by doing so, we might have to disregard considerations of coherence. However, this might lead to a better form of (long-term) coherence in the end, as it allows us to pick up on deeper problems with our conceptual frameworks than we would if we always tried to achieve maximal coherence in our thinking in the moment itself. This led us to acknowledge the standard of goodness of creativity for good thinking—in the sense of being led by these feeling-based directional hunches—which is ultimately an aspect of the virtue of flexibility. Hence, I showed, the feeling states play an analogous role in thinking well to the role they play in ethical decision-making.

I made a final observation that this also shows us something about what it means to be a good philosopher. Good thinking, and thus good philosophy, is not only done with our cognitive capacities but also with our feeling capacities. That means, in turn, that in order to be good philosophers, we not only have to train our cognitive capacities, but also our feeling capacities. Considering the role of feeling capacities and the virtue of flexibility, thus, also in the end led us to have an insight about our own activity and methodology as philosophers.

As mentioned in the introduction, I take the argument of this book to be a first step toward the larger hypothesis that, in general, how an action *feels* can itself be an ethically justifying reason to perform or not perform it. This larger hypothesis also has its parallel in the theoretical sphere. That is, we can think of the argument in the last chapter as a first step for the larger hypothesis that, in general, feeling-based thinking is per se better than thinking where no such feeling-states are involved, no matter whether this has any other advantages, such as, for example, a more long-term kind of coherence.

While I was not able to address this larger question for either sphere within the scope of this short book, I hope I was able to make it plausible that emotional responses and feelings in general play a significant and independent role in normative guidance and in thinking well. They keep the subject's character flexible and her thinking creative, in that they disrupt her engrained habits and beliefs in an educated and directional way whenever it is needed.

Bibliography

Achtenberg, Deborah (2002): *Cognition of Value in Aristotle's Ethics: Promise of Enrichment, Threat of Destruction.* New York: State University of New York Press.

Anscombe, Gertrude E. M. (1957): *Intention.* Cambridge: Harvard University Press.

Aristotle (1984): *Rhetoric.* In: Barnes, Jonathan (Ed.): *The Complete Works of Aristotle: The Revised Oxford Translation.* Princeton: Princeton University Press.

Aristotle (2002): *Nicomachean Ethics.* Sarah Broadie and Christopher Rowe (Eds.). Oxford: Oxford University Press.

Azevedo, Ruben T., Garfinkel, Sarah N., Critchley, Hugo D., and Tsakiris, Manos (2017): „Cardiac afferent activity modulates the expression of racial stereotypes". In: *Nature Communications* 8.

Baier, Annette (1990): „What Emotions are about". In: *Philosophical Perspectives* 4 (*Action Theory and Philosophy of Mind*).

Barlassina, Luca and Hayward, Max Khan (2019): „More of me! Less of me!: Reflexive Imperativism about Affective Phenomenal Character". In: *Mind* 128. No. 512, 1013 – 1044.

Barney, Rachel (2008): „Aristotle's Argument for a Human Function". In: *Oxford Studies in Ancient Philosophy* 34, 293 – 322.

Barney, Rachel (2016): „Colloquium 2: What Kind of Theory is the Theory of the Tripartite Soul?". In: *Proceedings of the Boston Area Colloquium of Ancient Philosophy* 31. No. 1, 53 – 83.

Bayne, T. & Montague, M.(eds.) (2011). *Cognitive Phenomenology.* Oxford University Press UK.

Bell, Macalester (2013): *Hard Feelings: The Moral Psychology of* Contempt. Oxford: Oxford University Press.

Ben-Ze'ev, Aaron (2000): *The Subtlety of Emotions.* Cambridge and London: MIT Press.

Betzler, Monika (2007): „Making Sense of Actions Expressing Emotions". In: *Dialectica* 61. No. 3, 447 – 466.

Betzler, Monika (2009): „Expressive Actions". In: *Inquiry* 52. No. 3, 272 – 292.

Betzler, Monika (2012): „The Normative Significance of Personal Projects". In: Kühler, Michael and Jelinek, Nadja (Eds.): *Autonomy and the Self.* Dordrecht: Springer, 118 – 101.

Betzler, Monika (2014): „Enhancing the Capacity for Autonomy: What Parents Owe Their Children to Make Their Lives Go Well". In: Baggatini, Alexander and MacLeod, Colin (Eds.): *The Nature of Children's Well-Being.* Dordrecht: Springer Science and Business Media.

Betzler, Monika (2016): „Evaluative Commitments: How They Guide Us over Time and Why". In: Altshuler, Roman and Sigrist, Michael J. (Eds.): *Time and the Philosophy of Action.* New York: Routledge.

Blackburn, Simon (1988): „Attitudes and contents". In: *Ethics* 98. No. 3, 501 – 517.

Block, Ned (1995): „On a confusion about a function of consciousness". In: *Brain and Behavioral Sciences* 18. No. 2, 227 – 247.

Block, Ned (1996). „Mental paint and mental latex". *Philosophical Issues* 7:19 – 49.

Block, Ned (2003). „Mental paint". In Martin Hahn & B. Ramberg (eds.), *Reflections and Replies: Essays on the Philosophy of Tyler Burge.* MIT Press. pp. 165–200.

Block, Ned (2007). *Consciousness, Function, and Representation: Collected Papers.* Bradford.

Boghossian, Paul (2014): „What is inference?". In: *Philosophical Studies* 169. No. 1 1 – 18.

Bordini, Davide (2017): „Not in the Mood for Intentionalism". In: *Midwest Studies in Philosophy* 41. No. 1, 60 – 81.

Boyle, Matthew (2016): „Additive Theories of Rationality: A Critique". In: *European Journal of Philosophy* 24. No. 3, 527 – 555.

https://doi.org/10.1515/9783110780932-010

Brady, Michael S. (2013): *Emotional insight: The epistemic role of emotional experience.* New York: Oxford University Press.

Bratman, Michael (1987): *Intention, Plans, and Practical Reason.* Cambridge: Harvard University Press.

Bratman, Michael (1990). „Dretske's desires," *Philosophy and Phenomenological Research*, 50: 795–800.

Bratman, Michael (1999). *Faces of Intention: Selected Essays on Intention and Agency.* New York: Cambridge University Press.

Brentano, Franz (1874): *Psychologie vom empirischen Standpunkte.* Berlin: Duncker und Humblot.

Broadie, Sarah (1991): *Ethics with Aristotle.* Oxford: Oxford University Press.

Brook, A., (2006). „Desire, reward, feeling: Commentary on Schroeder's *Three Faces of Desire*," *Dialogue*, 45: 157–164.

Broome, J., (1991). „Desire, belief and expectation," *Mind*, 100: 265–7.

Burnyeat, Myles F. (1980): „Aristotle on learning to be good". In: Rorty, Amélie O. (Ed.): *Essays on Aristotle's Ethics.* Berkeley: University of California Press, 69–92.

Burnyeat, Myles F. (1997): „Culture and Society in Plato's Republic". In: *Tanner Lectures on Human Values.* Salt Lake City: University of Utah Press.

Burnyeat, Myles F. (2000): „Plato on Why Mathematics is Good for the Soul". In Smiley, Timothy (Ed.): *Mathematics and Necessity: Essays in the History of Philosophy.* Oxford: Oxford University Press, 1–81.

Burnyeat, Myles F. (2002): „De anima II 5". In: *Phronesis* 47. No. 1, 28–90.

Burnyeat, Myles F. (2006): „The Presidential Address: The Truth of Tripartition". In: *Proceedings of the Aristotelian Society* 106, 1–23.

Butler, K., (1992). „The physiology of desire," *Journal of Mind and Behavior*, 13: 69–88.

Byrne, Ruth M. J. (2005): *The Rational Imagination: How People Create Alternatives to Reality.* Cambridge: MIT Press.

Byrne, Ruth M. J. (2016): „Imagination and Rationality". In: Kind, Amy (Ed.): *The Routledge Handbook of Philosophy of Imagination.* New York: Routledge.

Byrne, A. and Hájek, A., (1997). „David Hume, David Lewis, and decision theory," *Mind*, 106: 411–28.

Caston, Victor (2015): „Perception in Ancient Greek Philosophy". In: Matthen, Mohan (Ed.), *The Oxford Handbook of Philosophy of Perception.* Oxford: Oxford University Press, 29–50.

Charles, David (2004): „Emotion, cognition and action". In: *Philosophy* 55, 105–136.

Charles, David (2009): „Colloquium 1: Aristotle's Psychological Theory". In: *Proceedings of the Boston Area Colloquium of Ancient Philosophy* 24. No. 1, 1–49.

Charles, David (2011): „Desire in action: Aristotle's move". In: Pakaluk, Michael and Pearson, Giles (Eds.): *Moral Psychology and Human Action in Aristotle.* Oxford: Oxford University Press.

Chislenko, Euegene (2016): „A Solution for Buridan's Ass". In: *Ethics* 126. No. 2, 283–310.

Chudnoff, E. (2015). *Cognitive Phenomenology.* Routledge.

Cohon, Rachel (2018): „Hume's Moral Philosophy". In: Zalta, Edward N. (Ed.): *The Stanford Encyclopedia of Philosophy* (Fall 2018 Edition). https://plato.stanford.edu/archives/fall2018/entries/hume-moral, last accessed April 6, 2023

Cooper, John M. (1998): *Reason and Emotion: Essays on Ancient Moral Psychology and Ethical Theory.* Princeton: Princeton University Press.

Cooper, Neil (1968): „Morality and importance". In: *Mind* 77. No. 305, 118–121.

Damasio, Antonio R. (1985): „Understanding the mind's will". In: *Behavioral and Brain Sciences* 8. No. 4, 589.

Damasio, Antonio R. (1994): *Descartes' Error: Emotion, Reason, and the Human Brain.* New York: Putnam.

Damasio, Antonio R. (2000): „A second chance for emotion". In: Lane, Richard D. R., Nadel, Lynn, Ahern, Geoffrey L., Allen, John, and Kaszniak, Alfred W. (Eds.): *Cognitive Neuroscience of Emotion*. Oxford: Oxford University Press, 12–23.

Damasio, Antonio R. (2003): *Looking for Spinoza: Joy, Sorrow, and the Feeling Brain.* London: William Heinemann.

Davidson, Donald, (1980). *Essays on Actions and Events*, Oxford: Oxford University Press.

Davidson, Donald (1982): „Paradoxes of Irrationality". In: Davidson, Donald: *Problems of Rationality.* Oxford: Oxford University Press.

Davis, W., (1982). „A causal theory of enjoyment," *Mind*, 91: 240–56.

Davis, W. (1986). „The two senses of desire," in J. Marks (ed.), *The Ways of Desire*, Chicago: Precedent.

Deonna, Julien A. and Teroni, Fabrice (2015): „Emotions as Attitudes". In: *Dialectica* 69. No. 3, 293–311.

Descartes, René (1925): *Discours de la Méthode.* Hamburg: Felix Meiner.

Dewey, John (1933): *How We Think.* Lexington: D. C. Heath and Company.

Dewey, John (1997): *Experience and Education.* New York: Touchstone.

Dohrn, Daniel (2008): „Epistemic Immediacy and Reflection". In: Brun, Georg, Dogluoglu, Ulvi, and Kuenzle, Dominique (Eds.): *Epistemology and Emotions.* Farnham: Ashgate Publishing Company, 105–124.

Dorsey, Dale (2021): „Francis Hutcheson". In Zalta, Edward N. (Ed.): *The Stanford Encyclopedia of Philosophy* (Summer 2021 Edition). https://plato.stanford.edu/archives/sum2021/entries/hutcheson, last accessed April 6, 2023.

Dretske, F., (1988). *Explaining Behavior: Reasons in a world of causes*, Cambridge, MA: MIT Press.

Dreyfus, Hubert (1992): *What Computers Still Can't Do.* Cambridge: MIT Press.

Engstrom, Stephen and Whiting, Jennifer (1998): *Aristotle, Kant, and the Stoics: Rethinking Happiness and Duty.* Cambridge: Cambridge University Press.

Feldman, Fred (2004): *Pleasure and the Good Life: Concerning the Nature, Varieties, and Plausibility of Hedonism.* Oxford: Clarendon Press.

Festinger, Leon (1957): *A Theory of Cognitive Dissonance.* Redwood City: Stanford University Press.

Fiecconi, Elena C. (2019): „Aristotle's Peculiarly Human Psychology". In: Kreft, Nora and Keil, Geert (Eds.): *Aristotle's Anthropology.* Cambridge: Cambridge University Press.

Frankena, William K. (1966): „The concept of morality". In: *Journal of Philosophy* 63. No. 21, 688–696.

Frankfurt, Harry (1971): „Freedom of the will and the concept of a person". In: *Journal of Philosophy* 68. No. 1, 5–20.

Friedman, Jane (2019). „Inquiry and Belief". *Noûs* 53 (2):296–315.

Galton, Antony and Mizoguchi, Riichiro (2009): „The water falls but the waterfall does not fall: New perspectives on objects, processes and events". In: *Applied Ontology.* 4. No. 2, 71–107.

Gaut, Berys (2017): „Educating for Creativity". In Paul, Elliot S. and Kaufman, Scott B. (Eds.): *The Philosophy of Creativity.* Oxford: Oxford University Press.

Geach, Peter (1956): *Good and Evil.* In: *Analysis* 17. No. 2, 33–42.

Gendler, Tamar (2010): *Intuition, Imagination, and Philosophical Methodology.* Oxford: Oxford University Press.

Gerrans, Philip and Sander, David (2014): „Feeling the future: Prospects for a theory of implicit prospection". In: *Biology and Philosophy* 29. No. 5, 699–710.

Gewirth, Alan (1968): *Reason and Morality.* Chicago: University of Chicago Press.

Goffin, Kris (2021): „Better Scared than Sorry: The Pragmatic Account of Emotional Representation". In: *Erkenntnis* 76. No. 1, 73–89.

Goldie, Peter (2008): „Misleading emotions". In: Brun, Georg, Dogluoglu, Ulvi, and Kuenzle,
    Dominique (Eds.): *Epistemology and Emotions*. Farnham: Ashgate Publishing Company, 149–165.
Haidt, J. and Keltner, D. (1999). „Social Functions of Emotions at Four Levels of Analysis." *Cognition and Emotion* 13 (5):505–521.
Haidt, J. and Keltner, D. (2003): „Approaching awe, a moral, spiritual, and aesthetic emotion". In:
    Cognition and Emotion 17. No. 2, 297–314.
Haidt, Jonathan (2005): „Invisible fences of the moral domain". In: *Behavioral and Brain Sciences* 28.
    No. 4, 552–553.
Haidt, Jonathan and Bjorklund, Fredrik (2008): „Social intuitionists answer six questions about
    morality". In: Sinnott-Armstrong, Walter (Ed.): *Moral Psychology*. Vol. II. Cambridge: MIT Press.
Haidt, J., Graham, J., Nosek, B. A., Iyer, R., Koleva, S. and Ditto, P. H. (2011). „Mapping the moral
    domain." *Journal of Personality and Social Psychology* 101 (2):366–385.
Hajek, Alan (2014): „Philosophical Heuristics and Philosophical Creativity". In Paul, Elliot S. and
    Kaufman, Scott B. (Eds.): *The Philosophy of Creativity*. Oxford: Oxford University Press.
Hare, Richard (1955): „Universalizability". In: *Proceedings of the Aristotelian Society* 55, 295–312.
Harte, Verity (2004): „The philebus on pleasure: The good, the bad and the false". In: *Proceedings of
    the Aristotelian Society* 104. No. 2, 111–128.
Harte, Verity (2014): „The Nicomachean Ethics on Pleasure". In: Polansky, Ronald (Ed.): *The Cambridge
    Companion to Aristotle's Nicomachean Ethics*. Cambridge: Cambridge University Press, 288–318.
Hayward, Max Khan (2018): „Non-Naturalist Moral Realism and the Limits of Rational Reflection". In:
    Australasian Journal of Philosophy 96. No. 4, 724–737.
Hayward, Max Khan (ms): *Terrestrial Ethics*.
Heyd, David (2019): „Supererogation". In: Zalta, Edward N. (Ed.): *The Stanford Encyclopedia of
    Philosophy* (Winter 2019 Edition). https://plato.stanford.edu/archives/win2019/entries/
    supererogation, last accessed April 6, 2023.
Heyes, Cecilia (2018): *Cognitive Gadgets: The Cultural Evolution of Thinking*. Cambridge: Harvard
    University Press.
Horgan, T. and Graham, G. (2012). „Phenomenal Intentionality and Content determinacy". *In Richard
    Schantz (ed.) Prospects of Meaning*. De Gruyter.
Horgan, T. and Tienson, J. (2002), „The Intentionality of Phenomenology and the Phenomenology of
    Intentionality". In Chalmers, D (ed.) *Philosophy of Mind: Classical and Contemporary readings*.
    Oxford University Press.
Jaggar, Alison M. (1989): „Love and knowledge: Emotion in feminist epistemology". In: *Inquiry* 32.
    No. 2, 151–176.
James, William (1884): „What is an emotion?". In: *Mind* 9. No. 34, 188–205.
Jaworska, A. (1999). „Respecting the margins of agency: Alzheimer's patients and the capacity to
    value," *Philosophy and Public Affairs*, 28: 105–38.
Jaworska, A. (2007a). „Caring and internality," *Philosophy and Phenomenological Research*, 74: 529–68.
Jaworska, A. (2007b). „Caring and full moral standing," *Ethics* 117, 460–97.
Jost, John T., Banaji, Mahzarin R., and Nosek, Brian A. (2004): „A Decade of System Justification
    Theory: Accumulated Evidence of Conscious and Unconscious Bolstering of the Status Quo". In:
    Political Psychology 25. No. 6, 881–919.
Kahneman, Daniel (2011): *Thinking, Fast and Slow*. New York: Farrar, Straus and Giroux.
Kant, Immanuel (1920): *Grundlegung zur Metaphysik der Sitten*. Hamburg: Felix Meiner.
Kant, Immanuel (1990): *Die Religion Innerhalb der Grenzen der Blossen Vernunft*. Hamburg: Felix Meiner.
Kenny, Anthony (1963): *Action, Emotion and Will*. New York: Humanities Press.

Kind, Amy (2013): „The Case Against Representationalism About Moods". In: Kriegel, Uriah (Ed.):
	Current Controversies in Philosophy of Mind. New York: Routledge.
Kitcher, Philip (2005): „Biology and ethics". In: Copp, David (Ed.): *The Oxford Handbook of Ethical
	Theory.* Oxford: Oxford University Press.
Kitcher, Philip (2006): „Ethics and evolution. How to get here from there". In: Macedo, Stephen and
	Ober, Josiah (Eds.): *Primates and Philosophers.* Princeton: Princeton University Press.
Kitcher, Philip (2011): *The Ethical Project.* Cambridge: Harvard University Press.
Korsgaard, Christine (1996a): *Creating the Kingdom of Ends.* Cambridge. Cambridge University Press.
Korsgaard, Christine (1996b): *The Sources of Normativity.* Cambridge: Cambridge University Press.
Korsgaard, Christine (1999): „The Sources of Normativity". In: *Philosophical Quarterly* 49. No. 196,
	384 – 394.
Korsgaard, Christine M. (2008): *The Constitution of Agency: Essays on Practical Reason and Moral
	Psychology.* New York: Oxford University Press.
Korsgaard, Christine (2009): *Self-Constitution: Agency, Identity, and Integrity.* New York: Oxford
	University Press.
Kriegel, U. (2015), *The Varieties of Consciousness*, Oxford University Press.
Kripke, Saul A. (2011): „Two Paradoxes of Knowledge". In: Kripke, Saul A.: *Philosophical Troubles.
	Collected Papers.* Vol I. Oxford: Oxford University Press.
Laird, James D. and Lacasse, Katherine (2014): „Bodily Influences on Emotional Feelings: Accumulating
	Evidence and Extensions of William James's Theory of Emotion". In: *Emotion Review* 1, 27 – 34.
Latham, N., (2006). „Three compatible theories of desire," *Dialogue*, 45: 131 – 138.
Lawrence, Gavin (2001): „The Function of the Function Argument". In: *Ancient Philosophy* 21. No. 2,
	445 – 475.
Lawrence, Gavin (2006): „Human good and human function". In: Kraut, Richard (Ed.): *The Blackwell
	Guide to Aristotle's Nicomachean Ethics.* Malden: Blackwell.
Lawrence, Gavin (2011): „Acquiring character: Becoming grown-up". In: Pakaluk, Michael and Pearson,
	Giles (Eds.): *Moral Psychology and Human Action in Aristotle.* Oxford: Oxford University Press.
Lazarus, Richard (2003): „From Appraisal: The Minimal Cognitive Prerequisites of Emotion". In:
	Solomon, Robert C. (Ed.): *What is an Emotion?* Oxford: Oxford University Press.
Leunissen, Mariska (2013): „Becoming good starts with nature: Aristotle on the moral advantages and
	the heritability of good natural character". In: *Oxford Studies in Ancient Philosophy* 44, 99 – 127.
Lewis, D., (1972). „Psychophysical and Theoretical Identifications," *Australasian Journal of Philosophy*, 50:
	249 – 58.
Lewis, D., (1988). „Desire as belief," *Mind*, 97: 323 – 32.
Lewis, D., (1996). „Desire as belief II," *Mind*, 10: 303 – 13.
Liao, S. Matthew (2006): „The right of children to be loved". In: *Journal of Political Philosophy* 14. No. 4,
	420 – 440.
Lipton, Peter (1991): *Inference to the Best Explanation.* London and New York: Routledge.
Lorenz, Hendrik (2006): *The Brute Within: Appetitive Desire in Plato and Aristotle.* Oxford: Oxford
	University Press.
Macintyre, Alasdair (1957): „What Morality Is Not". In: *Philosophy* 32. No. 123, 325 – 335.
Mackonis, Adolfas (2013): „Inference to the best explanation, coherence and other explanatory
	virtues". In: *Synthese* 190. No. 6, 975 – 995.
Maclean, Ian (2006): *René Descartes, A Discourse on the Method. A new translation by Iain Maclean.*
	Oxford: Oxford University Press.

Marks, J., (1986). „On the need for theory of desire," in J. Marks (ed.), *The Ways of Desire*, Chicago: Precedent.

Mason, Elinor (2018): „Value Pluralism". In: Zalta, Edward N. (Ed.): *The Stanford Encyclopedia of Philosophy* (Spring 2018 Edition). https://plato.stanford.edu/archives/spr2018/entries/value-pluralism, last accessed April 6, 2023.

McCready-Flora, Ian (2014): „Aristotle's Cognitive Science: Belief, Affect and Rationality". In: *Philosophy and Phenomenological Research* 89. No. 2, 394–435.

McDowell, J., (1978). „Are Moral Requirements Hypothetical Imperatives?" *Proceedings of the Aristotelian Society* (Supplement), 52: 13–29.

McDowell, John (1998a): „Deliberation and Moral Development in Aristotle's Ethics". In: Engstrom, Stephen and Whiting, Jennifer (Eds.): *Aristotle, Kant, and the Stoics: Rethinking Happiness and Duty.* Cambridge: Cambridge University Press, 19–35.

McDowell, John (1998b): „Some Issues in Aristotle's Moral Psychology". In: Everson, Stephen (Ed.): *Companion to Ancient Thought 4: Ethics.* Cambridge: Cambridge University Press, 107–128.

Millikan, R., (1984). *Language, Thought, and Other Biological Categories*, Cambridge, MA: MIT Press.

Mitchell, Jonathan (2021): *Emotion as Feeling Towards Value: A Theory of Emotional Experience.* Oxford: Oxford University Press.

Moore, George E. (1903): *Principia Ethica.* Mineola: Dover Publications.

Moore, George E. (1942): „A reply to my critics". In: Schilpp, Paul A. (Ed.): *The Philosophy of G. E. Moore.* Chicago: Open Court.

Morillo, C., (1990). „The reward event and motivation," *Journal of Philosophy*, 87: 169–86.

Nagel, Thomas (1979): *Mortal Questions.* Cambridge: Cambridge University Press.

Nanay, Bence (2014): „An Experiential Account of Creativity". In Paul, Elliot S. and Kaufman, Scott B. (Eds.): *The Philosophy of Creativity.* Oxford: Oxford University Press.

Neves, Vitor, Babb, Rebecca, Chandrasekaran, Dhivya, and Sharpe, Paul T. (2017): „Promotion of natural tooth repair by small molecule GSK3 antagonists". In: *Scientific Reports* 7. No. 39654.

Nussbaum, Martha C. (2001): *Upheavals of Thought: The Intelligence of Emotions.* Cambridge: Cambridge University Press.

Oddie, G., (2005). *Value, Reality, and Desire*, New York: Oxford University Press.

Olsson, Erik (2021): „Coherentist Theories of Epistemic Justification". In: Zalta, Edward N. (Ed.): *The Stanford Encyclopedia of Philosophy* (Fall 2021 Edition). https://plato.stanford.edu/archives/fall2021/entries/justep-coherence, last accessed April 6, 2023.

Papineau, D., (1987). *Reality and Representation*, New York: Basil Blackwell.

Papineau, David, (2021), *The Metaphysics of Sensory Experience*, Oxford: Oxford University Press.

Paul, Elliot S. and Kaufman, Scott B. (2014): *The Philosophy of Creativity.* Cambridge: Oxford University Press.

Paul, Laurie A. (2014): *Transformative Experience.* Oxford: Oxford University Press.

Pautz, Adam (2020): „The puzzle of the laws of appearance". In: *Philosophical Issues* 30. No. 1, 257–272.

Peters, Richard S., and Mace, Cecil A. (1961): „Emotions and the category of passivity". In: *Proceedings of the Aristotelian Society* 62, 117–142.

Pitt, David (2004): „The Phenomenology of Cognition or What Is It Like to Think That P?". In: *Philosophy and Phenomenological Research* 69. No. 1.

Plato. (1997a): *Philebus.* In: Plato: *Complete Works.* John M. Cooper (Ed.). Indianapolis: Hackett Publishing Co.

Plato. (1997b): *Republic.* In: Plato: *Complete Works.* John M. Cooper (Ed.). Indianapolis: Hackett Publishing Co.

Price, H., (1989). „Defending desire-as-belief," *Mind*, 98: 119 – 27.

Prinz, Jesse J. (2004): *Gut Reactions: A Perceptual Theory of the Emotions.* Oxford: Oxford University Press.

Putnam, Hilary, (1981), *Reason, Truth and History*, Cambridge: Cambridge University Press.

Quine, Willard V. O. (1960): *Word and Object.* Cambridge: MIT Press.

Rabinowicz, Wlodek and Rønnow-Rasmussen, Toni (2004). „The strike of the demon. On fitting pro-attitudes and value". In: *Ethics* 114. No. 3, 391 – 423.

Rapp, Christof (2009): „Nicomachean Ethics VII. 13 – 14 (1154a21): Pleasure and Eudaimonia". In: Natali, Carlo (Ed.): *Aristotle: Nicomachean Ethics.* Oxford: Oxford University Press.

Rapp, Christof (2010): „Aristotle's Rhetoric". In: Zalta, Edward N. (Ed.): *The Stanford Encyclopedia of Philosophy* (Spring 2010 Edition). https://plato.stanford.edu/archives/spr2010/entries/aristotle-rhetoric, last accessed April 6, 2023. Metaphysics Research Lab, Stanford University.

Reisenzein, Rainer and Stephan, Achim (2014): „More on James and the Physical Basis of Emotion". In: *Emotion Review* 6. No. 1, 35 – 46.

Rorty, Amélie O. (1998): „How to Harden Your Heart: Six Easy Ways to Become Corrupt". In: *The Yale Review* 86. No. 2, 104 – 112.

Rossi, Mauro and Tappolet, Christine (2019): „What kind of evaluative states are emotions? The attitudinal theory vs. the perceptual theory of emotions". In: *Canadian Journal of Philosophy* 49. No. 4, 544 – 563.

Roughley, Neil (2001): „Michael E. Bratman, Faces of Intention: Selected Essays on Intention and Agency". In: *International Journal of Philosophical Studies* 9. No. 2, 265 – 270.

Roughley, Neil (2016): *Wanting and Intending: Elements of a Philosophy of Practical Mind.* Dordrecht: Springer.

Russell, Bertrand (1917): „Knowledge by acquaintance and knowledge by description". In: *Proceedings of the Aristotelian Society* 11 (1910 – 1911), 108 – 128.

Scanlon, T., (1998). *What We Owe to Each Other*, Cambridge, MA: Harvard University Press.

Scarantino, Andrea and Griffiths, Paul (2011): „Don't Give Up on Basic Emotions". In: *Emotion Review* 3. No. 4, 444 – 454.

Schellenberg, Susanna (2013): „Belief and Desire in Imagination and Immersion". In: *Journal of Philosophy* 110. No. 9, 497 – 517.

Scherer, Klaus, Schorr, Angela, and Johnstone, Tom (Eds.) (2001): *Appraisal Processes in Emotion: Theory, Methods, Research.* Oxford: Oxford University Press.

Schroeder, Tim, (2004). *Three Faces of Desire*, New York: Oxford University Press.

Schroeder, Tim, (2020) „Desire", In: *The Stanford Encyclopedia of Philosophy*, Edward N. Zalta (ed.), URL = <https://plato.stanford.edu/archives/sum2020/entries/desire/>.

Schueler, George F. (1991): „Pro-attitudes and direction of fit". In: *Mind* 100. No. 400, 277 – 281.

Sherman, Nancy (1989): *The Fabric of Character: Aristotle's Theory of Virtue.* Oxford: Oxford University Press.

Siewert, Charles (1998), *The Significance of Consciousness.* Princeton University Press.

Siewert, Charles (2022): „Consciousness and Intentionality". In: Zalta, Edward N. (Ed.): *The Stanford Encyclopedia of Philosophy* (Summer 2022 Edition). https://plato.stanford.edu/archives/sum2022/entries/consciousness-intentionality, last accessed April 6, 2023

Singer, Peter (1972): „Famine, Affluence, and Morality". In: *Philosophy and Public Affairs* 1. No. 3, 229 – 243.

Smith, M., (1987). „The Humean Theory of Motivation," *Mind*, 96: 36 – 61.

Smith, M., (1994). *The Moral Problem*, Cambridge, MA: Blackwell.

Sosa, Ernest (1991): *Knowledge in Perspective*. Cambridge: Cambridge University Press.

Sosa, Ernest (2007): *A Virtue Epistemology: Apt Belief and Reflective Knowledge*. Oxford: Oxford University Press.

Sosa, Ernest (2014): „Knowledge and Time". In: Matheson, Jonathan and Vitz, Rico (Eds.): *The Ethics of Belief*. Oxford: Oxford University Press.

Sousa, Ronald de (1987): *The Rationality of Emotion*. Cambridge: MIT Press.

Sousa, Ronald de (2002): „Emotional Truth". In: *Aristotelian Society Supplementary Volume* 76. No. 1, 247 – 263.

Spelman, Elizabeth V. (1989): „Anger and Insubordination". In: Garry, Ann and Pearsall, Marilyn (Eds.): *Women, Knowledge, and Reality*. London: Unwin Hyman.

Sprigge, Timothy L. S. (1964): „Definition of a Moral Judgment". In: *Philosophy* 39. No. 150, 301 – 322.

Stampe, D., (1986). „Defining desire," in J. Marks (ed.), *The Ways of Desire*, Chicago: Precedent.

Stampe, D., (1987). „The authority of desire," *Philosophical Review*, 96: 335 – 81.

Stanford, P. Kyle (2018): „The difference between ice cream and Nazis: Moral externalization and the evolution of human cooperation". In: *Behavioral and Brain Sciences* 41.

Stich, Stephen (2018): „The Quest for the Boundaries of Morality". In: Jones, Karen, Timmons, Mark, and Zimmerman, Aaron (Eds.): *The Routledge Handbook of Moral Epistemology*. New York: Routledge.

Strawson, Peter F. (1962): „Freedom and resentment". In: Watson, Gary (Ed.): *Proceedings of the British Academy*. Vol. XLVIII. Oxford: Oxford University Press, 1 – 25.

Strawson, G., (1994). *Mental Reality*, Cambridge, MA: MIT Press.

Street, Sharon (2006): „A Darwinian dilemma for realist theories of value". In: *Philosophical Studies* 127. No. 1, 109 – 166.

Tappolet, Christine (2000): *Émotions et Valeurs*. Paris: Presses Universitaires de France.

Tappolet, Christine (2011): „Values and Emotions: Neo-Sentimentalism's Prospects". In: Bagnoli, Carla (Ed.): *Morality and the Emotions*. Oxford: Oxford University Press.

Tappolet, Christine (2012): „Emotions, perceptions, and emotional illusions". In: Clotilde, Calabi (Ed.): *Perceptual Illusions. Philosophical and Psychological Essays*. London: Palgrave-Macmillan, 207 – 224.

Tappolet, Christine (2015): „Values and Emotions". In: Hirose, Iwao and Jonas Olson (Eds.): *The Oxford Handbook of Value Theory*. Oxford: Oxford University Press. 80 – 95.

Tappolet, Christine (2016): *Emotions, Value, and Agency*. Oxford: Oxford University Press.

Tappolet, Christine and Rossi, Mauro (2015): „What is Value? Where Does it Come From? A Philosophical Perspective". In: Brosch, Tobias and Sander, David (Eds.): *The Value Handbook: The Affective Sciences of Values and Valuation*. Oxford: Oxford University Press, 3 – 22.

Taylor, Paul W. (1978): „On taking the moral point of view". In: *Midwest Studies in Philosophy* 3. No. 1, 35 – 61.

Tenenbaum, Sergio (2007): *Appearances of the Good: An Essay on the Nature of Practical Reason*. Cambridge: Cambridge University Press.

Teroni, Fabrice (2016): „Emotions, Me, Myself and I". In: *International Journal of Philosophical Studies* 24. No. 4, 433 – 451.

Teroni, Fabrice and Deonna, Julien A. (2017): „Getting Bodily Feelings into Emotional Experience in the Right Way". In: *Emotion Review* 9. No. 1, 55 – 63.

Teroni, Fabrice and Deonna, Julien A. (2020): „Emotional Experience: Affective Consciousness and its Role in Emotion Theory". In: Kriegel, Uriah (Ed.): *Oxford Handbook of the Philosophy of Consciousness.* New York: Oxford University Press, 102 – 123.

Toulmin, Stephen (1981): „The Tyranny of Principles". In: *Hastings Center Report* 11. No. 6, 31 – 39.

Vadas, M., (1984). „Affective and nonaffective desire," *Philosophy and Phenomenological Research*, 45: 273 – 80.

Velleman, J. David (1992). „The Guise of the Good". *Noûs 26* (1):3 – 26.

Vogt, Katja M. (2010): „Why Pleasure Gains Fifth Rank: Against the Anti-Hedonist Interpretation of the Philebus". In: Dillon, John and Brisson, Luc (Eds.): *Plato's Philebus* (250 – 258). Sankt Augustin: Akademia.

Vogt, Katja M. (2012): *Belief and Truth: A Skeptic Reading of Plato.* Oxford: Oxford University Press.

Vogt, Katja M. (2017): *Desiring the Good: Ancient Proposals and Contemporary Theory.* Oxford: Oxford University Press.

Vogt, Katja M. (forthcoming-a): „Deliberative Imagination and Practical Truth". In: Frey, Jennifer (Ed.): *Practical Truth.*

Vogt, Katja M. (forthcoming-b): „What is Hedonism?". In: Harris, William (Ed.): *Pain and Pleasure in Classical Antiquity.*

Waal, Frans B. M. de (1996): *Good Natured: The Origins of Right and Wrong in Humans and Other Animals.* Cambridge: Harvard University Press.

Waal, Frans B. M. de (2006): *Primates and Philosophers: How Morality Evolved.* Macedo, Stephen and Ober, Josiah (Eds.). Princeton: Princeton University Press.

Wall, D., (2009). „Are there passive desires?" *Dialectica*, 63: 133 – 55.

Whiting, Demian (2006): „Standing up for an affective account of emotion". In: *Philosophical Explorations* 9. No. 3, 261 – 276.

Whiting, Demian (2011): „The Feeling Theory of Emotion and the Object-Directed Emotions". In: *European Journal of Philosophy* 19. No. 2, 281 – 303.

Whiting, Demian (2012): „Are emotions perceptual experiences of value?". In: *Ratio* 25. No. 1, 93 – 107.

Williams, Bernard (1966): *Morality and the Emotions: An Inaugural Lecture.* London: Bedford College.

Williams, Bernard (1981): *Moral Luck: Philosophical Papers 1973 – 1980.* Cambridge: Cambridge University Press.

Williams, Bernard (1982): „Practical necessity". In: MacKinnon, Donald M., Hebblethwaite, Brian, and Sutherland, Stewart R. (Eds.): *The Philosophical Frontiers of Christian Theology: Essays Presented to D. M. Mackinnon.* Cambridge: Cambridge University Press.

Williamson, J. (1970): „Pro- and con-attitudes". In: *Philosophical Quarterly* 20. No. 81, 357 – 367.

Williamson, Timothy (2018): *Doing Philosophy: From Common Curiosity to Logical Reasoning.* Oxford: Oxford University Press.

Wittgenstein, Ludwig (1929). „Some Remarks on Logical Form". *Aristotelian Society Supplementary Volume 9* (1):162 – 171.

Wolf, Susan (1992): „Morality and Partiality". In: *Philosophical Perspectives* 6, 243 – 259.

Wolf, Susan (2012): „'One Thought Too Many': Love, Morality, and the Ordering of Commitment". In: Heuer, Ulrike and Lang, Gerald (Eds.): *Luck, Value, and Commitment: Themes from the Ethics of Bernard Williams.* Oxford: Oxford University Press, 71.

Worsnip, A. (2018a). „What is (In)coherence?" *Oxford Studies in Metaethics* 13:184 – 206.

Worsnip, A. (2018b). „The Conflict of Evidence and Coherence". *Philosophy and Phenomenological Research* 96 (1):3 – 44;

Worsnip, A. (2021). *Fitting Things Together: Coherence and the Demands of Structural Rationality.* New York: Oxford University Press.

Index

https://doi.org/10.1515/9783110780932-011

www.ingramcontent.com/pod-product-compliance
Lightning Source LLC
Chambersburg PA
CBHW030830090426
42737CB00009B/951